LONGMAN PROFESSIONAL DEVELOPMENT SERIES IN COMPOSITION

Comp Tales

AN INTRODUCTION TO COLLEGE COMPOSITION THROUGH ITS STORIES

Richard H. Haswell
TEXAS A&M UNIVERSITY–CORPUS CHRISTI

Min-Zhan Lu
DRAKE UNIVERSITY

and

Contributors

PEARSON
Longman

New York San Francisco Boston
London Toronto Sydney Tokyo Singapore Madrid
Mexico City Munich Paris Cape Town Hong Kong Montreal

Senior Sponsoring Editor: Virginia L. Blanford
Executive Marketing Manager: Megan Galvin-Fak
Production Coordinator: Scarlett Lindsay
Senior Cover Design Manager: Nancy Danahy
Text Design: David Munger, The Davidson Group
Senior Manufacturing Buyer: Roy L. Pickering, Jr.
Electronic Page Makeup: Dianne Hall
Printer and Binder: R. R. Donnelley & Sons Company/Harrisonburg
Cover Printer: R. R. Donnelley & Sons Company/Harrisonburg

Cataloging-in-Publication Data on file at the Library of Congress

Please visit our website at http://www.ablongman.com

ISBN 13: 978-0-205-57635-7
ISBN 10:   0-205-57635-4

Printed in the United States of America
1 2 3 4 5 6 7 8 9 0—DOH—10 09 08 07

To students of writing, present and future.

On your work depends the life of each comp tale.

Contents

Contributors

FOREWORD

⤶

MIN-ZHAN LU

AND

RICHARD H. HASWELL

This project to collect oral stories of college composition teachers hopes to carry on its collaborative effort on many levels through all stages of its life. And it hopes to produce the kind of collaborative work among and between editors, contributors, and readers that acknowledges rather than erases the diverse and ever-changing interests and practices in the post-secondary teaching of composition.

Originally, it was the possibility of working with someone of different experience and expertise in composition which encouraged Rich to approach Min-Zhan with the idea of putting together a collection of comp tales and which intrigued Min-Zhan to sign on. In retrospect, it seems that this collection would not have materialized but for the willingness of both of us to speak our minds and to use the differences in our viewpoints and work styles constructively as we thought, negotiated, and otherwise worked our way through the project.

More importantly, the project would not have been possible without the collaboration of contributors from across a whole range of institutional divides—old-timers and newcomers, tenured and tenure-track and adjunct and teaching assistant, research and four-year and two-year institutions, etc. When we sent out our call for oral narratives of the field, "stories that college writing teachers like to tell and retell," we said they could deal with "anything connected with college composition" (see Appendix A for the original call). Together, the contributors brought us oral-based tales depicting a variety of professional relations—writing teachers working with, for, alongside, and sometimes despite one another, co-working with students, with colleagues in other fields within and outside English, and with the public, addressing issues central to the teaching of writing, including the production and reception of texts, the work of professionalism, and the confrontation with all systems of discrimination. Furthermore, the tales illustrate the broad range of beliefs, interests, and desires as well as tones, registers, and modes populating writing teachers' narratives. Rich has sorted the tales into eleven chapters, roughly tracing the career trajectory of a writing teacher. In sequencing the tales within each chapter, rather than aiming for unity or flow from tale to tale, he has left visible the often conflicting and temporal nature of the dialogue internal to the tales. That is, the chapters show how storytelling indeed works in collaboration to define and redefine relations and issues central to the field. But it is collaboration resulting from shared commitment to the profession and shared willingness to examine and change established knowledges and practices rather than from any desire for uniformity and fossilization.

Given the performative nature of oral storytelling, the future life of this project will depend finally on the collaboration of readers, on the way they go about making use of the tales gathered here. As editors, we have made several decisions concerning the format of the book. First, to ensure that individual readers get a chance to encounter the tales with as little editorial interference as possible, Rich has kept the introduction to each chapter brief. Second, the contributors' commentary on their own tale follows it. And instead of using editorial comments to guide the reader through the tales, we have placed our occasional individual responses to tales at the end of chapters. Third, instead of jointly writing a foreword and an afterword, we have each written an essay articulating our thoughts on the genre and use of comp tales. These two essays follow the eleven chapters of tales. Rich has also indexed the topics in the tales, and provided an introductory bibliography of studies. Our overall concern is to invite a broad range of writing teachers to experiment with as many ways as possible of interacting with the tales at different points of their careers.

This unusual format recognizes that some readers will be more interested in using these tales to get a sense of the range and kinds of stories others tell and to get a sense of the differences in their own and others' conditions of work or in the way they and others tell and use comp tales. These readers can skip, if they so desire, the editorial notes and the essays by editors and instead go directly to the tales themselves. At the same time, some readers may also be interested in how others are interpreting and planning to use these tales. These readers can get two viewpoints from the notes and essays after their initial encounter with the tales. We hope that the dialogical tension between our notes and essays will stimulate some readers to generate readings and uses alternative to those posed by us.

We have offered a variety of options for readers using these different components of the book—the contributors' stories and their commentary, the notes of each editor, the two essays, the topical index, and the bibliography. We hope to open this book to a broader range of uses by diverse readers in different forums: for the pleasure of reading, for getting the pulse of the profession, for developing teaching strategies, for teacher training, for forums on faculty development, and in ways we can't imagine.

ACKNOWLEDGMENTS

As folktale analyst Vladimir Propp would have predicted, the making of *Comp Tales* did not lack helpers, providers, and magical donors. David Schwalm, moderator of the writing program administrators listserv (WPA-L), encouraged us to use his list to send out the original call for teacher tales. Similar help later was given by Lady Falls Brown of the writing center list (WCENTR-L), Karl Fornes of the peer-tutor list (WRITINGC), and Terry Collins of the basic writing teachers list (CBW-L). Ben R. Wiley of St. Petersburg Junior College–Clearwater did some special canvassing among teachers in the two-year colleges. Susanmarie Harrington sent us a sheaf of tales from her instructor workshop at Indiana University–Purdue University at Indianapolis. Michael Greer offered us early editorial advice. And throughout, there was always the wand of Lynn Huddon, our editor at Longman, when we needed it.

We're truly grateful for the advice given by the reviewers of the manuscript: Kristine Blair, Bowling Green State University; David Blakesley, Southern Illinois University; Linda Breslin, Texas Tech University; William Condon, Washington State University; Beth Daniell, Clemson University; Sara Garnes, The Ohio State University; Joseph Harris, University of Pittsburgh; Rebecca Moore Howard, Syracuse University; David Kann, California Polytechnic State University; Carrie Leverenz, Florida State University; Barry Maid, University of Arkansas at Little Rock; Elizabeth Metzger, University of South Florida; Keith Miller, Arizona State University; Meg Morgan, University of North Carolina, Charlotte; Donna Qualley, Western Washington University; Christopher Thaiss, George Mason University; and Peter Vandenberg, DePaul University.

Above all, we thank all those folk who sent us tales, bits of their lives, and especially those many whose stories, for lack of space in this slim volume, we had to return—good stories all. Finally, our thanks to Jan Haswell, Elizabeth Robertson, and Bruce Horner for their intellectual, emotional, and moral support.

Introduction
to the Tales

RICHARD H. HASWELL

These eleven chapters offer only one possible arrangement of the tales. I thought about ordering chapters by topic, but we ended up with so many topics I finally had to sort them by means of an index (see Appendix D). More tempting was a classification by subgenres: The Student as Ugly Duckling, The Blessing Disguised as a Classroom Observer, The Dark Night of the Final Grades, and so forth. Subgenre provides an insightful entry into comp tales (see Tale 134), but finally I felt it made tales simpler and less performed than they really are.

As the chapters now stand, tales are sorted into the major dynamic encounters of a comp teacher's life: colleagues, the classroom, the writing, students, the public, professional dilemmas, mentors. The chapters also sketch out a rough biographical storyline, the career trajectory of a writing teacher. If that storyline takes on a dramatic shape, a beginning with complications (Chapters 2–4) that grow into major crises (Chapters 5–7) that resolve themselves into a professional life (Chapters 8–10), it only writes large the narrative shape of many a tale. Finally, the first and last chapters remind us that oral stories have life trajectories too, which shape and parallel the lives of storytellers, lives which in turn shape the developing life of the profession. All told, I have arranged the tales, and discussed them in my brief chapter headings, in the narrative spirit of all anecdotes that are both personal and professional, a spirit both life-formative and field-enhancing.

In rather the same spirit, each chapter ends with occasional notes by Min-Zhan Lu and myself to some of the tales.

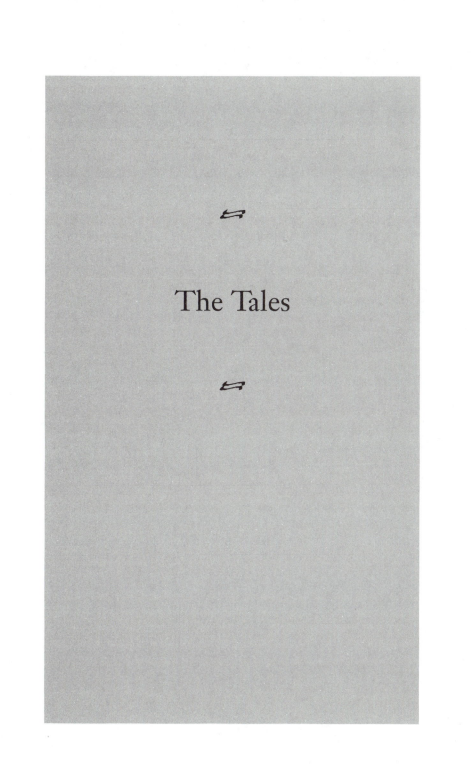

The Tales

CHAPTER 1

ↄ

Entering into Story

I was asked to play in the little orchestra in Blackfriars chapel, the Dominican house in Oxford, for the Christmas Day mass. I noticed that as I agreed I thought of how I would tell my friend Robinson about it. Here I work for the Jesuits and play for the Dominicans.

—Rom Harré (1997, p. 332)

As any oral story, a comp tale has an eventful life which can, with luck, be recorded (see Tales 129-133). But when did a tale get born? Even the authors have a hard time remembering when they first created an anecdote. It's like jokes, whose cleverness admirers pass on but whose birth no one seems to have experienced. With the following two stories, we catch a rare glimpse of the events and the motives that first push writing teachers on stage, encouraging them to take a piece of their private lives and make it public in narrative form. (RHH)

ↄ ↄ ↄ

1

It was 6:15 p.m., only a few minutes before students in my evening comp class were to convene for our fourth session of the semester. I was working at my desk when the figure of a large man, with scarred face and imposing tattoos, appeared at my open office door and questioned, "You're Newman, aren't you? Can you tell me where our class meets?" Astonished, I replied, "Yes, I am Newman, but who are you?" "Johnson," came the reply, "I'm in your class." Indeed, I did have a "J. Johnson" on the roll, but since this student had never come to class, I assumed that he had dropped the course before our first class meeting. Exasperated that a student expected to enter class so late, I replied, "I'm afraid you have missed too many classes to enter at this point. Only three hours of absence are permitted, and you have already missed nine. It would be impossible for you to catch up at this point." "I know I've missed," J. Johnson persisted, "but I couldn't help it—I was in jail! My sister had to register for me." Then he added, "I done all the work though. McCurry showed me the assignments." "D. McCurry?" I squinted, recognizing the name but puzzling over the connection. McCurry, with his highly polished shoes and short, military-style haircut, was the antithesis of the man standing at my office door. "Yep," J. Johnson replied, seeming pleased, "He's my jailer!"

The following week when a university professor conducting a course on "Teaching in the Community College" called for papers to describe the "typical" community college student, I presented the narrative of Johnson and McCurry. Where else but in the composition classroom of a community college could boundaries be so visibly crossed? Where else could such a plurality of voices find expression? What better example of the democratic classroom? Collaborative learning? The university professor (who had never been in a community college) expected me to cite the research data of such scholars as Patricia K. Cross and John Rousche ("the average age of a community college student is . . .", etc.). Narrative was unacceptable for scholarly writing in the academy. Oral storytelling certainly had no place. Sadly, too, in my own composition class that term, the common course syllabus called for exposition and argumentation. Narrative was unacceptable there, too, unless disguised, of course, as extended illustration. J. Johnson failed the course that semester.

I may have failed J. Johnson in not providing him the opportunity I take now to tell his story.

I generally tell this story to fellow two-year college educators in workshops—for a touch of humor as well as for the purpose of underscoring the value of narrative and the possibilities for cooperative learning. I sometimes share the story with colleagues informally (over dinner, etc.) in a "school stories" round-

table. I have also told the story to both two-year college and university col-
leagues to celebrate the democratic classroom of the community college and to
illustrate the validity of teaching experience as one form of scholarship.

—Georgia A. Newman

2

As new assistant professors at a mid-size regional institution in the Southeast, we entered with a clear sense of direction and stability and were excited to be part of a writing department. Given the hierarchical support from both the chair and the dean for our fledgling department, we have been intrigued by and puzzled by a story that each of us has heard repeatedly in a variety of situations that seemed designed to make us wary and concerned about our jobs.

Usually set within the oppressive literature department frame from which we have since split, the tale begins by saying that once upon a time there were a few people interested in (and even specialists in) composition who quietly went about the business of teaching within the literature department, and then a whole gaggle (three or four?) of composition specialists were hired, and as they rocked the boat, many of them were fired. The level of expertise of the hires is unclear, but the worst (or best) perpetrator was a woman who was fired after only one quarter because she reportedly "gave" all A's.

We are most interested in the high number of repetitions this story receives, and we are interested in the oblique references to the story. It's almost as if they count on each other to fill us in on the story so that their allusions resonate. We have heard this story at the gym, playing tennis with colleagues, in general meetings, in orientation meetings, and in conferences with our mentors and supervisors. Sometimes we wouldn't know what they were talking about unless we had already had the full version of the story. The allusion is murky. Not only is the story often opaque, but the participants are also unnamed. The woman who gave all A's was only named with hesitation, and her story given different spins based on the narrator.

Sometimes she's a representation of what all composition theorists must think particularly about standards and grammar. Sometimes she's characterized as crazy, an exception who has nonetheless caused quite a bit of trouble (what with a lawsuit for wrongful dismissal–the department has instituted many hoops for teachers in their first year of service). She's a justification for oversight by the first-year writing program administrator. Sometimes she's used as a wary warning, almost a justification for current silences, for survival strategies: "We should be careful what we say about writing because our positions may come back to haunt us." Sometimes the story is told when either of us expresses excitement about the possibilities here—hope seems a difficult concept that triggers this unhopeful story. Interestingly, our chair never has told this story, and when one of us mentioned the woman and the urban myth around it, he wasn't even aware of her name, though he acknowledged a vague awareness of the story.

However, in all accounts and uses of the story, the woman remained nameless. The details of her trauma—moving to this community at her own expense to begin her job here, her joblessness in the middle of an academic year, the blot on her professional record, the lack of due process, the humiliation, and the implications for all writing teachers and the field of composition (she was hired and fired by traditional literature faculty)—all go unspoken.

We have tried to deflate the narrative's power by creating our own narratives to read against the narratives we hear. We have tried to give the no-name woman back her name, to force people to recognize what happened and why and to force them to see the repercussions of this event not just in terms of the department's administration but also in terms of their own teaching and professionalism. The results of our revising of the tale are not yet known.

One of us has relayed bits and pieces of the story to friends from home or grad school colleagues, and the responses have often been dismay and incredulity. The topic of the conversations has been adjusting to a new place. The other of us has discussed the story in detail with a spouse and tried to figure it out, or more realistically tried to figure out how to respond to it.
—Names of authors withheld

⌂ ⌂ ⌂

NOTES

TALE 1 (p. 5). A story full of twists and turns, each adding a layer to our understanding of the work of teaching writing. It asks us to examine the potential disconnect between standard representations of "community college"—who goes there and how they should be taught—in scholarship and teaching training offered in universities and the lived experiences of those teaching in two-year colleges. It illustrates the danger of judging students—their work as well as their attitudes towards learning—through visible markers: physical features, manners, and dress codes. It is a heartening story of the power of collaborative learning between a most unlikely pair of students, jailer and jailed. It is also a story of the teacher's responsibility to design writing assignments and formulate responses which acknowledge and invite students to make use of rather than dismiss or undercut the interests, knowledge, and expertise they bring to the classroom. The last sentence of the tale also depicts the life of a story as extending beyond the frame of the narrated event, to how the narrator reviews it in retrospect, in the context of the narrator's developing experience in and understanding of teaching (see also "Tracking Comp Tales," p. 212). (MZL)

TALE 2 (p. 7). I interpret the narrators' attempt to give the no-name woman back her name as also an effort to combat the tendency to decontextualize a narrated event, thus stripping it of all its social and historical contingencies. By draping the event in the discourse of myth, the storyteller also deflects attention to the narrative event, from questions of how, why, when, where is the event narrated by whom, to whom. By elevating the tale above the dual material contexts of story and storytelling, the listener is put in the position of receiver—imbibing the moral of the tale or what the teller has extrapolated from the narrated event—rather than being put in the position of a co-author, someone who not only ask questions about both the narrated event and each narration of that event but also composes new versions of the event. I am particularly taken by the narrators' conclusion that "the results of our revising of the tale are not yet known." I read the narrators to be saying that the results cannot yet be known because that would depend on how others hear and make use of the revisions offered by the narrators, which cannot be separated from the materiality of the situations when the narrators' versions would be told and retold. (MZL)

TALE 2 (p. 7). This is the kind of institutional tale that sociolinguist Charlotte Linde calls "the unspeakable." Told only to the closest of friends, "difficult to speak because there is no sanctioned public occasion for it," the story is half private and therefore institutionally only a "potential narrative" (1997, p. 287). As most of the tales collected in Chapter 11, this tale is not conventionally shaped because the situation described is still in the shaping. In contrast is the tale within the tale, the story of the unnamed woman, which as told by department members serves as an initiation or cautionary tale to new members. The woman is unnamed, in part, so that the third story, her story, will remain untold. (RHH)

CHAPTER 2

☞

Beginnings

I remember I was on this job putting this bridge over the seaway and this new s.o.b. is up there and he had his hat on backwards, so this wind comes and lifts the peak up and the hat starts flying off his head. So this guy comes and reaches up with both hands and grabs his hat and goes overboard with it. So there he is falling down through the air about 100 feet still holding on to the damn helmet.

—Jack Haas (1977, p. 163)

Tales of first-semester teaching, understandably, often take the shape of anxiety dreams. The teacher sees a cigarette smoldering in the classroom trash can, steps on it, gets his shoe stuck in the can. The teacher is projecting a topic search on the Net and stumbles onto a pornography site. The teacher is out shooting birds on Saturday (I heard this from my first director of writing), forgets he has a set of essays in the car trunk, and gets quail blood all over them. I recall writing my office number at the top of my lecture notes in case I couldn't remember it, and then forgetting to give students the next day's assignment. My deskmate in the TA bullpen got herself into the wrong classroom and gave five minutes of a cheery introduction on the joys of writing to a set of astonished agronomy majors.

Telling these misadventures later, of course, turns them into learning moments. As we will see, comp tales of the novice semester take not only the shape of adversity overcome, but also of relief, enthusiasm, and a career found. If that were not the case, I suppose, the tellers of comp

11

starts would not be around to tell them. But as we will also see, the underlying moral of these tales has to do with a commitment qualified with a growing sense of complications. For novices, it seems that teaching composition ends up easier than first imagined and then starts becoming more difficult. (RHH)

3

When I was first teaching basic writing at Rutgers University, I was sure that the students were uniformly lazy and passive because they did not know any other way to be in a classroom. During my initial classes, I asked them to read essays from *Rereading America* and to come in ready to discuss a myth of American identity: race, gender, equal opportunity, the American Dream, etc. Each day I came in armed with dozens of provocative questions about the text. Each day I went home sure that my students would never care enough about the texts to respond to my questions.

So I decided to put them to work. I asked groups of two students to take charge of a single sentence in a very long paragraph by Gloria Anzaldúa. They had to decide what the sentence said in their own words and what words they thought were most important in that sentence and why. They were then to go to the board and transcribe their answers to these questions in note form. After each group had finished writing, they sat down and prepared a one-minute report on their sentence. Working from the first sentence to the last, they began to discuss their ways of reading this paragraph. And soon after, they started to argue with each others' interpretations. In the end, we mapped our competing interpretations on the board, and they wrote for five minutes about what they thought was the "right" reading and why. The ninety minutes flew.

I always think of this as the day I learned that it was me, not my students, who had the most to learn in basic writing.

I tell this story to new teachers in the course I teach for MA candidates in English at Boston College (Composition Theory and the Teaching of Writing).

—Dawn Skorczewski

4

I was teaching advanced composition for the first time in a class with a wide range of lived experience (usually, but not always, a function of age), writing/thinking ability, and political orientation. The heart of the course was the essay with its abiding spirit of "essayism" or discovery. Students wrote in response to prompts in *Reading Culture*, using strategies they felt best suited their subject matter, purposes, and audience—including as much or little personal experience and narrative as they thought was effective. The idea that students are writers in their own right, responsible for their choices, appealed to the libertarians among them, particularly those who were against affirmative action, multiculturalism, and the welfare system. But the focus on popular culture seemed irrelevant to some, especially to one of the best writers in the class, who complained that she wasn't getting the hard knowledge she needed for her major in composition, though I tried to explain that rhetoric was something people *did*—an act, one we as a class were engaging in.

About eleven weeks into the term I showed them the documentary film *Koyaanisqatsi*, which consists strictly of images and minimalist classical music—no dialogue, in order to teach the enthymeme. I thought it was also time for a change of routine. But the one bright student balked, turned in her chair and talked to her friend; others, sitting in the same part of the room, also protested. The more aesthetically sensitive and politically leftist watched in silence. Finally, disappointed, I fast forwarded to the end, explained that *koyaanisqatsi* is a Hopi word that means "life in turmoil, life out of balance," and hurled together a couple of enthymemes on the board (we'd already studied the syllogism). And then I confronted them, asking what was going on. They said that they thought the moviemaker was a hypocrite, using technology to denounce technology. They thought I was propagandizing them. One asked what made me ever consider showing the thing in the first place.

I decided not to defend the film. I told a story instead. I told them about how depressingly polluted the beaches in California had been when I'd returned recently to visit them after living in the desert for several years. I used the descriptive catalogue to its fullest effect, detailing the broken glass, styrofoam of half-eaten fast food, cigarette butts, plastic bags, condoms, tampons. I could tell that it moved them. I successfully used narrative persuasion, drawing in the most resistant among them. And then I closed by speaking their language, asking what each of them could do to ease the problem, eliciting answers from the few who were already doing something, taking responsibility.

The class was a challenge, and, probably as much because of guilty conscience as any mistakes I made, I've always felt a bit remiss in how I taught them. Even though they were juniors and seniors, I aimed too high. Some—most—needed work writing standard thesis-driven papers. Others wanted simply to learn how to write a convincing personal statement in a professional school application. (Others said they liked the course a lot.) I tell this story to other teachers because I'd like a second chance to teach the class, yet I know that the best lesson for all involved is to leave differences unresolved and move on.

—Andy Crockett

5

During the first year of my master's-level teaching assistantship, our university got its first computer labs. Therefore, early in the spring semester, I gave a pep talk to my students about using the computers for their writing. I was trying to explain how much easier it was to revise using computers. After describing the laborious practice of handwriting, at which they all nodded appreciatively, I said, "With computers, all that prep work isn't necessary. All you need to do is . . ." What I wanted to say was "slip your disk in." What I said was "slip your dick in." Of course, I froze in mortification for a moment. The class was as silent as a tomb. Somehow, however, I had sufficient instinct (or desperation) to begin laughing. The whole room exploded with hilarity and we couldn't get any work done after that, but the pressure was off. The incident became a kind of bond between us, and afterwards I could always get a laugh by referring to it in a self-deprecating sort of way. I learned, or at least began to learn, that as a teacher you can't always take yourself too seriously.

I sometimes tell this story to TAs and new teachers to empathize with them about mistakes/missteps/misspeaks in the classroom.

—Jackie Wheeler

6

I was conferencing with freshpersons on early drafts, and with each I was trying to praise something, identify where revision might help, and to close with praise—the ubiquitous "but" sandwich. One of my students, Bill, came in wearing blue jeans with a snoose-can imprint on the right hip pocket, a plaid flannel shirt, and a yellow baseball cap with "Ortho Nitrates for Better Yields" inscribed above the bill. I quickly read his brief draft, searching for something, anything, to praise. "Well . . . ," I began, "I . . . you really . . . uh. . . ."

"It's a piece of shit, isn't it?" he blurted.

"Yes, Bill," I replied, "it is."

I have told this story for years in TA training sessions when the topic was formative feedback. It reminds us that one of the worst things a writing teacher can do is lie to students.

—Dana C. Elder

7

One of my novice TAs told me this story, laughing the whole while. He had been getting after his comp students all semester to look up words they did not understand in the anthology of readings. "Use the dictionary," he kept telling them. "That's what it's for." Then late in the semester he was conferencing with a student over a first draft of a research paper. The student, obviously very competent in the topic, had indulged in much technical jargon with no explanation of the terms for lay readers. "You have to keep your audience in mind," said the TA to the student. "I have no idea what these words mean." "Look 'em up," said the student to the TA.

I have told this story often to young instructors, especially when the issue arises of unequal power relationships between teacher and students. The story also comes readily to mind when TAs first start complaining about how badly students read academic prose.

—Rich Haswell

8

A colleague asked me to substitute in her class on a day she was going to be out of town. The day before she left, she came into my office with an elaborate list of instructions for me and a stack of handouts for her students. "There's just one more thing," she added before she left. "I don't want you to dress like THAT." I glanced down at my outfit worriedly.

Just before I had left my apartment that morning, I had realized that, depending upon the lighting in the room, the green in my top didn't seem to match the green in my skirt as well as I had thought. If Kim—who usually teaches in jeans and T-shirts or sweatshirts—was commenting on my appearance, I figured my clothes must really clash. Then Kim added, "If you go into my classroom with a skirt and blouse and pantyhose and makeup, my students are all going to be afraid of you."

I use this story in working with teachers (particularly new teachers) who are concerned about authority issues in the classroom. The wardrobe story can be a neat segue into a discussion of various elements that impact our authority in the classroom. In addition to discussing dress, we often end up discussing things like what to have our students call us, when it is OK to cut class a few minutes short, whether it is OK to cancel the last class before Thanksgiving, and how to respond to inappropriate classroom behavior.

—Debra S. Knutson

9

I once had a male student, roughly the size of a vending machine, try to hand me a used Kleenex while I was speaking to the class, so he wouldn't have to get up to throw it away. Was he testing me to see if he could gain the upper hand? Return the serve. I made gagging noises and said, "Yuck, Marvin, throw away your own snotty Kleenex!" The class laughed, and we had a good relationship thereafter. No more tests.

This sort of thing happens all the time and new TAs don't even realize they're being "called out." True, young men shouldn't try to dominate their female teachers, but the teachers need to be aware of the game that's being played and know how to return the first serve.

I've told the story to a number of colleagues and to my husband. Mostly I tell it for laughs, but it's also a good example of dealing with the unexpected, and I've used it as such in teacher development seminars, orientation, etc.

—Gail Hapke

1 0

This event took place in my first semester of teaching English composition as a graduate student. Near the beginning of the semester,

I told my students to go home and choose a topic for an argumentative essay. The topic was to be one that had an impact on their own lives and the lives of people around them. In the next class, I did a topic check. I asked each student to describe their topic to the class and explain how this topic was connected to their personal experience. One of my students—a tall, male student—said he wanted to write on the issue of rape. He said that he was connected to the issue because he has a mother and sister and mumbled something else after that. I didn't ask any further questions. Assuming he chose this topic for sensitive personal reasons, I went about the rest of my duties.

A week or so later, I received a draft of his essay and as I read it I became quite numb. His claim was something like "Rapists should not receive the death penalty." He went on to argue that "the nature of the crime of rape is really theft, not violence, in that something is stolen from the man the woman belongs to." Other points he made were "rape isn't a violent crime" and "if a mugger doesn't get the death penalty, a rapist shouldn't either."

Obviously I had a huge problem on my hands. Every point he made was unsound (rapists do not normally get the death penalty, rape is in fact a violent crime, etc.), but I was very clearly in a situation where anything I said against his argument could be misconstrued as bias. I decided to be very open and tell him that his paper made me angry. I pointed out to him how ridiculous it was to write this type of essay for a young woman instructor. Then I tried to explain how his reasoning was faulty. All of these comments came out in our conference, where I gradually became painfully aware of the fact that I was in a small office (with the door open, of course) with two young male students who were quite successfully backing me up against a wall. They saw nothing wrong with the argument. At one point the writer asked me, "Have you ever been raped?" Both students accused me of being biased against a point of view different from my own. I felt trapped.

After that incident I noticed that out of twenty-five students in my class, twenty were male. I did all I could to keep face, but my heart was no longer in that class.

I tell this story to my students now so that they will be more aware of me as an audience. Somewhere in the telling of the tale they learn that I am a human being with attitudes, opinions and feelings. They understand that while it's my job as a comp instructor to put aside my biases in order to evaluate their work objectively, they still need to be aware of me as an audience.

—Linda Kaastra

1 1

When I was in grad school at the University of Michigan, I got a part-time job teaching writing for Jackson Community College. My classes were at Jackson State Prison, a high-security facility that was said to be the largest walled prison in the world.

When I showed up for my first class, I had to pass through five or six different locked gates and doors between my car and my classroom. Once in the classroom, I found myself faced by two dozen inmates, all convicted murderers, rapists, armed robbers, all in drab prison uniforms, all in the bizarre haircuts, beards, and tattoos that you find only on cons and ex-cons.

When I introduced myself, none of them responded, not even with a nod. So I began the in-class writing assignment that I had used successfully in the on-campus writing classes I had taught.

"It's ten years from now," I said, "and you have appeared on the cover of *Time* magazine for something you have done. You have won a Pulitzer Prize, perhaps, or an Academy Award, or an Olympic gold medal. Write the story about yourself that's inside that issue of *Time*."

No response. Blank stares. Some men started to write, but most just studied the ceiling. Oh, shit, I thought. This isn't going to work at all. My whole course isn't going to work at all. What have I got myself into?

Then a hand went up, from one of students. "Yes?" I said eagerly, even desperately.

"How do you spell integrity?" he asked.

I laughed. He laughed. Everybody laughed. The semester was underway.

Over the years, I've told this story to new teachers I've helped prepare, either in orientation sessions or in grad courses, as a way to break the ice with them about discussing their own fears and problems in the classroom. I've also told this story to other veteran teachers when we swap stories about our classroom experiences. I suppose I like telling the story because it's self-deprecating but also kind of "macho."

—Kenneth W. Davis

1 2

I just started working for the local community college as a composition instructor when the department coordinator called me for a new assignment. The local sheriff's office had contracted the school to provide a few remedial writing courses for its employees. I happily accepted the appointment, firmly believing that non-traditional (i.e., old) students were the most motivated, cooperative, and rewarding. I composed a syllabus by mapping out a plethora of homework assignments, quizzes, and essays.

The first day of class I walked into a silent room and looked out from a wobbly podium at a room full of stern faces and piercing eyes. My nervousness was exacerbated by the realization that not only were all of my new students clearly unhappy, but they were all in uniform and fully armed. I hesitantly handed out the syllabi and began to go over the course expectations and requirements. Each sentence I spoke seemed to elicit more animosity. Some of the students never unlocked their hard stare from me, never glanced once at the syllabi in front of them.

I stopped mid-sentence, pulled out a chair, plopped down in it in front of the podium, and looked at all of the deputies in the room. One man, sitting in the front row, slowly crossed one leg over the other, resting his ankle on the opposite knee. While conducting this performance for my benefit, he hiked up his pant leg just enough to expose the small firearm strapped underneath.

I simply asked, "What's going on here?"

After a few minutes of discussion, I discovered that the sheriff's office had forced all employees to take a placement test. Those students that received low scores were subsequently required to attend courses. Furthermore, this class was the group of students who had performed the lowest. They knew it. Their colleagues knew it. Their supervisors knew it. Their subordinates knew it. Unfortunately, until that very moment, their teacher did not.

I stood up, collected the course syllabi, and chucked them in the trash. We spent the remainder of the class discussing what they wanted to accomplish, what realistic goals we could set, what kind of time limitations they had in and out of the classroom, and what would encourage them to leave their sidearms at home.

I learned a valuable lesson about the necessity of teacher adaptability. My idealistic notions of educational outcomes collided with the reality of classroom and student circumstances. By devising a plan that fit the circumstances, we were all able to reach the goals we set and still retain a modicum of pleasantness throughout the course. All students passed the placement exam when they re-took it at the end of the quarter, and I don't think I have to worry about getting a speeding ticket again as long as I live in this county (I'm just kidding, Sheriff).

Being the natural talker that I am, I tell the story orally. This was the first time I put it down on paper. I have shared this story with a few other novice composition teachers, particularly during discussions that focus on how our initial classroom experiences were very different from what we expected. I think some of us approached teaching with the expectation that we would have a class full of ourselves—you know, students who thought, acted, and performed as we did when we were Comp 101 neophytes. My jarring experience with the officers was a quick and dirty indoctrination into the real classroom. Because this story is a success story, so to speak, it has turned discussions, which may have been gripe sessions between teachers, into constructive analysis of classroom planning. Of course I also tell the story for entertainment value. When I hear other instructors complaining about difficult students, I'm quick to ask if they've ever been the only unarmed person in the classroom, with everyone aware of that fact. Retelling the story also reinforces the personal lesson and reminds me how much fun teaching and accomplishment can be.

—Traci E. Augustosky

1 3

I saw that a new TA had given all A's. I called him into my office and asked, "What does this mean? These are freshman writers. How could you give all A's?"

"I guess it means I'm a good teacher," he said.

Told to me by my chair not long after he had talked me into directing the writing program. He told it in a kind of wonderment at such a clever reply, but I have told it since in a different vein, to complicate the discussion when people are ranting about grade inflation.

—Rich Haswell

1 4

I was working on an MA in history and was asked to teach a section of composition because I wrote well and because there was need and because my own department had no support for me. At the end of the semester I sat on my bed with the final grade sheet, my students' last papers spread around me. Grades were due the next day. I lost it. I couldn't decide on one student. My gradebook, badly kept, just made things worse—the grades I had recorded were all over the place. All I knew was that every student had sometimes written well, sometimes not, sometimes got better, sometimes got worse. But on second thought I wasn't even sure of that. What was better written, worse written? In a panic I started marking final grades, if not at random at least for the flimsiest reasons. A girl in a dirty parka, hair put up in a pony tail with a rubber band, turning in her last essay late because she "had been blown away by it": A-. A boy seated in the back corner who once pretended not to hear me when I called on him: C-. At the end, I went back through and altered some grades so my distribution wouldn't too much offend department guidelines. I signed my name and I felt terrible. I swore I would never teach writing again.

For seven years now I've been running a composition program at a large two-year school. I've never told anyone this story. I help teachers as best I can.

—Author's name withheld

1 5

The men from the physical plant had just finished moving a new desk and chair into my office. Karen came by.

"Isn't this desk too big for this room?" I asked.

"I don't think so," she replied.

"Are you sure? There seems to be less floor space."

"Well," she said, as she got up and walked toward the door," it could be worse. You could be sharing. . . ."

It was something I had heard over a decade ago.

I was working as an adjunct for a technical college where I was assigned to teach three sections of composition at 8, 9, and 10 a.m. Student conferences were required and they were to be held in the humanities building, which was sectioned off into three areas: an office for the chair of the humanities division; cubby holes where the full-time faculty worked; and three rectangular tables, located near the back of the building, where part-time faculty were to meet with students. Teachers and students squeezed together at the tables, talking quietly, some almost whispering as they leaned over papers. By my fourth conference, I was getting used to the cramped quarters. I was speaking to a student about her paper when I noticed she was looking at neither the paper nor me. I asked if she felt uncomfortable working here, and she said, "I guess it could be worse." Fearing that if we continued I would never hold her attention, I asked if she knew of another place where we could work. She described a grassy section of campus with benches.

The autumn air was brisk and the maple leaves were beginning to turn red and gold. After a very productive conference, I thanked my student for introducing me to the place.

"From now on," I said, "I think I'll hold conferences here."

She replied, "Sure! At least until November or the first snow. . . ."

I find myself telling this story in a variety of contexts, but mostly at professional conferences in response to an old friend who seems to have talked too long, and in exaggerated ways, about how we as tenured teachers of writing are not appreciated. I offer this story not to point out how fortunate we are, but as a prompt for our thinking more historically about our immediate positions, our careers, and the status of the discipline.

—*Jody Swilky*

1 6

When I was a new graduate teaching assistant, I entered the composition classroom with more than my share of nervousness and insecurities. The experience caused me to reflect on the composition instructors I had in my first year of college. The realization that I had two excellent teachers moved me to write a letter of thanks to them in appreciation for their wonderful examples of good teaching, and I also wanted to let them know how I wished I had some of their experience to guide me. Although I never expected a reply from them, I should have known better. They were individuals who never ceased to encourage and support a student. One wrote, "I know you, and I know you are a wonderful teacher. How I would love to be in your classroom." The second teacher responded with similar words of reassurance: "Your letter was all the thanks any teacher could ever hope for. Thank you. You will be a fine teacher, because you're smart, you care, and you don't use your intelligence to take power trips. Lastly, you love the subject, so I know you'll be fine."

I repeat this anecdote when talking to new graduate teaching assistants to reassure them that we all suffer from the anxiety of walking into the classroom as first-time instructors. What I try to impress upon them is the same sentiment that my composition teachers tried to convey to me: We have confidence in you; you have to believe in yourself. My instructors taught me another lesson: I hope that I can inspire students in the classroom the way they continue to inspire me.

—Patrice Hollrah

ꙮ ꙮ ꙮ

NOTES

TALES 3 (p. 12) AND 6 (p. 14). It seems that tales of first-semester teaching are almost always also tales about the differing perceptions of student needs or capabilities and of the "images" of good teaching one initially brings to and/or eventually takes away from that experience. First-time teaching is tough because it is often the first time when our preconceived notions of good teaching and of the typical student are tested, even contested. But it is exhilarating because it is also where real revision of our sense of self, of the student, and of how to teach take place. Tales of first-semester teaching are useful for disseminating and interrogating competing images of student needs and capabilities. Teacher training is one site where this work is being currently carried out. (MZL)

TALE 4 (p. 13). Nested in this tale are two stories of first-time experience—the encounter with the polluted beaches (told to the class) and the encounter with the class (told to writing teachers). Both tales convert the past experience of the teller into an ethical act that lives on as a remembered step in his ongoing professional life ("I'd like a second chance to teach them"). But notice the inclusion of a variety of student stories as well, voiced by students who also want to make sense and make use of the classroom event. For everyone involved, including the current teacher-listeners, the tale begins with "discovery," suffers through "differences unresolved," and ends with the need to "move on." Ultimately, teaching as movie-making and storytelling can only present, never coerce. (RHH)

TALES 5–8 (pp. 14–15). It's no accident that so many of these first-time teaching stories are told to first-time teachers. The message is not that I was nervous, stupid, inexperienced, but that I learned, not that you should avoid these novice mistakes but that I survived and so will you. The story lives on because the troubles are not solved once and for all but continue to complicate the lives of young hands and old hands alike. (RHH)

TALES 8, 9, 10 (pp. 15–16). I'm intrigued by the possibility of telling Tale 8 back to back with Tale 9, or Tale 10. All three tales indicate that, as a result of sexism, racism, class elitism, nationalism, homophobia, etc., teachers and students tend to use physical markers—wardrobe (Tale 8), body size (Tale 9), sex (Tales 9 and 10), and I might add, skin color or facial features—to construe one's authority. Yet, certain markers (such as sex or skin color) cannot be put on or taken off like wardrobes. So, how might we use our experiences in combating the prejudices resulting from one set of markers to inform or complicate how we deal with the discriminations resulting from another set of markers? For instance, since experiences of discrimination as a result of not bearing the "right" wardrobe are something almost all teachers and students can relate to, we might use stories similar to Tale 8 to motivate students such as the ones depicted in Tales 9 and 10 to reflect on and critique their own sexist beliefs and behaviors. Or, we might use tales similar to Tale 9 or 10 to extend the scope of discussions initiated by tales similar to Tale 8. (MZL)

TALE 11 (p. 18). The last sentence reminds me, when sharing tales, to also reflect on why we are more invested in telling certain stories than others. Furthermore, the ideal image of the teacher shaping our teaching practices and our narration of these practices is never asexual but subtly mediated by our sense of our gender (or racial, class, sexual, ethnic being). (MZL)

TALES 11 (p. 18) AND 12 (p. 19). This pair of law-enforcement comp tales are perhaps an appropriate setting for the issue of security and authority. For new teachers, who often are only a few years older than their students, authority may be their largest worry (see Tales 9 and 10). But as hard as establishing authority is learning when to relinquish it. When do you abandon the security of a lesson plan and let students have their say? Compare Tale 101. (RHH)

TALE 12 (p. 19). See "Tracking Comp Tales," p. 224. (MZL)

Tale 13 (p. 20). Originally, it was no accident that the story about a new TA was told to a new Writing Program Administrator. My chair may have displayed wonderment, but the cautionary message to me was clear— allying this tale with Tale 2. Both tales strike me as confirmation of an observation made by sociologist Max Gluckman: "A most important part of gaining membership of any group is to learn its scandals" (1963, p. 314). But I would note that as the new members of the group become old members, they can retell their own story as a resistance to the very group practices that the story originally upheld. Compare Tale 132. (RHH)

Tale 14 (p. 20). My guess is that the event recounted by Tale 14 is neither unique to new TAs nor to its anonymous author. The tale compels me to examine these questions: What concrete, institutional conditions continue to make not-telling-anyone or telling-only-in-anonymity the only credible options for those of us with similar experiences? What are the limitations and/or uses of keeping such stories underground? (MZL)

Tale 15 (p. 21). Compare with Susan McLeod's anecdote (1990), another story of desks, space, and part-timers. "Desks are signs," writes McLeod, "emblematic of power and status." (RHH)

Tale 15 (p. 21). A reminder of another aspect of our work about which we could use a few more stories: the different conditions of work spaces allocated to different ranks of English teachers and, more importantly, the impact these material conditions have on student learning. (MZL)

CHAPTER 3

↤

Colleagues

I can remember, we had a lady admitted to the hospital who had a diaphragm. She had put it in the drawer. I called every nurse in the place, 'cause we had never seen one. We would sneak in at night with a flashlight to look at it.

—Female respondent,
remembering the 1950s,
cited by Janelle Wilson, 1997 (p. 171)

As Tale 17 implies, new teachers often meet their colleagues before they meet their students. This is perhaps not by chance. Colleague, *com + legare*, "chosen to come together." To modern ears, the idea of colleague connotes team work and team play, and comp life seems to abet the idea. We team teach, substitute for one other, publicly support each other's grades even when privately we may not concur, say in the catalogue and to the dean that we teach equivalent sections, participate in "read-arounds" to "normalize" department standards. It is easy to forget that indeed we have been chosen to come together, and it is the institution that has done the choosing. There are no walk-ons teaching composition. Our institution—whether it functions as comp committee, academic unit, department, or professional field—operates as any other institution, with complexity and inner tensions. We get chosen simply to teach writing, and immediately things get complicated. We are chosen to play a part, but the parts have to be different, and with the differences come rank, turf, seniority, prestige, and power. Our new colleagues turn out to be assigned mentors, program administrators, classroom observers, academic advisors, a whole crew of varied players. We're asked to row in unison, but there is more than one boat.

Everything supports the institutional hierarchy, including the stories told within it. In the form of rumor, gossip, scandal, anecdote, and exempla, and more cryptically in the form of faculty files, visitation reports, annual reviews, and letters of recommendation, narratives initiate, sort, exclude, show power, shape information, and authorize public image (see Crashaw, 1974; Gluckman, 1963; Linde, 1997; Martin and Powers, 1983; Pondy, et al., 1983; Shotter, 1993). One of the enlightening features of the comp tales about colleagues in this chapter is the way many of them repeat the story-versus-story conflict within Tale 2 (and within Tale 1, come to think of it). Tale and countertale, initiation and change, institutional expectations and resistance to them, thus are narrated the tensions and contradictions of being a colleague. Thus speaks the Janus face of collegiality. (RHH)

☞ ☞ ☞

17

As a brand new adjunct (just hired, underqualified, and recently returned to the teaching world after a nine-year hiatus), one of my first group experiences in the English department was to participate in a "read-around." One of the composition instructors brought multiple copies of a dozen or so papers, and nine of us sat down to read and grade, then discuss the grade and why we awarded it.

After almost a decade away from the paper-grading game, I was insecure and quiet and became even more so when the discussion of one paper turned to "shun" words. I was puzzled and confused. What words could have gained such a reputation that they were now shunned? The paper I had just evaluated had no vulgarities, no gross misspellings. I did not want to reveal my ignorance to my new colleagues. The read-around moved on, and I kept my silence.

We began discussing the final paper. Again, my colleagues brought up the dreaded "shun" words. I looked diligently, still wondering what these evil words could be. Then a colleague's explicit spelling revealed their source: they were "-tion" words, nominalizations, the opponent of good writing.

I started laughing. My secret ignorance begged to be revealed and it was. My colleagues laughed with me (not at me as I had feared they might).

—Patricia Ericsson

1 8

One summer when I was in grad school, I team taught a composition class with another graduate student. Towards the end of the summer, a colleague asked me how John and I had managed to survive without killing each other: "Your styles are just so different. I don't know how you can possibly work together." Actually, John and I had very similar teaching styles—we were both easygoing and down-to-earth, and we had similar senses of humor. I knew our colleague was thrown by the fact that John almost always wore faded T-shirts and torn cut-offs, and I always wore my "teacher disguise"—a dress or skirt and blouse. Because John was a man with a full beard, he didn't need to dress up to establish his authority in the classroom, but I did. However, when our colleague talked about our "styles," I didn't want to let on that I, too, was thinking about anything as superficial as our wardrobes, so I just let on that there really had been one sticking point in our collaboration: "I know," I said, "John's writing is a lot more formal than mine." My colleague gave me a strange look and walked away shaking her head, obviously assuming I just didn't understand her point.

This story is useful in the undergraduate composition classroom because it is one way to address the problem of tailoring one's work for an appropriate audience. For example, at the end of each semester, when my students are composing reflective introductions to their portfolios, someone always asks who is going to read their reflections. At Illinois State, all introductory composition students must submit one copy of their final portfolios to their teachers, and another—an electronic copy—to the writing program. And some of my students figure they had better find out whether they need to address an audience of faceless professors, or whether they are writing to Deb. (Other students automatically assume they are writing to English department faculty, and they begin drafting papers that sound like they have swallowed thesauri. Still others automatically assume they are writing just to me, and they begin writing informally. One student even began with the title, "My Kick-Ass Introduction.")

—Debra S. Knutson

1 9

One day, during a brief question-and-answer session on anything students wanted to ask questions about, the discussion got onto collective nouns and mass nouns and how to decide the number of the verb that accompanied them. Somebody asked whether "lettuce" was a collective noun. I always have difficulty with collective nouns, too, so I was stumbling around in responding ("lettuce" had sort of come out of nowhere). One student, in an attempt to be helpful I suppose, stated that it depended on whether it was head lettuce or leaf lettuce that was being referred to. His rationale was that head lettuce seemed like a collective noun that could be treated as plural or singular depending upon whether he wanted to treat the lettuce as a single head or refer to the collection of leaves that made up the head. On the other hand, if it were leaf lettuce he would treat that as singular or plural, depending on the number of leaves he was referring to. As I attempted to regain control of the conversation, I was happy that Winnie Horner or Gus Reid were not in the class observing that day.

—Don Cunningham

2 0

I had sent an e-mail message to a TA, thinking I was mediating a dispute between the TA and a faculty member. I'd thought that I was really doing a fine job of helping this TA see that she might benefit more from clearing the air between them rather than from continuing to argue publicly (on a listserv). A couple of hours later, she wrote to me telling me that my message had gone to the whole list. I got messages from about five different sympathetic folks who understood my position but felt badly for me because they knew how it'd come down. I was scolded by a couple of my superiors.

Among some faculty members, my move wasn't seen as mediatory; rather, I was called "subversive," and I was advised, by two different faculty members, to avoid becoming friendly with TAs (Eek! I thought. I think TAs are the BEST, and I cultivate their friendship). Somehow, avoiding TAs would connote a greater commitment to senior faculty, allegedly where my allegiances should lie. I sort of see it, but I don't like it nor do I adhere to this policy in the extremes some would like. Oh, it was ugly.

Posted on a listserv. I still tell this story, particularly to close friends and family whenever work issues arise. Recently, my father has gotten WebTV and is all excited about e-mail. I tell him my story. I also recently told this story to a new colleague, in a conversation regarding the nature of academic hierarchies and how they can be destructive to a communal and intellectual spirit.

—*Bonnie Kyburz*

2 1

Just after I finished my doctorate, I published a pseudonymous piece, "Reflections of a Young Teacher," by D. Phillips, in *The Journal of General Education*, complaining about my graduate teachers' failure even to mention teaching. About ten years later, when the university was about to make me an offer to return, one professor, himself a fine teacher, insisted on interviewing me privately; he had figured out, behind the pseudonym, that I was the villainous attacker on his department, and he wanted to know if I was as strongly against it as D. Phillips had seemed! I told him, "It depends on whether the department now offers any help or advice about teaching." He said something like "No, except for setting a model," and for reasons I'll never figure out, he dropped his opposition.

I often tell this story when people are ignoring the neglect of teaching, in the name of higher-falutin lit crit.

—*Wayne Booth*

2 2

My first full-time job was a soft money, three-year appointment as a basic writing teacher at an open admissions university in the midwest. For the first two years, I taught four sections of basic writing per semester, working harder than I had ever worked in my life. During the summers, I served as director of the writing center; then, in my third year, when the long-time director retired, I became the new director. Near the end of my third year, the chair of the department told me he had managed to have my staff designation changed from academic to administrative so that they could keep me permanently on a year-to-year, contract basis, teaching three sections of basic writing each term with released time from one section to direct the center. At the next department meeting, the chair announced to my colleagues my change in status, saying how pleased everyone was to have found a way to keep me because I was such a fine teacher of BW, worked with "remedial" students so well, etc. Then in the next breath he said, "But, of course, we don't all have the personality of a Donna Dunbar-Odom; she can relate to them on their level." Everyone chuckled affectionately, and then moved on to the next item on the agenda. But I was left wondering why this good news had suddenly made me feel so bad. It took me a while to realize that I felt bad because, before I could even savor my compliments, they had been taken away—my ability to work so well with the students in my classes became a result of my personality, not of my intellectual and pedagogical skills.

When I first read your call for papers, I was stumped; my story-well seemed dry. Then, in the course I teach for each year's new group of graduate assistants, I found myself telling a story and, as I was telling it, realizing that I'd told this story again and again—that, indeed, it had become one of "my" stories. I tell this story now in order to talk about how it is important to remember that teaching well is the result of hard work, reflection, and serious intellectual labor—not just a matter of being upbeat and perky.

—Donna Dunbar-Odom

2 3

This is a simplest of tales, and I bet it is not unique. I earned my Ph.D. in literature (18th-century). Two years on the job and my chair asked me to direct the writing program. The Americanist who was hired with me took me aside and asked, with a look of the utmost concern, if the move wouldn't hold back my advancement in the department, jeopardize my career. That was his word, "jeopardize." Three years later during a financial crunch, he did not make tenure. That was all some time ago. Last year I was promoted to full.

I tell this to comp/rhet students when they have been snubbed by lit students, but on the promise that they won't pass it on. I've never told it to any of my literature colleagues.

—Author's name withheld

2 4

It was yet another small room at 4Cs, and yet another set of remarkable papers (one paper presaged a well-received first book growing out of the same research). The chair of the panel was a Big Name in the field, and most of those in the audience at the lightly attended session were also Big Names. None of the presenters was yet a Big Name, though all have the ability to be and one already is certainly a growing name. The papers raised many interesting questions, but the discussion afterward had turned, for nearly half the time, to banter among the Big Names on some point that one of the papers had only tangentially raised but that was currently a hot Big Name kind of topic. Finally getting called myself, I could not resist spending the first fifteen seconds of my question with a satirical barb at the nature of the preceding discussion. The chair, in high dudgeon, implied that I was at fault for not honoring the authors (two of whom were pretty good friends of mine) and spent a good minute chastising me for not getting right to the subject of the papers themselves—which I then did, the first to do so, as soon as he quit his harangue. Of course, shortly after, the discussion got back comfortably away from the papers once the Big Names were back in control. The moral: beware of Big Names gathering in small rooms.

I tell this tale when people are bantering about how to decide whether to go into a session or not when there seem to be several good choices, in part to problematize the "boutique" agenda of avoiding the big splashy sessions for the more quiet and out of the way ones.

—Author's name withheld

2 5

This is almost a mythic comp tale, drawn from several examples at once and none in particular. But did you ever notice that, at sessions at major conferences involving major figures, when a major figure in the audience addresses a major figure of equally exalted stature on the platform, the one in the audience often stands—especially if their reputations have been made on the issue under discussion? It's as if to signal that there is a battle going on in the heavens over the heads of us mere mortals.

Whenever I tell this one at a conference, someone always comes back, incredulously, to report that they have just seen confirmation of my thesis, even if they had never really noticed it before. Of course, if you publish this then perhaps nobody will do it any more, which would spoil all the fun.

—Keith Rhodes

2 6

I was in my first year of graduate school working on my Ph.D. in rhetoric and composition. I was also attending my *first* 4Cs conference—"Baby's first C's," my friends chanted. My mentor at my university encouraged me to network and meet people, and that's exactly what I intended to do. I come from a doctoral program that firmly believes in professional service; in fact, my being at the conference giving a paper as a first-year grad student is indicative of my mentor's wise advice. So, I hurried from session to session, meeting and listening to scholars; I chatted with folks in the bars, the elevators, and the lobby; and I was given a warm reception at the book exhibit. If you weren't there, just imagine thousands of colleagues with silly nametags worn proudly around our necks filling that plush Palmer House hotel. And Chicago blues was just moments away! So this, I thought, is what professionalism is all about.

It was Friday night, and the Allyn-Bacon Rock 'n Roll party was cooking in the posh Red Room. Eventually, I escaped to the vast elevator area to smoke a cigarette. And while there, a gentleman approached me to bum a smoke. We struck up a conversation, and finally I said, "Who are you? Your nametag is twisted backwards." Immediately upon his turning his tag around, I recognized his name—he's the editor of a journal in our field! Well, that deadly cigarette has added a new dimension to my professional life, for I am now a regular reviewer for that journal!

I love to share this story with other compositionists, for, too often, newcomers to the field find going to national conferences and meeting professionals an intimidating venture. This rather humorous story proves that compositionists are ordinary folk, and I find this fact most comforting.

—Judy Isaksen

2 7

"Ronald" was a teaching assistant in the philosophy department at a major research university in the Midwest, and he taught a course on contemporary ethics in the same classroom that I would use for my introductory composition course. During the break between his class and mine, we would often chat for a few minutes about our mutual interests in philosophy. Several weeks into the semester, I asked him if his students were "thinking philosophically" yet. To my surprise—and in a voice loud enough for my own students to hear—he replied matter-of-factly, "I'd just be happy if they thought at all." I uncomfortably smiled and then wished Ronald a good weekend.

Looking back on this incident, I wonder why I found it so surprising at the time. After all, I've encountered far too many instructors who—in private discussions—complain about their students' incompetence and indolence. And I've met instructors who not only laugh at the awkward expressions or naïve arguments of student papers but who also feel compelled to share their "jokes" with colleagues. Several times, these derogatory remarks took place in communal offices where the students of other instructors were present. I think what surprised me the most was Ronald's public display of arrogance and condescension. Perhaps he didn't intend for other students to hear what he said; perhaps he didn't even give a thought about who else might conceivably be listening—but that's precisely the point.

But what most disappoints me is my own reaction to his comment. By not challenging it, I tacitly sanctioned it; and even if Ronald's students would never hear what he said, my own students had. And they had also observed how I failed to react—just as I have repeatedly failed to act with conviction many other times, both before and after this event. It is understandable that colleagues may be frustrated with those students who are unwilling to work and bewildered by those students who do not appear prepared to handle college-level work; I have felt frustrated and bewildered, too. But I cannot sympathize with fellow instructors whose attitudes have hardened into cynicism and even hostility toward their students. What we say (or don't say) about our students says less about them than about us.

Until now, I have told this story only to a few colleagues and friends. It is my hope that, by writing about my experience and so publicly sharing it, I will find the strength of will to act not as I have but as I should. A shallow, private conviction is none at all.

—Kevin J. Porter

∽ ∽ ∽

NOTES

TALE 17 (p. 28). This story inspires me to look at a familiar scenario from the viewpoint of someone new to and on the periphery of the profession. I wonder how often I have participated in conversations where I and others have relied on jargon to describe students' use of jargon. I wonder too if, on those occasions when I try to be collegial by laughing with the newcomer rather than at her, I ought to be really laughing with her at myself, at the discrepancies between what I require of my students' writing and what I allow in my own language use. (MZL)

TALE 18 (p. 29). The institutional story, fostered by the colleague and by the department rule that a copy of the portfolio should go to the "Program," is that composition teachers are or should be alike. Neither Knutson nor her students, of course, believe that story. (RHH)

TALE 19 (p. 30). I was a fellow TA with Cunningham at the University of Missouri and remember these two observers well. Reid showed up in the back row on the second day of my teaching career, with a frown on her face. After class she told me that a student had misused *who/whom* as he was responding to one of my questions and that I should have corrected him, then and there, before the whole class. "He'd not forget." A month later, Horner (see Tales 105 and 121) shook hands with me at the door and asked if today was a good day for her to sit in my class. (This was more than a decade before she published *Historical Rhetoric: An Annotated Bibliography of Selected Sources in English*). Afterwards, she congratulated me and said I would turn out to be a fine teacher. Then she added, as if it were an afterthought, that I might think about not handing back a set of essays at the beginning of the hour. "Some students secretly studied your comments all class long." I've never corrected a student in class, and I always hand back papers at the end of the hour. So when I tell this story to my colleagues, is it an institutional or a counter-institutional performance? (RHH)

TALES 20-22 (pp. 30-31). Tales of colleague relations are good places for studying the competing notions of the identity of an English professional. Should we relate to TAs as students or colleagues? Should we be friends with our colleagues? Are teaching and teacher training important to professional development? What is involved in the teaching of writing: hard work, reflection, and serious intellectual labor or perky and upbeat personality? As my questions indicate, we tend to approach these issues through either/or questions, which lead us to reduce the complexity of the issues at hand. Rather, if we pose the question differently—i.e., "to what extent should we (should we not) be friends with students or colleagues, when, where, and why?"—colleagues with different ideas of the profession might begin to relate to one another differently. (MZL)

Tale 20 (p. 30). In remarkably few sentences, this tale warns the new colleague how complicated an English department is. The narrative is like a children's puzzle: how many hierarchies can you find in this tree? Student and professor, WPA and TA, friend and foe, superior and subordinate, senior and junior faculty. And the next tales depict more. (RHH)

Tale 22 (p. 31). As many other tales in this collection, this narrative follows the stages of telling that can be inferred from Patricia Stock's unique account of the genesis of a comp tale. A moment happens that we are "eager to relive," we "shape the moment for an audience of colleagues who hadn't been there," and eventually we "translate the anecdote into . . . a significant occurrence within one of the larger narratives that define our teaching practice," (1993, pp. 173, 174, 185). A "larger narrative" I see in this tale is the ongoing professional battle to get outsiders to recognize that "soft money" appointments still require "hard work." (RHH)

Tale 24 (p. 33). Interestingly, the divisive nature of scholarly fame did not appear often in our submissions to *Comp Tales*, and then mainly in stories set in that parallel world to the academic department, the professional conference (but see Chapter 9). This tale sets up a question—are the tales institutional or counter-institutional?—but then suggests that the question probably assumes a false dichotomy. As Rhodes implies, the very telling of a conflicted scene may be an act tending to resolve it. All personal narratives, argues Richard L. Ochberg, contain two versions: a preferred reading and a suspicion of the preferred reading: "One version tries to overcome the voice of a suppressed alternative" (1994, p. 140). (RHH)

Tale 25 (p. 33). I am struck by the serious conviction embedded in the playful tone of the concluding sentence: Once someone has heard or

read this mythic comp tale, they might never again look at the same conference scene nor participate in it in the same manner. (MZL)

Tales 25-27 (pp. 33-35). Any story tends to highlight the villain, of
course, and voices of mentor, collaborator, or secret donor tend to be
muted. Marginal in the comp tales of this chapter—indeed throughout
the book and especially in Chapter 9—are non-hierarchical colleague
relationships: friend, fellow novice, confidant, spouse, companion-in-
arms, office-mate. But they are always implicit in the *listeners* to the tale,
who gather around with the teller and, as the group of nurses in the epi-
graph to this chapter, peer into the drawer of this ever strange comp life
at night with a flashlight. Further, not all comp tales tell of institutional
barriers enforced. Some recount barriers between colleagues crossed,
as in Tale 26. But note how this tale of team spirit also transmits the
voice that says such collegiality is exceptional. (RHH)

Tale 27 (p. 35). The tale questions collegiality built on shared cynicism
and hostility towards students. The narrator concludes: what we say (or
don't say) about our students says less about them than about us. This
poses a strategy for reading other tales featuring students. I like the fact
that the narrator uses the event of composing this tale to turn the critical gaze on himself, to review what he has failed to do and what he
should have done. I'm intrigued by his belief that one of the potential
outcomes of publicly sharing this tale in print could be his finding the
strength of will to act out his convictions in ways he has hitherto failed
to do. (MZL)

CHAPTER 4

☞

Classrooms

I had a discussion with another tuner, who is a great guitar man. He said, "Why are we tuners?" I said, "Because we want to hear good sounds."

—Eugene Russell, piano tuner,
interviewed by Studs Terkel (1972, p. 318).

By "classroom" I mean all the apparatus that comes with the trade. A writing teacher has to do many different things right, they all interconnect, and the wires all travel through that actual classroom or writing center or computer lab or teacher office, that institutional space of four walls and (if we're lucky) a window or two. We have to enforce the attendance policy to get the students into a common room to clarify the assignment to individualize the topic to avoid the plagiarism to legitimize the first draft to rationalize the conference to deepen the thinking to raise the grade to fulfill the course requirements to justify the attendance policy. And this particular ring-around-the-policy is only a tenth of the total practice we think, on good days, that we have under control. There is commenting, tutoring, testing, grading, creating assignments, managing the computer and the library, conducting the course evaluation—a relentless tide whose tricky navigation the tales in this chapter amply show.

Often there is a Kafka-esque voice inside these tales of the classroom. It is as if the antagonist is rules-and-regulations itself, a multi-cloaked villain appearing in the guise of seating charts, attendance policies, grading standards, paper guidelines, usage rules, citation styles, commentary expectations, evaluation forms, curricular structures, mandated testing—a persistent and subtle villain who outmaneuvers the innocence of the learner and the experience of the teacher. But there are tales of victory as well, and out of the Laocoon entanglement with apparatus come moments of insight and learning, for students and teachers alike. (RHH)

☞ ☞ ☞

2 8

A student I once had wrote almost entirely in clichés. For two or three papers, I would write "cliché" each time I saw one, and they kept proliferating. I finally asked her if she couldn't reduce their numbers, but she gave me a puzzled look, and said, "I thought you kept marking them because you liked them."

I usually tell this story to TAs in an effort to illustrate that they cannot always be sure that what they're writing on students' papers will be taken in the way it is meant. A discussion with students is highly desirable to make sure.

—Leon Coburn

2 9

This is about a student who labored long and hard to improve his writing but who despite all his effort seemed determined to ignore my directions to straighten out his invariably faulty sequencing of verb tenses. Finally I got him in for a conference to discuss his writing. I pointed to the margins of his most recent essay and asked why he persisted in ignoring my advice. "I've tried and tried to relax," he exclaimed, "but it never seems to work!"

Of the morals to be drawn from this episode, the most obvious are that we should never assume our students share our vocabulary, and that it's important to hold conferences. A less obvious insight may be that other kinds of experience also determine how students understand writing. Perhaps my student had previously taken a personal writing class and was there urged to find his own voice, to write naturally in a relaxed way. In this context, he indeed would have known what "tense" meant. Students don't arrive in our classrooms unformed and uninformed: we need to discover their existing framework of knowledge, and perhaps we must do so before they can appreciate our own.

I almost always share this tale from my early years of teaching during the session on "responding to student essays" in Cornell's "Writing 700" training seminar for new instructors of writing.

—Katy Gottschalk

3 0

Here's an incident that I'm sure more than one technical writing teacher has experienced. After receiving the first set of papers in all manner of formats (folded, written on front and back, handwritten, etc.), I decided that I would be very specific in setting the requirements for the next paper. I guess my biggest peeve was receiving papers that were written on both front and back. So I carefully stated, "Be sure that you write on one side of the page only."

When the next assignment was handed in I discovered that four students had turned in papers in which each page had a vertical line drawn down the middle and they had typed on the right side of the vertical line. I asked why they had done that and they all responded that I had told them to write on one side of the page only. They went on to say that it made perfect sense to them because they assumed that I wanted to use the other side of the page for my comments.

I occasionally recount this incident to illustrate that readers and listeners create meaning, not writers and speakers. We in technical writing have collected many such examples of the slipperiness of our language and what happens when writers and speakers don't take into account that others might interpret what we say and write in ways different from what we mean. And their interpretations always make sense to them.

—Don Cunningham

3 1

Back in 1958, when I first taught at the University of Missouri, my students had a terrible time with pronoun references. Finally I got so mad I told them that in their next paper they had to state, in parentheses after each pronoun, the antecedent to the pronoun. One student put in parentheses, "(by 'they' I mean the dog)."

Told over the phone.

—Bernie Warren, remembered by Rich Haswell

3 2

About mid-semester in one class, finding myself frustrated with a batch of papers in which students seemed to jump from topic to topic as they moved from paragraph to paragraph, I made an impassioned plea for transitions. I returned the papers to be rewritten with the admonition that every paragraph in the body of a paper needed to look back to the previous writing and make a clear connection. The reader, I said, had to be guided through the paper, and moved from point to point. When the revisions were turned in at the next class, one student had rewritten his paper so that every paragraph after the first started with the following transition: "Moving right along to the next paragraph. . . ." This was not at all what I had in mind, although as he pointed out to me, I could not fault him for not following directions.

I tell the story to my tutors-in-training, to students in my course in teaching writing, and to my colleagues. My point is to remind them of the disjunction between what we say about writing and what students may hear and to urge them to avoid a "cookbook" approach to teaching writing. I also often tell these stories to students in my writing classes to convey the idea that they need to look for the spirit of what teachers say about writing, rather than trying to follow the letter of our "laws"; that they need to use common sense—and their own experience in reading—to put into practice what they hear us say; and that writing is an intellectual process, not a mechanical act.

—Linda S. Bergmann

3 3

On the first day of an introductory course in teaching composition for graduate assistants, as I went over the outline for our course, I explained the assignment sequence and called their attention to the way in which the assignments were designed to build on one another and gave several examples. Throughout the semester, as I returned each evaluated assignment and explained the next one, I discussed the ways in which the new project could build on work from the previous one. As the semester drew to a close and students began preparing their course outlines, I emphasized again the ways in which they could build on work they had done for previous assignments in their final project.

I assumed they got my point that the assignments built on each other—I had reiterated it often enough—too often, I thought. But on the last day of class, while we were munching cookies and discussing what they had learned and how I might change the course in the future, one of my best students mused, "I don't know if you intended it this way, Professor Rose, but it was interesting how, in a way, each of the assignments could kind of build on the preceding ones and they all turned out to be useful when I was putting together the final course project."

Now I tell this story to the teachers I am working with as an illustration that sometimes it is simply not possible to repeat to students too many times something that seems obvious to you as the teacher. Your course design may make perfect sense to you, but it won't necessarily be clear to students, especially if it is different from their previous experience. And sometimes, it won't make sense to students until they figure it out for themselves.

—Shirley K Rose

3 4

After striding briskly into the lab that mid-semester day, I directed the students to access Class Assignment on their computers, locate the guidelines for creating their research proposals, and begin working. After this announcement, I checked attendance and passed back papers, not paying too much attention to the students.

Once these tasks were completed, I began looking around the room to see if students were engaged in their writing task. The clacking of the keys had already indicated that most were busily typing away. However, when my eyes rested on Shelby, seated in the first seat of the first row— right under my nose—I was appalled to see tears trickling down her cheeks. I leaned over and asked if everything was okay, and she shook her head "no." I motioned to her to step out in the hallway, where I said, "What's the matter?" (After all, I had clearly *told* them what to do.)

Her voice trembling, she said, "Everyone else just jumped right in and started typing, but I have no idea what you want!"

I felt like the wind had been knocked out of me. Shelby was a produce manager at Kroger who had returned to school to earn a business degree. If she was having trouble, chances were good others were as well. Why had I assumed my directions would be enough to get them started? Why hadn't I put a sample proposal on the projection screen and gone over it? Why hadn't we looked at some good proposals and some not-so-good proposals? Why didn't I TEACH them how to do a proposal?

I felt bad about Shelby, and ever since I have focused on showing, not telling, on teaching, not directing.

I share this story with other instructors in the writing program, especially new instructors, to show them that even as a veteran instructor—maybe especially as a veteran instructor—I have to engage continually in practice and stay "in touch" with my students by determining their learning styles and creating a supportive classroom environment.

—Julie Freeman

3 5

We were in the early stages of the research paper in my freshman comp class. All semester long, I'd been emphasizing the importance of an arguable thesis, and the necessity of presenting and refuting opposing views. Nick, an attentive student, had internalized this lesson well. When it came time for the research paper proposal, he wrote: "My research topic is high school education. I will be reading articles, magazines, and journals, and interviewing a high school teacher. My audience is this class. In my research paper, I will be analyzing the pros and cons of high school literacy, to see whether it is a good idea or not." My mind boggled; so did those of my colleagues.

I tell this story to students in my comp classes before they write their own research paper proposals in order to encourage them to think more deeply about what makes a good debatable thesis.

—Theresa Conefrey

3 6

ESL students often focus on technical revision because it's easy to spot, easy to fix, and, most likely, how they first learned English. As a teacher, I've worked to help ESL students understand the importance of conceptual revision before technical. As a new faculty tutor in the university writing center, I was delighted to find the tutoring protocol supportive of my approach, and I found it fairly easy to slip this concept into my tutorials. That is, until a late afternoon tutorial with a first-time composition client from Africa.

Although it was semester's end, I was amazed at the student's writing: obviously "borrowed" passages, incomplete thoughts, disorganized support for an unclear thesis. We began exploring his understanding of conceptual concerns—surely his instructor was praying for more than this!—and I was greatly encouraged when he paused for a moment and said, "Okay, I have a question." Beaming like only an instructor can when she believes she's helped a student to see the light, I said, "Great. What is it?" He replied, "So, do I need a hyphen in cooperation?"

I tell this story to remind myself, and to share with people new to ESL, that for some ESL students, grammar focus is so ingrained that the road to conceptual concerns is long and hard (maybe even permanently closed). But perhaps more importantly, I tell it as a reminder of the importance of remembering to meet the student where he's at.

—Susan Mayberry

3 7

Ten years later, I still recall the incident with remorse.

A young man who was both a star basketball player and a student in my basic composition class came to my office to discuss a paper he had written about the recent death of his brother. Though heartfelt, it was a poor piece of writing. I had given him a D.

As we talked about the paper and its shortcomings, he became more and more agitated. Finally, he jumped to his feet and, towering over me and waving his arms frantically as though guarding an opponent on the court, he yelled, "You gave a D to my feelings!" His shout reverberated through the busy office.

I don't remember what either of us said subsequently, just that my colleagues praised me later for restoring calm. But I made a vow that day: I would never again put a D or an F on a paper. Now, if a paper is not yet C level, I simply put no grade on it and tell the writer that the paper is unfinished. Here's the kind of work remaining to do.

I instituted the change immediately and explained to the class, without giving names or identities, why I was doing so.

I've been pleased with this decision because it reflects my true attitude toward writing and toward students. Most of the writing I see in class or in the writing center is not so much "bad" as "raw." Many students have not yet realized that good writing requires time, care, and reflection. That's what they need to learn from us.

The semester ended well for this student and me. I still have his end-of-semester evaluation of himself as a writer, and it speaks positively of what he learned in my class about the need for revision in writing. So, another lesson: don't escalate conflict with students. Speak softly. Hear what they have to say, and they may hear you.

When I share this story in staff meetings of writing tutors and of composition instructors, I make a point that has been crucial to my own professional life: nothing we teach students is more significant than modeling the problem-solving approach of reflecting on our experience and making appropriate changes based on those reflections. We expect it of them. We must be willing to do it for them.

—Mary Mortimore Dossin

3 8

Though my teaching load at a large public university in the Midwest included both writing lab and classroom teaching, I spent most of my time in the writing lab and frequently taught the same students over successive semesters, working individually with them on papers for other classes—lit, history, the composition course—as well as on papers for the lab credit course itself. Thus I came to know both the students and their writing quite well. Many of these students had unusually low ACT scores and were generally underprepared for college. I found myself spending time explaining to them what a syllabus was and helping them "read" it. The book store, the library, the final exam schedule were all equally mysterious and, like most teachers in the lab, I conducted *de facto* "college orientation" courses—individualized instruction—in addition to work with their writing.

One semester when I saw my class list for the beginning first-year composition course, I saw several familiar names, students I had worked with individually over a two-semester period the previous year. I was pleased because I knew exactly where I could begin with them in their writing and felt sure I would be able to insure their continuing attendance in the lab. Because students just sign up for a class and a time-slot in pre-registration, I was aware that the students hadn't known I was the teacher for that course, and therefore had not chosen me in particular.

Even so, I assumed they would be reasonably pleased to see I was the teacher, since I considered I had had good relationships with them. On the first day of class, as the students came in, each of my familiar students did a shocked double-take. I was amused, thinking that their dismay—feigned or real—probably had to do with the fact that they thought I would make them work hard. After class, the student I knew the best and had worked with the longest came up to me and told me, hesitantly, eyes downcast, that he wanted to drop my course. I felt astounded. "Why?" I asked.

"Because," he said, "if you are the *teacher* of this course, who will help me?"

I told this story at first—mostly to people who knew both me and the student and how the writing lab worked—to illustrate how dismal must be the state of our teaching where students see classroom teachers as adversaries— out to expose student weakness—and how clearly the student in question had accepted me as "helpful" only because he knew me as a lab teacher. It was, I thought, both a poignant comment and a disguised plea for the help he and I both knew he needed. Of course, I assured him that nothing essential would change, and that I would teach the class much as I had taught in the lab. He was—at least for awhile—unconvinced.

Later, I read both his response to me and mine to him quite different-ly. He was neither ignorant nor naïve about teaching, nor was he neces-sarily being cynical. His response reflected, I think, his conviction based on experience that the classroom demanded a kind of impersonal demeanor from me and less involvement from him. His sense of social distance depended on his knowledge of "roles" rather than of individual people. In my ready assurance to him that "nothing would change" I was not only ignoring deeply ingrained cultural expectations in reference to teaching— and the opportunity to examine such expectations and their implications— but was "essentializing" my concept of my own teaching, imagining indeed that it was always and everywhere "the same." He was perhaps more instinctively aware than I that the complicated student-teacher relation-ship we had negotiated over the previous semesters had now to be renego-tiated—and at a cost.

—Elizabeth Robertson

3 9

A colleague of mine once told me that her precocious five-year-old was diagnosed as not ready to move on to the next stage of learning because, when told to "outline a square" with a crayon, he asked if one could "inline" a square, and if so, how.

I tell this story often because it illustrates the child's ability to question the obvious, to imagine alternative ways of viewing and representing an object. And it illustrates the tester's inability to hear the student. Instead of sensing the child's boredom with repeating a familiar classroom activity, the tester mistook his question as proof of his (in)ability to comprehend and execute a command. On certain occasions, I also speculate whether the tester might have been more ready to "recognize" his verbal and intellectual playfulness had the child looked white and been known as the son of an English professor.

I often tell this story to my first-year composition students, using it as a prompt to ask them to consider the use and abuse of conventional activities, such as underlining and highlighting a text when reading. We'd begin by comparing with one another the sentences in a particular passage a majority of the class has highlighted, and discuss how and why we underlined it. Then we'd practice what I have termed "reverse highlighting." That is, we examine the parts—phrases, words, or sentences—we have not underlined, and how and why we tend to overlook such parts. We ask what particularly about our personal, social, and educational histories may have led us to gloss over such parts (and to highlight certain other parts). We would thus use reverse highlighting to contest the ways in which our socially constructed values and assumptions constrain how we highlight (or gloss over) a text when making sense of it.

—Min-Zhan Lu

4 0

This story has its origins in the five years (1985–90) that I directed the Writing Center at Oregon State University. It was told to me by an experienced writing assistant who was troubled by both its facts and by the implications behind them.

The story involves one particular student, an older student (i.e., not 21 or 22 but perhaps someone in her 30s), a non-native speaker who wanted to work in English as a Second Language instructor. She was both timid and determined. She had failed the essay-writing section of the teacher certification test (C-BEST) at least five times. This writing assistant began to work with her as intensively as she would allow. He showed her how to think of an essay as a structure of ideas supported by explanations. She drilled using various sentence-level exercises in the effort to increase her mastery of punctuation and grammar.

In the process, she wrote a number of sample essays responding to C-BEST-like questions such as: "Recall a significant teacher in your own past and explain why this teacher's impact remains important to you" or "Write about a learning situation that was difficult for you. Explain the situation and show how you managed to succeed despite the difficulties." The writing assistant saw these practice essays. They were often unfinished, often very short, and often filled with what seemed like mere generalities. The two of them would discuss the need for detail, and they would work yet again on quirks of verb tense and preposition usage. The student writer professed to understand the need for details, the need to avoid overly-broad generalizations. And her grammatical skills, never seriously deficient, steadily improved.

Over the course of at least six months, this Vietnamese woman became a regular in the writing center. She adopted an English nick-name, and her diligence and friendliness made us all want to help her succeed. Yet she failed the writing portion twice more. But at last, she did pass. She came into the Writing Center a last time to tell the writing assistant who had worked so often with her. They sat down as usual, she told him she had finally passed the writing portion, he congratulated her and asked her what she thought had finally made the difference. She replied that she had finally decided to pretend she was a 19-year-old American girl with a Vietnamese name. She invented a past for herself—an American past—and wrote a fictional answer to the essay questions. She said she tried to imagine herself in some tele-vised version of the past (based on cable TV reruns). Her fictional answers were good enough to yield passing marks.

This disturbed the writing assistant, who relayed the story to me as writing center coordinator.

I tell this story to new writing assistants (I'm still a writing center director, now at Linfield College). I ask them to speculate as to why a Vietnamese woman in her thirties might have needed to do this in 1988. I'd like them to remember the story for the same reasons that I do: because it suggests to me the routine privilege of many, many American lives, because it calls into significant question the effort to use two thirty-minute essays as genuine indica-

tors, and because it emphasizes the fact that behind any prose (or poetry, for that matter) written by an individual there resides just that—a human individual working to make sense of what may well be a difficult subject.

—Lex Runciman

4 1

The first time I taught honors composition was not a good experience. I had gone in expecting accomplished and enthusiastic writers and found half the class were engineering hopefuls who saw the course as a hurdle, their instructor as a sappy female, and their writing as much better than the C it would have earned in my regular first-year course.

They were, however, very accomplished at pressuring me into giving them B's and A's at the end of the semester. And I suspected that they also had done a fine job of damning me with faint praise in their course evaluations. But all this doesn't excuse what I then did.

I took the students' final exams, an in-class essay, and used the handwriting to try to identify the authors of the evaluations.

I still cringe when I think about it, and that is every time I have administered course evaluations since.

It was harder than I had thought. Some students had block printed their evaluations, and the handwriting of others changed radically depending on whether they were writing fast or slow. But I had managed to match about two-thirds of the class when I quit in a spasm of self-revulsion.

Not, however, before I had made a discovery that amazed me. From what I knew about students, there was no way to predict the evaluation! Some of the students I thought hated me and the course gave us the highest praise. A student who knew he was going to get a C and who had left my office in a fury when I let him know it wrote that he had learned more in my course than in all the other courses he had taken that semester. A woman who had sat all semester in class with a frown on her face said I had inspired her to change her major to English.

The severest evaluation, a real hatchet job, was written by a student who—I realized—had been the teacher's pet and had asked for my teaching schedule next semester in order to take another course from me "right away."

For a while I associated course evaluations with human hypocrisy (including my own). Now I think my discovery justifies course evaluations. Maybe they really are the only way that some students can say what they truly think.

I have never told anyone, not even my husband. But I wonder how common a practice it is.

—Author's name withheld

4 2

I was a graduate teaching assistant, teaching two courses, writing my master's thesis, and working a part-time job at night because I couldn't make ends meet on the subsistence pay of the university. I had fallen behind on responding to student papers, had two stacks on my desk and two more coming in. I realized that there was no way I could "do it all." So I took the two stacks on my desk and returned them, unread, to my students with this commentary: "I've read your papers and have decided to return them to you without comments or grades. I was very disappointed. This is your worst effort this semester, and I don't think you would really want to see what I would say about them. So I'm going to give you another chance to revise them. This time, you'd better take them seriously. If you really don't know what you can do to improve them, then come see me." I said this sternly, and then dismissed the two classes. No one had said a word. No one came to see me for help. I despised myself for lying, and I decided that I would quit after that semester, as I had no business being a teacher. But here's the strange part. When the papers came back, they were the best I'd received that semester. It taught me a little something about asking my students to make better use of their own resources and made me wonder how much as teachers we do and say that our students already know. But the happy ending has never freed me from that dishonest moment, nor from questioning the exchange that occurs between teachers, students, and the act of responding to student writing.

—Author's name withheld

4 3

Working the morning shift in the writing center, I looked up as a thirty-something woman moved tentatively through the entrance.

Recently divorced—a white, untanned stripe circled her wedding finger—she wore inexpensive, out-of-date, clothing, and straggly, half-bleached hair, overdue for a touch-up. Without a book bag, she clutched two notebooks and three texts before her, apparently shielding all her vital organs from our attack.

Joni—a thirty-something, junior, special-ed major in her third semester tutoring—rose to greet the timid writer. I looked at Joni's close-cropped hair, T-shirt and Wranglers, remembering that I had first met Joni when she walked, timid and oddly dressed, into my comp class two years before.

Joni took the woman's elbow and guided her toward the couch. "Hi, I'm Joni," she said and, barely pausing, added, "and I used to be as scared as you look. What can I do to help?" The woman looked a little more at ease. "Hi," she responded. "I look this way because I just came from Dr. Jones' office. I have him for history, and I have to write a combination book review and biography. I went to ask him what to do, and he totally overwhelmed me with his explanation. I'm so frustrated I'm about to quit, but I thought I'd come see if you can help?" It was clear to me that this woman's future hung on Joni's response, and I pushed my chair back a little nervously. An experienced and polished tutor, Joni still might lack the skill to pull this one off, I worried. I was ready to step in if anything went wrong.

"Well," Joni drawled before stopping. I watched her closely, trying to decide if she was thinking or panicking. "I've never written a biography book review, but three years ago I'd never written anything and I'm still here," Joni finally continued and I relaxed. "Let me look around. I think we may have an example from Dr. Jones, and some of these books will probably help, and the boss"—she motioned over her shoulder with her thumb—"probably has a handout in the file drawer. I'm sure we can figure this out. But it may be like the blind leading the blind."

"Oh, Joni," the woman said, "Dr. Jones could see everything and he couldn't help me a bit. Maybe a blind woman's just what I need."

I tell this story to tutors in a writing center training course, hoping to illustrate two points to them: first, that no matter how little they think they know, it usually is enough to help a struggling writer; and second, that instead of another teacher many writing center clients need a friend, a helper. Sometimes, only another "blind" person can help you learn to see.
—Kevin M. Davis

4 4

One of my favorite teaching moments came while I was teaching College Writing 113 at the University of Massachusetts, Amherst. The course met in a networked-computer classroom, and all papers, drafts, brainstorms, class Interchange (online discussion software) transcripts were saved on the server. This allowed students who missed a class to come in and catch up in virtual space and time; when no classes were in sessions, students who took classes in that room could come in and work on their own.

While we were doing the research paper assignment, discussion drifted into why citation guidelines were so particular, and why it mattered to get citations correct. To help students see the matter from the point of view of authors who get cited and who cite colleagues, I held an Interchange discussion on a set of letters that offered diametrically opposed accounts of how Ezra Pound was treated while in a military stockade in Italy. Both writers claimed to be there at the time and to have been in charge of overseeing Pound as part of their duties.

The discussion was long and intense. The assignment after it was for students to write an essay that explored the different accounts (thereby needing to cite the letters), but also to make sure they referenced something—anything—from the class discussion transcript. As part of the assignment, we looked at the elements that go into a citation: author, date, title, etc., and told students they had to come up with some way of citing the Interchange so that a person who was not in our class would be able to find it.

So it went, class ended, and I left to go to the library. About six hours later, I swung into the lab (it was close to 10 p.m.), to pick up some files to take home. I looked in and saw twelve of the fourteen members of my class in the lab. One of the students was writing on the melanin board, while two others offered comments, others were clustered in groups around terminals. I went in to see what was up. The writer on the board was drafting ideas for the citation and the kids at the terminal were testing it out to see if the information made sense.

They hadn't planned to be together, but they had all ended up in the lab that night, had logged into the class documents, and had come together and conducted, on their own, without a teacher, an impromptu class. Serendipitous collaboration. I bought them all pizza for the next class.

I tell the story when I do workshops on networked pedagogy, workshops or teaching on research requirements, and when people who aren't teachers ask me what I do.

—Nick Carbone

4 5

While teaching freshman comp several years ago, I had a student who had one of the worst cases of "academic garble" I had ever seen. Tom was a lanky farm kid who smiled a lot and spoke up clearly in class discussion, but when it came to writing, his sentences were painfully unclear, twisted wrecks of prepositional phrases and nominalizations. During a quick after-class conference, I taught him a scaled-down version of Richard Lanham's "Paramedic Method" for reviving sick sentences: circle the prepositions and the forms of "to be" verbs; if you find two or more prepositional phrases in a row and lots of weak "is" forms, sound the sentence alarms and rewrite. Most of us learned to identify prepositions in second grade: teachers had different tricks for helping students to find them. My second grade teacher, Mrs. Wagoner, taught me that a preposition was "anything you can do to a cloud" (you can fly over, under, to, from . . .). So I taught Tom this cloud-preposition trick and sent him off to try revising some of his garbled, unclear prose. The next week he came into class beaming, waved his paper in the air and announced, "No more clouds!" And it was truly amazing: there were no more clouds; his prose was remarkably clearer. Every time I ran into Tom during the next year, he would give me a thumbs up sign and say, "No more clouds." Still makes me smile.

I tell this story to other teachers who complain about the pseudo-academic mumbo jumbo they find in some student papers—I remember sharing it with a group of new TAs recently who were sharing drafts of troublesome student essays in a seminar.

—Jennie Nelson

4 6

When I served as director of composition at a large university a few years ago, a teaching assistant's middle-aged mother died suddenly. After providing her grading norms and conferring with me, two assistant directors, and two substitute teachers, the teaching assistant flew away, never to return. Each substitute agreed to instruct one class. Because the substitutes had to continue filling in for sick teachers—their regular job—I requested extra money from the dean to hire substitute paper graders.

When the students received their first set of graded papers, they exploded, complaining vociferously to the substitutes, the graders, and our assistant directors. Two students were angry at the mother of their teacher, who had the temerity to die at such an inauspicious moment in their lives. Several were outraged that the teacher had deserted them so heartlessly. Most students were simply mad about their grades. While the graders were very carefully following the norms that the teacher had explained to us, we soon realized she had been grading far more leniently than other teachers and far more leniently than she had indicated to us. Many of her grades were outright gifts.

But what grades did the students deserve? If the graders marked papers as generously as the teacher had, then we would be inflating grades just as much as she had. That would not be fair to students in other classes, whose work was being judged more rigorously. But, as the students complained, if we graded with more toughness than the teacher, we were holding them to a different standard than their teacher had presented. What should we do? There seemed to be no good answer. We decided to continue grading according to the norms that the teacher had supplied us.

But we had an enormous problem. We were running the classes by committee, and the students were so hostile that both sections seemed on the verge of cratering. I ventured to each class to discuss the entire situation, explaining that, yes, we were sorry their teacher had to leave. After informing students that we were grading as the teacher had instructed us, I handed each of them a copy of the norms that the teacher had supplied us. Fortunately, the anger subsided somewhat.

When the graders were tabulating final grades for the term, they consulted with the assistant directors and me. For each student, we followed our standard grading formula when averaging the grades of the original teacher with the marks given by the grader. Then we deliberated over students whose grades teetered on the borderline. Unsure of what to do, we bumped up those students' grades. On a Saturday I called the teacher, talking to her about each student's final grade. She agreed with the grades.

One day a young man came in, bringing along a small, well-behaved dog whose breed I did not recognize. Never having seen a dog in our building before and happy to recognize a friendly pet, I welcomed the student and his dog into my office. He had been in one of our committee-run classes. As he told stories about his low-income urban neighborhood, he impressed me as tough and streetwise. After pouring out his grade complaint, he casually informed me that his pet was a pit bulldog. Suddenly the friendly animal did not seem so soothing. I promised to read his papers carefully myself and invented an excuse for not reading them on the spot. Smiling, I escorted him and the pit bull out of the office, then muttered to myself that I had been stupid to allow the dog into the office. Then I decided that I was not being paid enough to do my job.

Now, several years afterward, I tell this story to anyone interested in writing program administration. The tale explains my subsequent gratitude any time all our teachers would finish the semester. The tale also illustrates the problems that a director of composition faces and calls into question the fairness, value, and existence of grades.

—Author's name withheld

▱ ▱ ▱

NOTES

TALES 28-36 (pp 40-44). Stories of misunderstanding between teacher and student are fairly popular. Communicating in the classroom is harder than it seems—not a fact that ought to surprise teachers of written communication. Surprise always makes a good tale, of course. These stories may be construed as demeaning the student, but that is not how I read them, nor is it how these teacher-narrators read them, judging from their commentary. The tales resonate from a faultline in the natural geography of student and teacher, the unavoidable disparity between age, knowledge, and interest. When two parties don't "share a vocabulary," as Katy Gottschalk notes (Tale 29), both have to work to solve the problem. (RHH)

TALES 36 (p. 44) AND 40 (p. 48). If we tell Tale 36 back to back with Tale 40, we hear a hidden script in the ESL student's concern over "technical" revision. That is, it is probably his sense of the credible options he faces—his knowledge of the predispositions of the "audience" grading his paper—rather than his passivity as a learner which has led him to remind the tutor that for him to pass in the face of such an "audience," what he most urgently needs to worry about is, indeed, "technical" revision. (See "Tracking Comp Tales," p. 213.) (MZL)

TALE 38 (p. 46). The narrator changes her view concerning the narrated event as she tells and retells it through the years. This indicates that the life of a story depends as much on what happened during the narrated event as on what the teller makes of that event as her understanding of the field and of her work evolves. In this case, the narrator turns the critical gaze inward, to the different relations she negotiates with students when teaching a course in writing and when tutoring in the lab, and she turns the gaze beyond the personal (helpful/indifferent teachers) to the ways in which diverse institutional settings constrain and enable different kinds of student-teacher relationships. (MZL)

TALE 40 (p. 48) . This tale generates some long thoughts about what writing assessment does to non-native writers. On the one hand we decry social forces that work to de-story people—educational curriculums designed to squelch the natural impulse of the young to invent and tell tales (Bamberg & Damrad-Frye, 1991), or in the nightmarish extreme, POW camps designed to deprive political prisoners of stories by which they can make sense of their imprisonment, so that even if they survive, their sense of identity does not (Amos Funkenstein, 1993). But on the other hand we have to allow individuals the right to refuse to story their lives. If stories are social constructs to some degree, to be storied is to be partly locked into a prefigured meaning. In an unforgettable moment at the end of her autobiography, sociologist Carolyn Kay Steedman thinks about her anomalous life and hopes that it will never be turned and thereby falsified into a sociological tale (1994). To what extent did the C-BEST exam put the woman from Vietnam, if she wanted to pass, into an impossible dilemma, forcing her either to tell her own story, that she may not have wanted to tell, or to tell a story which was not hers? (RHH)

TALE 41 (p. 50). See "Tracking Comp Tales," p. 201. (MZL)

TALES 41 (p. 50) AND 42 (p. 51). A pair of unspeakables (see note to Tale 2) about methods of student response to teacher and teacher response to student. In the public world of comp, more unorthodox stories can hardly be imagined. There the orthodoxy, of course, is honest and open dialogue between students and teachers in course evaluation and paper commentary, not the deception and silence recounted by these two tales. So should the tales, with their questioning of the conventional, be made more public? Should they be retold to students? (RHH)

TALE 42 (p. 51). One of the few stories in this collection pointing to the incredible amount of work we put into reading and commenting on student writing. It is ironic but not surprising that we lack the discourse to detail this part of our labor except through a confession of "guilt"—of being short of what we are supposed to do and be. This lack is most probably related to the institution's lack of interest in having us talk about the discrepancy between what we are contracted to do and how that labor is compensated. The narrator's speculation that we spend more time saying what students already know also suggests the usefulness of "sideshadowing" (Welch, 1998, p., 374): having students rather than teachers begin the commenting process. (MZL)

TALE 43 (p. 51). This tale whets my curiosity about what "the woman" might look like upon graduation. The metamorphosis of the writing center tutor, Joni, in not only her confidence as a writer and a student but also, her hairstyle and dress code, is something I have both experienced and witnessed in so many others surviving and thriving in the academy. I have often gossiped with trusted colleagues about changes in the physical aspects we notice in this or that writing student. I have yet to explicitly include this part of the work of composition into any of my teaching narratives, especially those intended for tenure and promotion reviews. (MZL)

TALE 44 (p. 53). This tale touches on several issues often overlooked in narratives of our work. First, it asks us to view what happens in the classroom in terms of what takes place outside of it, in terms of the work individual teachers devote to selecting course materials and composing writing assignments. And it reminds us that this type of discursive work is as important as the work we accomplish through face-to-face encounters with students. Done right, it can significantly impact the motivation and performance of writing students. Stories of this type of work are fewer probably because they are less dramatic and thus, more difficult to tell. Secondly, the story challenges a false dichotomy between the "mechanical" (citation guidelines) and "conceptual" (diverse interpretations and presentations of the cited text) aspects of writing, one which continues to dominate many of our stories concerning the work of teaching writing. Thirdly, it offers an account of students and teachers working to break down the divisions between two media, print and computer interchange. (MZL)

TALE 46 (p. 54). In the final tale of this chapter, the authority figure barely escapes alive in a battle with apparatus. Rules-and-regulations keeps coming back. Its conflict with spontaneity, creativity, and other joys of the craft betrays one of the major contradictions of the profession. One of the subplots in career tales (e.g., Tales 115 and 117) is a Wordsworthian closing in of the "shades of the prison-house" that comes with repeated practice, administrative duties, and maybe just age. The other half of the picture, how teachers maintain their enthusiasm over years of practicing comp, is little narratized. Is that story too dull, or too improbable? (RHH)

CHAPTER 5

〜

The Writing

The first English course I had ever taken at the university had turned me away from any thought of a formal career in that subject. The teacher had read my first assignment and told me bluntly, "You didn't compose this; it is too well written." Good or bad, it happened to be my own.
—Loren Eiseley (1975, p. 80)

It is odd that from a profession that has approved process over product came so few comp tales about the act of writing. Is the process of writing so internal that it does not lend itself to stories? The hours absorbing secondary sources, the moment when the right phrase comes to mind, the drafting and redrafting until an argument feels solid—how do you turn that into a catchy comp tale?

I would put a different construction upon it. There *are* tales in the writing process, especially now that we understand that process to be deeply social and cultural. But so far the profession has tended to process process through the largely non-narrative mode of the scholarly paper or the scholarly monograph, studies of writer's block, for instance, or of composing at computers. Maybe the subject is just too new for the oral anecdote. Without an intuitive, shared, and historicized understanding of a phenomenon, the vernacular tale hesitates to deal with it. Sociolinguists Aylin Küntay and Susan Ervin-Trip once documented this. Their students had the presence of mind to record remarks of Californians just after the 1989 Loma Prieta earthquake, as they were surveying the damage done in their houses. The discourse is pre-narrative—no protagonist, no conflict, no clauses of time, just a report of what they found. Two months later the same people offer up "full-fledged narrative structure" in talking about their experiences of the earthquake (1997, pp. 117–118).

Anthropologist Charles A. Briggs, who provides other examples (1997), generalizes that the more an event is temporalized, ordered in causal and other time sequences, the more it has been understood and coped with.

As a profession, we all know that writing is our area, whether the word refers to process or product, or as I prefer, act or consequence. The writing is our field of study. As a profession, however, don't we still understand and cope with the consequences of writing better than we do with the acts of writing? It would seem so, judging by the number of stories submitted to *Comp Tales*. At least, if we divide this chapter into two parts—first, stories about the consequences of writing (Tales 47–53), and second, stories about the acts of writing (54–58)—it is clear we have a scarcity of the second. This very division between writing as an act and writing as a consequence reflects one of the profession's current crises—"crises of character," as Gerend-Meinking puts it (Tale 57)—in the sense that as teachers we feel a compulsion to commit ourselves to one side or the other, and as teachers we cannot completely do so. (RHH)

🖙 🖙 🖙

47

When I was a graduate student, I had the opportunity to work in the writing center of an urban university in the Midwest. The center director was asked to present information to the English department at its first fall meeting, and she asked me to come along to help.

As I distributed dittoed copies of information (remember the purple masters?), I saw thirty hands reach into thirty suit/sport coat pockets, remove thirty red pens, and begin circling typos.

This is a story I tell to my students and new faculty to emphasize the dangers of professional, habitual actions, and to point out that faculty members sometimes respond by rote instead of thought. And when they respond by rote, they are not responding to content but to surface error.

—*Jay Wootten*

48

My friend, who is originally from England, was sitting on a hiring committee. The candidate with the best qualifications, references, etc.

had made a so-called comma splice error in his letter of application. He also happened to come from England. My friend tried to explain that in England, the comma is accepted in places where in North America it is not. She could not persuade one of the committee members who felt that this comma splice error indicated complete unsuitability. The person was not hired.

This story was told by a colleague who teaches legal writing at the University of British Columbia, and I like to tell it to my classes and workshops when we discuss the so-called usage rules or conventions and their history. Come to think of it, I try to tell these stories to faculty members—if they appear to be open or if they are complaining about certain kinds of student writing.

—Mieke Koppen Tucker

4 9

When I was teaching composition and working in the Writing Lab at Cal State Fresno, I worked with a Vietnamese student whose writing just amazed me, it was so quiet and moving and lyrical. Binh had been a writer and storyteller back home in Vietnam and especially loved writing tales for children. I told him that his gift for writing shone through, despite the language barrier. It was gratifying to feel I could connect with Binh as a writer of stories, even though our work together usually focused on preparing him to write a passing essay for a basic competency test.

One week Binh wrote a story about a friend he had loved dearly who was killed trying to escape from Vietnam. For some reason, the families were not supposed to associate with one another, so the friends would meet in the forest to play together and tell stories and dream about going to America. I won't even try to do the story justice, but I remember being so moved that I got goosebumps, and I told him so. I even felt a little bit jealous at his storytelling skill.

Since I was editing the college literary magazine at the time, I told Binh I wanted to publish his story. His face flushed with pride. Then he asked me if I was going to be the one to edit the paper for publication.

"Oh, well, it's ready to be published just as it is," I told him.

Binh looked confused. He knew and I knew that it was full of "second-language errors." And he didn't want his name to represent an article containing such errors; he wanted his first publication in English to look like everybody else's English.

"But the story reads like poetry, Binh. Poetry often isn't standard English."

No, no, no. He want it be proper English, proper English.

That's when I clearly understood for the first time that how you say a thing is as important as what you're saying—that language is not just a container for the package, it *is* the package. What I loved most about the story was the telling, itself—the voice that spoke in "incorrect" but beautiful, powerful language. To standardize the English would greatly diminish its impact. But I couldn't find a way to convince Binh that the story worked best the way it was.

In the end I couldn't justify asking Binh to publish the piece in his "authentic" voice. In his view, publishing what he saw as his "bad" English made his achievement different, and lesser, than that of the other contributors. He didn't want to be a token voice, and I had to respect that. I can only hope he came to learn in some other time, in some other way, that he was a gifted user of the English language.

I've told the story several times. I never plan to tell it, and my stories usually arise sort of in the thick of other things going on—very spontaneously, you know. So it's hard to track the "why," exactly. But it seems to arise when I am talking about stylistic and sentence level concerns—and in two ways: 1) when I want students to know that "correctness" isn't everything, and that Standard English isn't necessarily proper for every occasion. I want them to be aware of the rhetorical demands of each writing situation and to know that they should command a repertoire of stylistic voices depending on the writing task; 2) when I want students to think about the integration of form and content—to see that how you say something is crucial to what you say. I want them to see language as concrete, manipulable, and not as transparent and neutral. 3) I also want them to see that I respected the student's intentions, even when I disagreed with him. It was his piece.

—Carol Roh-Spaulding

50

I was correcting the English in a report written by my roommate (who is Swiss-German and is here doing postgraduate work in educational psychology). She had written: "Mike prevented William from working by putting his hand over William's keyboard. Mike found this very sparingly and did it again and again."

I asked her, "What do you mean by 'sparingly'?" She replied that she had originally written "funny," but when she ran the report through the grammar-checker on her computer, it told her that "funny" was trite and suggested "sparingly" as a substitute. Baffled, I crossed out "sparingly" and wrote "amusing."

The next morning, it hit me: the grammar-checker must have said something like "The word 'funny' is trite. Use sparingly."

Posted in the writing program administrators listserv by a third party during a discussion of editing software.

—Mark Israel

5 1

Let's call the student Jane. Jane was one of my students several years ago, and she was a strong writer, a rather fussy person who tried hard to shape and edit her work. When she turned in a personal memoir essay, I expected a well-written piece. It was well-written with lots of description of some days of personal anxiety and uncertainty which left her feeling unsettled and supposedly "neurotic." However, throughout the essay, she used the word "necrotic." When I returned the essay and told her it had a major problem, she was genuinely surprised. She truly did not know the word "neurotic," thought she had spelled it correctly, and assumed that it was okay because spellcheck didn't spit it back to her.

I always tell my first-year writing students this story to emphasize that their own knowledge of words is important and they must proofread after they spellcheck. In this case, most students didn't know the word "necrotic"; some biology students did. I happen to be very familiar with the term because I teach at Omaha's Henry Doorly Zoo as a volunteer and necropsies on animals are part of zoo life. So, you can imagine that I was a little stunned when I first read this essay about my necrotic student.

—Maria Anderson Knudtson

5 2

I remember well the student who handed me a paper copied from a book I mentioned frequently in class, helpfully beginning with the page number 212 at the top of the first page. "I don't understand why you would plagiarize a book you know I know," I asked her later. She looked at 'her' paper, dumbfounded. "Goddamn him!" she said under her breath. "Goddamn who?" I asked. "The sonofabitch I paid for this paper, that's who!" she replied.

The best plagiarism stories have levels that go beyond witlessness or dishonesty into suggestions of causation, hinting at a society in which getting ahead is all that matters. When I was teaching first-year composition at an elite school with a strict honor code, I received a paper in March copied from an obscure essay by John Updike. I went back over the term's output of that student to discover that every paper that year had been plagiarized cleverly from similarly out of the way writings of the famous. Before turning the case over to the college's disciplinary committee, I asked the student why she had done this, when she knew how severe the punishment would be. "I had no choice," she replied. "Last year, as a high school senior, I won the American Legion National Americanism Award for my writing. So this year I have to give talks on Americanism to high schools all over the country. I just don't have time to write my own papers."

The coincidence award must go to one of my young colleagues in the political science department. When he was an undergraduate, a term paper he wrote was in a pile that the professor naïvely put outside his office door for the students to retrieve. The pile disappeared. A generation later, now a professor, my colleague discovered that long lost paper when one of his own students handed it in to him, copied off the Internet word for word, including misspellings, except, of course, for a new title page with the student's name on it.

I tell these tales when teachers gather over meals or drinks to talk about Moments They Remember from their classes. I can usually top them all by telling them that I (so the FBI informed me) was the Unabomber's freshman comp teacher but sometimes I resort to these plagiarism memories, filled with nice ironies.

—Edward M. White

5 3

It is the University of Louisville, back in the days when athletes worked for their scholarships. A young man is cleaning out the office of his writing teacher, and finds in the wastebasket the back to the mimeographed in-class essay assignment for the next day. He takes it to his fraternity, and his buddies write up a terrific essay. Next day in class, he pretends to be writing the essay and then hands in the piece his friends had composed. A week later, the teacher returns all of the in-class pieces except for the athlete's. "Where's mine?" he asks. "See me after class," says the teacher. The student knows that the game is up. "How did you know?" he asks the teacher after class. "Well," says the teacher, "it wasn't hard. Yours was the only essay that was typed."

He told it whenever he could, whether the topic was plagiarism, athletes, fraternities, or the good old days.
—Richard E. Haswell, remembered by his son

5 4

One of the writing proficiency test essays appeared to be total gibberish. Then one of the readers suggested she read it out loud, phonetically. To our pleasant surprise, the essay made perfect sense: it was well-organized, developed with support, and written in good, even complex sentences. It turned out that this writer suffers from extreme dyslexia. His father, a successful lawyer, has the same problem. The reader, who is also a writing center tutor, worked with the student to develop certain editing strategies, but he will always need an editor. However, he is a good reader, as his essay test showed, and he knows how to use the written language.

I like to tell this story to both my basic writing classes as well as the students in my writing workshops (which I give weekly for anyone interested, which turns out to be mainly students who did not pass the writing proficiency test).
—Mieke Koppen Tucker

5 5

When I was a teaching assistant at a large midwestern university, one of the students in my first-year composition class had a habit of submitting papers where words were omitted. And I'm not talking here about leaving out a word here and maybe another word down the page: I'm talking constant omission of words so that sometimes the meaning was totally obscured. Oh, I gave all the usual advice: before you submit a paper (these were in the days before portfolios, incidentally), proofread and look for, among other things, missing words.

Read your work aloud to see if you have written what you think you've written. I even marked his drafts to indicate where words were omitted and queried him about the holes in the text. Nothing worked. Paper after paper brought missing words ad infinitum.

Then one day this student was in the office conferring with me. One of his classmates waited just outside the door because I had fallen behind in the schedule of appointments. As I read the first student's paper, I found the same major problem as always: missing words, a lot of them. I asked this student to read aloud a passage where quite a few words were omitted, and he read the passage to include the missing words! He read words that were NOT on the page. So, I quietly called in the classmate sitting outside the door, asked him to help us with an experiment, and invited him to read the passage that the first student had just read but not actually read.

To the surprise of the word omitter, the second student wasn't able to fill in the blanks and read the passage exactly as it was in cold print on the page. For the first time ever, the first student was forced to confront the fact that he hadn't really been reading what he had written at all, but what he thought he had written and indeed what he persisted in believing he had written. Thereafter, he learned really to read his writing, and that problem was solved.

I tell this story to my writing classes to emphasize to them the difficulty of getting what is in one's head accurately on paper and to emphasize how symbiotic reading and writing really are. What we think we are writing is sometimes not what we are actually writing: and I'm not even talking about nuance, tone, attitude toward audience, or relatively elevated ways of thinking about the relationship of thought to text. This story also underscores the important point that writers need readers and that instructors need the synergy of peer relationships to make a difference in the class. After all, I had told this student many times that words were left out, but he did not hear me: he heard, however, the voice of his friend and colleague.

—C. Beth Burch

5 6

One semester I decided to try a different approach to tutoring. Actually, it was inspired by a classroom observation I had made during my training seminar many years ago. I had observed Vicki Hale's

W131 class. She used writing as a focus to get the class started. I decided to adapt her process into my tutorials.

The first time I tried it was with a W231 student. From the very first tutorial, I would read what this student had written aloud. Then I would have her write on scrap paper ideas, concepts, approaches, sometimes using complete sentences and paragraphs for her to use in her work. While the student was writing, I was silent, which everyone will tell you is a stretch for me. During this silence, I would work on tutoring paperwork or monitor the phones. This use of silence enabled the student to actually work on her writing and get instant feedback. After about ten minutes or so, I would look at what she had written. We would revise it and it would be included in her work. The student liked this approach; therefore, I continued using this method in other tutorials.

This technique worked with most students. They found it helpful for honing their proofreading skills. However, one student in particular found the process strange. She had wanted me to do the writing. At the end of the tutorial she went to the desk to schedule another appointment. She told the tutor at the desk that she would not reschedule an appointment with me. The student added that she didn't care who she worked with, she didn't want to work with me because, and this is the actual quote, "He makes me write!" Imagine that—a writing center that makes a student write.

When writing center tutors get together they like to tell stories about the weird things that happen to them during tutorials. This story is one I like to relate because it shows the difference between students and why they come to the writing center.

—Kitty Flowers

57

As a former corporate writer, editor, and occasional legal proofreader, I've become a grammar witch. (I even dress as one for class Halloween parties.) From years of professional experience, my focus in a composition course is readability: creativity of content, clarity and coherence of thought, natural style, and standard usage. I believe that no matter how brilliant in insight, a paper that ignores linguistic conventions will confuse—and lose—the reader. To address this issue, I allow students who receive a C or worse on a paper to try for a B in a revision.

From my neuro-linguistic standpoint, I'd been unable to under-stand how some professors could reward creativity and critical think-ing at the expense of grammar and usage. Until recently.

As an experiment in an advanced composition class, I assigned a creative satire. Admittedly, I was concerned that students would have trouble with this genre. However, their essays and short stories were stunning. I was amazed with the level of creativity, insight, sarcasm, and irony. So much so, I experienced a crisis of character, similar to the situations in the class readings. My dilemma was whether to uphold my linguistic principles or to acknowledge the quality of the students' ideas.

Eventually, unlike the class models, I realized that I didn't have to choose, but that I could do both. To recognize insight yet reward read-ability, I offered everyone who hadn't received an A the opportunity to earn one in a revision. From the quality of the edited versions, I'm confident that I made a good decision.

Yes, I'm a grammar witch. And proud of it!

I tell part of this story as an introduction to all of my composition classes. Naturally, I save the crisis of character for classes to which it applies.
—*Kathy Gerend-Meinking*

5 8

I need help. I've exhausted all I know to do, so I'm hoping that some of you with more experience will be able to offer me some suggestions for working with one of our students. Here's the situation. The stu-dent is a nontraditional female who has not passed TASP, a basic skills test all students are required to take to enter college. My tutors have been working with her for nine weeks now on various writing assign-ments, but the student doesn't seem to be learning much of anything.

The student has been out of school for a number of years and writes the same way she speaks. She is still on the second writing assignment (she should be on #6 by now—they're writing fairly short assignments for the class) and has a number of errors in her papers. My tutors, at my suggestion, have tried a number of techniques to teach this student about the errors she's making and how to find them for herself. We've marked errors for her in a particular sentence or para-graph and had the student get the handbook out, explained the error to her as well as how to fix it, but the student could not find the same errors repeated in her paper. When we ask her to look at the next sentence or paragraph, she still saw nothing. My tutors have had her read her sentences out loud and have read them out loud for her, but they sound right to her. She cannot see the errors, and she cannot hear them. One of my tutors even wrote a sample paragraph and had the student try to find the errors in it, but the student still couldn't see. I'm not sure what else to do.

In her regular freshman composition course (she is in two writing courses—one in the writing center to help prepare her to pass TASP and the normal first-semester freshman comp course), she refuses to speak in class and has only recently begun to speak in small groups. On workshop days, she skips class.

There has to be a way to teach this student how to proofread her papers and find the errors in them, but I'm at a loss how to do it. I've exhausted all my strategies. I have a feeling that this is more complicated than the student's seeming inability to write Standard English. Could this perhaps be linked to a reading problem as well or a learning disability? I'd appreciate any suggestions or comments. I have experience tutoring, and this is my first year as director of our writing center, and I don't know what else to offer to my tutors who are working with this student. The tutor and the student are becoming frustrated at this point, and I'd like to find a way to address this before the student becomes alienated.

Posted to the writing center listserv.

—Jonikka Charlton

⌐ ⌐ ⌐

NOTES

TALE 47 (p. 62). Thanking Wootten for his tale, I mentioned that a student of mine told me his mother, an English teacher, returned his letters with spelling and punctuation corrected. Wootten replied that there must be an English teacher who had read every murder mystery in a suburban library he once patronized—all the typos in the books were corrected in ink. And—I'm thinking of the next tale—is there an English department hiring committee in the land that doesn't have one member who circles all the surface mistakes, even in the letters of reference? The presence of so many comp tales bemoaning the profession's fixation on surface errors (see the Index of Topics) shows how conficted we are over them. (RHH)

TALE 48 (p. 62). This tale suggests that what writing teachers say about "writing"—what they notice in the written texts produced by the students—says more about how they read than how the students write. A useful story to be told in relation to Tales 36, 40, and 49. Tale 48 suggests a possible rationale to the insistence of Binh in Tale 49 that the tutor/narrator help him tell his story in "proper English": Binh is aware that his foreign-sounding name would lead others (besides the tutor/narrator) to mark him as an ESL student and then, use any deviation in his use of English to automatically dismiss his authority as a storyteller. As the narrator of Tale 49 reminds us, teachers need to respect the intentions of students like Binh (and I'd add, the student's assessment of the material conditions surrounding the reception of his or her writing). (MZL)

TALE 50 (p. 64) AND 51 (p. 65). Many years ago I started a list of mistakes students made with comparatives and absolutes. The student boast that he "graduated in the top 90% of his class" I thought was good. So was the literary analysis, "Roland was brave and loyal above no other." Better was the course evaluation addressed to a teacher, "Sometimes I felt that you were impartial to some students in class." Even better was the student who wrote of the teacher, "She always ceases to amaze me." Best of all was the student who said that the TA "has no outstanding qualities that differentiate him from an abnormal person." Then one day a colleague of mine proposed including in the student literary journal "the best gaffes from freshman composition papers." This horrified me so much that I swore off my list. Lists and tales of verbal mistakes made by students are forever popular within all teaching disciplines, and now circulate in cyberspace. The practice casts a disturbing light on our profession, which prides itself as student centered. I notice that most of the tales of student gaffes in this volume illustrate students caught in circumstances for which they are not entirely responsible, as with these two stories about using spellcheck programs. No tale we received made unapologetic fun of honest student mistakes. In our world of comp tales, the teacher who belittles students for their mistakes is a villain (cf. Tale 27).

The two tales also show how stories may be ill judged and even meanly judged without appreciation of the situation in which the stories are told (see "Taking in Comp Tales"). Out of context, a tale of unthinking word-choice may make students appear as unthinking, but when told to a group of teachers or students it may come across as sympathetic and cautionary, an anecdotal means to better methods of instruction and techniques of composing for thinking students. (RHH)

TALES 52 (p. 65) AND 53 (p. 66). White's last story is identical twin to one I tell about the (apocryphal?) teacher who showed a student that the piece he had submitted was copied from an anonymous entry in a rather obscure encyclopedia. The student, who thought he had played it safe, asked in amazement how the teacher knew. The teacher had the enviable reply, "I wrote it." To interpret plagiarism stories as always demeaning students I think simplifies the stories. Certainly plagiarism tales can erase the situation of students who plagiarize unaware of the complex rhetorical conventions that govern use of secondary material, or who patchwrite in an effort to assume a sophisticated style. On the other hand, students who submit file or purchased papers as their own know pretty well what they are doing. When the teacher is taken in and responds to the paper as if it were the student's, then it is the teacher's situation that the student has erased. It is this second erasure that many plagiarism stories reflect, sometimes in near fairy-tale form, with the teachers as protagonists defending their natural rights ("I wrote it"). When the plot changes, and the plagiarizer becomes the hero, then the story loses this familiar form (see Tale 90). (RHH)

TALE 56 (p. 68). A powerful tale about the use of silence in the teaching of writing. The narrator's self-characterization—"I was silent, which anyone will tell you is a stretch for me"—points to a professional hazard common to writing teachers, myself included. This suggests yet again that most of the "weird" things which happen to writing center tutors probably say less about the tutees than about the teachers these tutees have had. The tutee was probably shocked that the tutor uses silence to "make the tutee write" because it does not match her previous experience with writing teachers. Writing teachers like to tell students what they should have written. It is often easier for us to write for the student than to "make" them write. (MZL)

TALES 54–58 (pp. 67–70). Three points worth noting in these tales of the writing act. They all begin with the familiar, with the product, and then switch to the act of writing (composing or rereading). They are longer than the typical tale of writing consequences, lacking that fable-like point. And their audience is students. The implication is that these are stories for the young in the profession, or for the old who are doubting the traditional. (RHH)

TALE 58 (p. 70). A narrative that lacks a resolution, and perhaps by rights should appear in Chapter 11. But I can think of no better story of how, in our profession tales of writing, consequences are sometimes no longer sufficient and tales of writing acts are not readily available. When this call for help was posted on the writing center listserv, it prompted some excellent advice, among which was to use "glorious, basic, old-fashioned patience." (RHH)

CHAPTER 6

⇔

The Student

*Once when Luther Lassiter was in Sacramento, Calif.
for a pool tournament, I asked him if he could find time
to give me a few lessons. He replied: "I don't give lessons
because I don't know what I'm doing."*

—Robert Byrne (1990, p. 27)

A colleague read just enough of a book of mine (the first page) to be disgusted at my comment that the focus of our profession is not writing, rather that our focus is the student, writing. "I don't teach students or anything they do," he told me. "I teach English, as my contract stipulates." In that encounter, I am happy to report, the huge majority of the contributors to *Comp Tales* would have lined up on my side. The bulk of their tales center on students. Students preoccupy their attention because students occupy the center of their discipline. It's right that this chapter, the longest, should lie at the center of the book.

Not that the contributors grow misty-eyed when they tell stories about students. They see students complexly, as innocent and captivating, captivating and naïve, naïve and brash, brash and illogical, illogical and youthful, youthful and emotional, emotional and adult (tallying only Tales 59–65). But they also see students as one of the profession's major contradictions, or crises, to put my theatrical spin on it. The understanding teachers have of students just does not go very far. Why does one student learn and another not? Why does one suddenly start getting it, another drop out? Why does one come with an enthusiasm for writing and another with a distaste for it? The crisis originates from being unable to decide whether to teach sure things, such as heuristics and texts and conventions, which teachers know go only partway, or to teach students, who are the true mission but often, as Churchill might have said, a question mark wrapped inside a curiosity. In many of these tales—some of which relate a mysterious success and others an equally mysterious failure—the teacher-protagonists commit to an unknown, their experience never capable of fully understanding the other. (RHH)

☞ ☞ ☞

5 9

A Southerner's revenge. When I taught English at a junior college in Japan, I taught the students phrases like, "Hi y'all" and "Bye y'all." Their perfect pronunciation of such things never failed to dazzle class visitors from the States. I also taught a special-topics reading class once, and the textbook was an ESL history of rock and roll. I brought in lots of records, passed out the words, and we practiced singing along with Mick Jagger, Bruce Springsteen, Janis Joplin, James Brown. It just slayed me every time they said, "Ow! Poppa got a brand new bag."

I tell this story a lot to other people who have taught ESL, especially in other countries, usually when we're sitting around reminiscing about funny stuff we've done in our classrooms. We generally share the urge to teach "real" English as opposed to textbook English. Especially in Japan, I always tried to emphasize to students that the U.S. has a lot of cultural and linguistic variety, and I think I relished teaching "non-standard" English in particular, such as my family's dialect.

—Clyde Moneyhun

6 0

I can vouch for the veracity of this story. An ESL student came into our department office wanting to sign up for a particular kind of writing course, but we were having difficulty understanding just what he was asking for. Finally we figured it out: he wanted to take a "suppository writing class."

A colleague who shall remain nameless opined that such a course should be just the thing for writer's block.

Posted on the writing program administrators listserv. I usually tell this story to colleagues in the context of my discussions of the ESL curriculum and how we need to do a better job serving our international students.

—Susan H. McLeod

6 1

A friend of mine was teaching at a large state university known principally for its athletic triumphs. In his comp class he had the entire starting freshman basketball team, five huge hulking boys totally innocent of the world of letters. For the first paper, he told me, all five handed in identical papers, word for word from that month's *Reader's Digest*. He called them in to his office, where he had all five papers and the magazine lined up. "How do you explain this?" he asked. Then he shook his head to me, sadly, summarizing: "To the very end, they maintained it was all some sort of bizarre coincidence."

—Edward M. White

6 2

I got an essay response on an hour exam that seemed to me garbled and incoherent. I wrote something like "unclear" or "I can't follow you here" on the margin and graded the paper accordingly. The student, a young woman, said nothing at the time, but I recognized the same handwriting on the course evaluation at the end of the term. Her parting comment, in a bold angry scrawl, was: "I don't care if you can understand what I write or not, as long as I get my point across!"

—Richard Law

6 3

During my student teaching days, I wrote a unit based on the variations of the Cinderella/Cinderfella tales from around the world. After studying several of the stories and identifying the common motifs, students took a motif and wrote a modern version. But the students were much more violent, with people cutting off body parts, even heads, or getting killed and eaten and being reborn. This violence was a real fascination for them; to put it politely, they loved it.

Later I chose to teach the unit to a group of sophomores who had flunked freshman English and were retaking it. One guy was having trouble writing his story, said he didn't know what to write about. I asked him what things he liked to do in his free time and if he had any hobbies. "Cars, I like to work on cars." Great, I told him, you could have your Cinderfella character be a mechanic and he could work on some rich girl's car. "Oh, okay." So off he went.

Well, when I got the finished story, I realized he had done what I asked, he wrote about what he knew, but he had taken my suggestion about how they meet and thrown it out the door. And good riddance, compared to his final version. In his version, the Cinderfella guy is driving his souped-up car down the street and hits the beautiful girl with his car. She goes flying off into another neighborhood from the force of the crash, and the Cinderfella guy, taken with her beauty, has to go around this neighborhood and knock on doors to find his princess. And how does he know it is really her? She has the hood ornament stuck in her forehead.

I usually tell this story every year to those students who don't think they have anything to write about. Everyone has a story to tell—in one form or another.
—Teresa Anne Ezell

6 4

Many years ago a young TA was waked up early one Monday morning by a telephone call from her comp director. "Don't leave your apartment. Wait for me to come pick you up for school. Keep calm and fix yourself a good breakfast." It turned out that one of her students had gone berserk Friday night and rushed out of his fraternity house with a pistol, saying he was going to kill all of his teachers. His brothers looked for him all Saturday, unsuccessfully, and finally called the dean of students. But by the end of the weekend he still hadn't been located.

Sure enough, the student was absent from the TA's morning class. Then along about noon she glanced up and there he was, standing in front of her desk. He looked at her and she looked at him. Then he began to cry. She took him by the hand and led him across campus to Health Services. Several days later she told her fortunate adventure to her professor of medieval literature. He nodded, stared at her abstractly across his desk, and said, "In 1840, a student at the University of Virginia walked into the office of his teacher and killed him with a shotgun."

I used to tell this story, I don't know why, to teachers of all sorts when the conversation turned to students with psychological problems. But I have stopped telling it since the recent schoolroom killings. I always thought the teacher was my TA buddy Bernie Warren. It certainly sounds like her. But she denies it. The professor of medieval literature, by the way, had his facts right. Ironically, four years earlier, in 1836, the unfortunate teacher at the University of Virginia had helped mediate a dispute between faculty and students. Students had gone on strike over a faculty decision to ban guns from campus.

—Rich Haswell

6 5

The homework from the night before was to write a descriptive essay about a common object that was personally important to the writer. I asked the students to get into groups and discuss how their objects could reflect their writing processes and/or repeated themes in their past essays. One group appeared to be having some serious problems, so I sat in to help prompt their brainstorming. I started asking a student about his object. He said it was a rock, and wouldn't say anything else about it. I asked him how big it was and if it had any distinguishing characteristics such as unusual color. He blushed and his group giggled at each of my questions. Finally, a friend of his says, "Why don't you whip it out for Teacher? She wants to see it."

Aware of the tension in our group, the whole class is listening when he blurts his response. "IT'S MY PENIS! MY OBJECT IS MY PENIS!!" Then, in a much lower voice, he asked me what I had expected, assigning an 18-year-old college student with raging hormones and away from his parents for the first time to describe a personally important object. I spent the rest of hour trying to refocus the class, asking him about other objects he might be more comfortable discussing in his group. After class he asked me if this meant that I thought his object wouldn't work. I know I shouldn't have, but I couldn't resist. I told him that maybe that was a question for his doctor.

It's a good story to tell over a beer.

I usually tell this to new GTAs as a good way to get them past being scared about teaching and to get them laughing instead. Actually though, when

they think about this story more, they tend to get even more scared. . . .
Maybe I should buy a couple rounds first.

—*Karen Schierhoff*

6 6

The class was coming up with topics. One lady, middle-aged and rather quiet, piped in and said it would be interesting to write a paper analyzing divorce in terms of the split of property and how housework does not count as work. Her audience would be the judges and the purpose would be to provide evidence that the full-time wife keeping the house should be considered as important as the husband making the wages that pay for the home. I agreed and was rather intrigued how someone would structure a paper like that.

As I began to read the paper, I saw she was arguing that housework is an integral part of a home and should be taken into account when property is being divided in a divorce. I was impressed with her thoughts and then all of a sudden she brought in a personal response about her own divorce, and as the paper went on her tone changed from concerned to upset to furious. She began badmouthing her ex-husband and called him and other men like him self-centered, woman-chasing asses. I had to laugh because by the end of her paper she brought it back to the point that women should be treated fairly in a divorce.

I tell this story to students because I start off explaining that if they have inter-est in the topic then the paper will be easier to write and they will probably have more to say about it. I let them know they can be emotional about something in process, but to make sure they stay on focus and not get too personal in the paper.

—*Teresa Anne Ezell*

6 7

John Fowles wrote that "all is hazard." The word "all" might be a lit-tle over-zealous, although a degree of accidental success or accidental failure appears even in our writing classes. J.B. was a reluctant, older learner in my first remedial writing course. His chair hugged the back wall, and every week he worked hard to avoid my eyes. Still, his assign-ments came in on time, although they were little more than disparate sentences thrown at the same page—like a Jackson Pollack painting.

Then one class, I noticed he had moved up two rows from the back. And the next week he moved another row, and I had no idea why. He began to stay after class to chat about writing. During a class discussion he announced that he was getting the hang of this writing stuff, and he was doing most of his composing while at work fixing car brakes. That worried me. But he was indeed getting the hang of it, and during the midterm conference, he said he might even major in English. He passed the class with no charity from me, and during registration for the next semester he was anxious to tell me he had signed up for the next writing course. He also had picked up a copy of *The Old Man and the Sea* (we had talked about Hemingway a lot that semester). He thought he was going to like it, he said. Several weeks later I heard from one of his classmates that he had dropped out of school, and no, he didn't know why. It was hazard.

At the start of each semester, I tell students it is impossible to predict all those "hazards" which might alter their sense of hope about the class. The good response is not to squeeze their eyes shut and take whatever comes, but rather to open them. If they could begin to recognize which hazards affect them—criticisms and compliments, workload, etc.—then they might do more than merely react; they could choose the wise response.

—Phil **Spray**

6 8

One of my least favorite, longest remembered students was a young man known to all of us who'd tried to encourage him to finish a semester of freshman English as The White Rat. This was not because we consciously regarded him as a laboratory specimen, though he provided an interesting example of galloping inertia, but because of his peculiarly pale, damp skin and his pink eyes.

To each successive class he was in, he contributed a leaden and determined loathing of writing, and would sit, sullenly limp at his desk, squeezing out a painful word or two at irregular intervals, but spending most of his time listlessly picking off pieces of skin from around his fingernails. This cowed defiance of any attempt to coax, heaven forbid, an essay, a paragraph even, out of him would last anywhere from two to eight weeks of the semester. Then he would disappear.

One spring, I had managed to keep him in my Comp I class for nine weeks, and I suppose I was becoming cocky. "This time you're going to make it," I told him encouragingly. "I'll help you all I can, and together we're going to get you through, okay?"

"I hate writing" was the predictable reply. "I don't see why I have to write."

"I know," I said, trying to keep my voice teacher-bright. "But wouldn't it be to your advantage to be able to do it? Just in case you ever need to?"

"I'm going into my father's business when I graduate," he volunteered suddenly.

It was the first remark he'd ever offered me of his own volition, and I was suckered. "Then that's the star to shoot for," I told him. "You'll have to write when you go to work there. You know," I went on rashly, "reports and letters and things."

He looked at me out of his little pink eyes in utter bewilderment, and spoke clearly and patiently, as if I were a particularly slow student of his. "But my father will give me a secretary, of course," he said. "And she will do any writing that needs to be done."

The next class day he had vanished again.

I've told this story to many of my fellow writing teachers, but perhaps particularly to those who are just starting out in the Freshman Writing business, and who've come to me discouraged by a student with whom they feel they've been less than successful. "You'll never succeed with 100%," I tell them.

—Vanessa Furse Jackson

6 9

You fail occasionally—just fail. And you can't say it was not your fault. And you can't forget, either.

It was the Friday before Thanksgiving vacation. Students had left in droves the day before because a storm had been predicted, and indeed it was snowing hard. It was late in the afternoon, and I too wanted to get home, to my wife and a fire. But a student, one I did not much like, had come into the office and was not picking up on my hints that it was time to go. A loner, the kind the women in class laugh about. He had brought a draft, but he had once before conferenced with me about it and done nothing to it in the meantime. Finally I got up, put on my coat. He followed me out into the snow. He was telling me how he had done well in the university chess competition. At the edge of campus I shook his hand, glove on glove, and pointed toward the street I had to go down. He said he would walk with me a ways. It was 5:30 and dark already and the snow was near-ly suffocating. He explained that his parents were divorced, that he was remaining in the dorms over vacation rather than deal with his stepfather. After several blocks, I stopped and said, "Look, you seem like you need someone to talk to about all this. You know, there are good counselors in Student Services. All you have to do is walk in." He said he would think about it. Then he said, "Thanks." We parted. I didn't turn around but I can still see him heading back through the snow to the dorms.

After vacation he wasn't in class. I never saw him again.

I've told my wife about this. A shrink. That's it.

—Author's name withheld

7 0

It was after the first day of class, in one of my first semesters of teaching, when Carol (not her real name) walked up to me and said, "I know I am going to do well in this class. My mother is an English teacher so I guess you could say I have English in my genes."

My initial response was delight at the prospect of having a student of what I assumed to be advanced abilities in the class. The delight, however, did not last long for either one of us. Carol's writing, while grammatically flawless and neat as a pin, was dry, cautious, and superficial. She could write six quite proper and professional-looking pages that ended up saying virtually nothing. I tried discussing this with her in conference—offering different strategies for revision, different essays to read as models, different kinds of assignments—hoping that I might strike on some idea or strategy that would get her to engage with a complex idea in her writing. Instead I kept getting the same clean and safe drafts with virtually no revision from one version to the next. The more I talked, cajoled, and eventually pleaded, the more she resisted. By the end of the semester she would sit in class and in conference, arms crossed, silently glaring at me.

After the last day of class I was going through writing portfolios when I discovered that Carol had included a draft I had never seen. It began with a story about how she had bought a plant at the halfway point of the semester, named it after me, and put it on the radiator in her dorm room to die. The essay went on to be a passionate, witty, perceptive, and complex defense of what she saw as the true uses of writing and how I should rethink the way I teach my course. Once I got over my initial shock at the opening anecdote and my defensiveness at having my teaching philosophy and practices attacked so thoroughly, I realized that not only was this the best writing Carol had done during the semester, but it was some of the best writing in the class.

I wrote Carol a long letter, which I enclosed with her portfolio when I mailed it back to her, telling her how strong her writing was now that she was writing about something that mattered to her. I told her how exciting it was to read a writer who was engaging with an idea in all its complexity, instead of worrying about neatness and formatting. I also tried to explain why I approached writing and my teaching as I did, but acknowledged that theories of composition were varied and that there were people in the field who certainly would have agreed with her argument. Finally, I told her that I was sorry we had not had this discussion earlier in the semester when we could have had some fruitful exchanges about the nature and purposes of writing.

Carol never responded to my letter and, in subsequent years when I saw her on campus, she would offer only a stiff but polite nod in response to my greeting.

I tell this story for two different reasons. First, it illustrates that some of our most challenging students are not basic writers, but the students who believe—and hope—that they already know everything there is to know about writing. The more important lesson for me, however, was realizing that writing and talking about writing and how it is taught was not something I should reserve only for my colleagues. Though Carol was a vivid example, all of my students would have benefited from the kind of ideas and questions Carol raised and I responded to in my letter. Because of this student and what happened with her writing and her frustration, I changed as a teacher. Since that semester I have spent more time trying to be aware of my students' writing and reading experiences and attitudes—my first assignment of the semester now is always a literacy narrative. I also spend more time in my course making explicit and open for discussion the questions and ideas that form the foundation of my views of writing and the teaching of writing, and I encourage them to think about, and write about, those ideas to help them understand what they want to be as writers.
—Bronwyn T. Williams

7 1

In one of my advanced writing classes, I once had this student whose writing skills were quite low compared to the other students. The work she turned in always had mistakes either in content or grammar.

It was quite obvious to me that she had slipped through the system because she was now in my advanced class and probably shouldn't have been. One of the criteria for students in the advanced writing class was for them to be able to proofread and edit their work thoroughly before they turned it in for a grade. This student had no clue how to proofread or edit her work in order to pass. As the quarter progressed, she became more and more frustrated with her lack of writing skills, and she began to take her frustration out on me. As her teacher, I was the obvious one to blame; after all, she had passed her first two writing courses with little or no problems. Toward the end of the quarter, the student's attitude toward me and the course had sunk to a level of pure belligerence. I had made a pledge to myself early in my teaching career that I wasn't going to pass a student from my advanced writing course who could not write; in my way of thinking, it would not have been fair to her. She failed the course and was forced to retake it the following quarter in order to graduate.

The second time around with this student in my advanced writing class began in the same belligerent fashion as the first had been. I simply did not understand why she had such a negative attitude toward me and this particular class. Sometime later that quarter, I began to notice what appeared to be a slightly positive change in her behavior. Her writing improved along with her attitude toward the course and me. When I asked her what had been the cause of her shift, she explained that she had recently acquired a new position at her job that required her to write letters. Her experience with writing up to that point had only been school related. Her skills were relative to her belief that writing was only an academic chore. Her livelihood had never been reliant on her having to write. The tide had turned for her practically overnight. On the final day of class, my student, who had once viewed me as her sworn enemy, approached me after class to tell me that she was glad that she had to retake my class because it had forced her to learn how to be a better writer, which in turn had helped her tremendously with her job.

A few weeks later I watched as she paraded across the stage to receive her diploma during graduation ceremonies. As I left the auditorium that night, she made a special point to stop me to talk. She actually thanked me for being so tough on her in my class. She said that she finally realized that I had had her best interest in mind throughout both classes; she just didn't see it at the time. When I got to my car and started driving out of the parking lot, I understood and appreciated the fact that I had just received the truest reward for my work as a teacher—a genuine compliment from a satisfied student.

I like to tell this story to people who wonder why I chose to teach and to those who suggest to me that I can find a job that pays better wages. I also like to tell this story to my colleagues when we all tend to fall into a mood of complaint or apathy as we sit and talk in the faculty lounge. My goal is always to reassure them and myself that our chosen profession has the potential for us to reap greater intangible rewards than many other professions despite the tremendous amount of time and energy we spend preparing lessons and grading students' work. We as teachers help others learn how to help themselves, and I can't imagine having a more satisfying job!

—David J. Sabol

7 2

Whenever I'm squirming with dismay during yet another ain't-it-awful complaint about students in first-semester remedial comp, I'll retell what my colleague Cindy Sabik calls my "wonnnnnderful" story about Metaphysical Sam.

His first writing sample baffled me. I'd asked the class to write about something—an object or experience—significant to them. His classmates wrote about prom pictures, lockets and rings, but Sam seemed to want to make me guess what he was describing. His tangled sentences were like black holes, but occasionally they would emit a little light. I could make out something "shallow blue" yet "rough as sandiest paper" and guessed the ocean. Wrong. After a third draft a frustrated and defeated Sam came to my office and explained that he was describing his girlfriend's eyes, "clustered with terrified tears." I was flabbergasted but hid it. How could I help Sam salvage confidence in his writing? How could I validate his poetic style yet get him to write clearer expository essays?

Then I had a crazy idea: had Sam ever heard of John Donne? Or metaphysical poetry? Nope, never. I pulled my new Longman anthology from the shelf behind Sam and opened it to "A Valediction: Of Weeping." Sam hitched his chair closer and looked on as I read the poem out loud. And then a miracle happened: before I'd done much more than start to explain what Donne was doing with tears, Sam took over and began explaining Donne's conceits to me! "No, see, his tear is 'pregnant' with her because her face is reflected in it." I shut up and watched the blinking lights. This eighteen-year-old, who had trouble putting three words together clearly, made sense of a poem that always stumps older students in my survey course.

Sam still can't write what he calls "dot-to-dot" (as opposed to "creative" writing), can't compose clear sentences. As one of our writing center consultants put it after hearing Sam's story, "He has the writer's eye, but not the hand, so to speak." But Sam is beginning to think of himself as a writer, and talks about taking a creative writing or poetry workshop course next year.

I'll tell this story to teachers who disparage remedial students as "stupid" because their writing skills are shaky. TAs especially are appalled by these students' writing; my current TA calls our students "MIAs." I'll also remind myself of Sam at the beginning of every semester. Identity formation is so important in the freshman year, and maybe thinking of oneself as a writer is prerequisite to writing better.

—Sally Joranko

7 3

Here is a simple, true story I tell my basic writing students when I talk to them about how students still working on basic skills can survive the first years of college. It's a little corny, perhaps, but I believe in its message.

Wendy showed up in one of my sections of ENG 100 about ten years ago. She was a pleasant, well-dressed eighteen-year-old whose writing was garbled and hopelessly incoherent. Even in a basic writing class, she stood out as far worse than anyone else. Although I had been teaching these classes for about twenty years, I couldn't understand how a sophisticated-looking teenager could end up this undeveloped as a writer. Then she told me her story. For the first few years of elementary school, she loved school and loved reading. Then in the fourth grade, the teacher began handing out reading books with different colored covers. Wendy hoped that she would get the purple one, because she liked that color, but instead got the ugly orange one. Then the teacher explained the meaning of the colors. When Wendy found out that she had been categorized as "a non-reader," she was devastated. She was stunned all day, and went home crying. This one experience destroyed all her interest in academics, and she turned off to the intellectual side of school completely, until her junior year of high school, eight years later. For whatever reason—she didn't inform me—she suddenly got interested in studying and reading again, and tried to catch up. When I met her she had been at it about two years. And indeed, her writing looked like that of an elementary school student.

Her story has a second part. I told her to use the Writing Center for all her work in my class and all the writing she had to do for her other classes. She did so. In fact, she became one of those people who "live in the Writing Center," known to all the tutors, eating her lunch there, stopping by to hang out even when she had no work to do. My office is in the same complex and I saw her there and in the word processing lab, which I ran, for years. Then one spring day I noticed her in the word processing lab, papers and books spread out, obviously writing a research paper at her terminal. I wandered over and said hello to her, and asked if she were graduating this spring. She was. Then I quietly lingered behind her for a moment. I wanted to see what her writing looked like. The fluent prose she was producing on the screen was above average for a college senior. I was very impressed. This young woman—who wrote far worse than any student in this class (I say to my students)—survived in college and became a competent writer. I don't insult her by saying that if she can do it, anyone can. It's not a matter of having or lacking some strange ability—it's a matter of wanting to.

I tell this "inspirational" story to my basic writing students on the first day of class in a short lecture on how to survive in college while they are trying to get their bearings. The drop-out rate for students placed in this course is rather high; sometimes almost half the class fails to finish the course, the students having dropped out of college or at least out of the composition course. While they take this course, which introduces them to writing in response to essays (about controversial social issues), they are also asked by teachers in other departments to write various other kinds of papers, including some that require research skills that the basic writing course only begins to touch on. How, then, can these weak writers handle those assignments? The best advice I can give them is to take advantage of our excellent writing center, run by a highly competent associate professor with a Ph.D. in rhetoric and linguistics and staffed by a dozen trained graduate and undergraduate students.

—William Murdick

7 4

In the late '80s, I taught in an ESL program at a southern, private university. Each class met four hours a day, five days a week. Enrollment was capped at six students. Most students enrolled for at least one year of study, moving through 6–8 levels of grammar, speaking, reading and writing until they reached the advanced course. As the advanced course had no set curriculum, students could repeat the course until they left the country. I taught the advanced course.

At the time, the Saudi government was working with many businesses in our city; consequently, there were many Saudis enrolled in our program. These were exotic people from exotic places. Some were members of the royal family; others had jobs that required perfect English. All saw themselves as ambassadors and loved explaining the intricacies of the Saudi political and social structure. We spent our days laughing at our cultural misconceptions. The exclamation, "You don't understand, Emily,..." still echoes in my thoughts.

On Friday nights, the Saudi men and women gathered in separate places to celebrate the beginning of a new week. As both a teacher and a friend, I was often invited to join the women. I can still hear the sound of limousines passing over wet pavement and see the drivers escorting passengers to the front door of a Saudi residence. And I can still see the beautiful dark features of the women's faces, highlighted with the tiniest bit of makeup, as they yanked off their veils the minute the door closed.

Mohammed and Salome, husband and wife, were two Saudis that I will never forget. Mohammed was in several of my advanced courses. Salome took charge of me on Friday nights, making sure that I was comfortable and understood the nuances of the conversation. They had three children: two daughters and a son. The girls attended a local elementary school. The son, a toddler with a heart condition, stayed home with a servant while his parents studied at the university. The family had come to our city to consult with an internationally acclaimed heart specialist. As I also had a two-year-old son, we often shared stories about our toddlers' latest antics.

Mohammed spoke fluent English. Salome spoke in broken, halting phrases. Whereas Mohammed's English improved throughout the year, Salome's did not. I saw her lack of progress as evidence of fossilization, a theory that non-native speakers learn only as much of the target language as needed. Salome's husband and children spoke for her; she had no reason to work on her English. It was as simple as that.

One gorgeous spring day, Mohammed didn't come to class. Another student told me that the couple's son had died during the night. I put off contacting the family that afternoon, supposedly because I was waiting for instructions about protocol. Actually, I was afraid. The next morning, a Saturday, I paced my kitchen floor for two hours and finally picked up the phone.

"Mohammed," I said, "this is Emily. I'm so sorry." "Emily," a broken voice responded, "…Salome…speak." There was a pause. "Emily," said Salome. "I am so glad you called. The baby's body has been wrapped for transport. We will leave tomorrow. I don't think we will ever return. I wanted to say good-bye."

Salome spoke for one hour, explaining all the details of the funeral arrangements, summarizing ancient and modern burial customs, comforting me while I sat speechless, crumpled on the kitchen floor, sobbing incessantly. I have often thought of that one-sided conversation and wondered how Salome could speak so fluently. After all, Salome's language had fossilized. Emotional events and telephones are supposed to impede communication, not improve it. Neither Mohammed nor I could say a word, but Salome spoke more eloquently than I thought possible.

Since that time, other theories have come into my classroom: feminism, social constructionism, post colonialism, etc. I love theory. It enriches my teaching by creating a context for my everyday interaction with students. But theory can also shape my expectations, stereotype my reactions, inhibit my thinking, and cause me to miss an important insight. And so, I am cautious when I teach theory. I try to keep myself open to other possibilities, for Salome taught me that just when I begin to believe a theory, it turns out to be wrong.

I usually tell this tale on the first or last day of an upper-division or graduate theory course.

—Emily Golson

7 5

The English department honored me by asking me to teach composition during the first coed summer session at Virginia Military Institute. The prospect of bringing women into the hallowed halls of this once all-male institution thrilled me. Admissions gave me my class list and I was disappointed to find only one female's name, Sally A. Once in the classroom, I discovered that the male students were receptive to her contribution to the class and respected her as a fellow classmate, so I ceased to worry that she would find it difficult as the only woman in the class. Another student presented a different challenge. Chin was a recent arrival from Taiwan and was very shy about speaking up in class; however, Chin always thanked me at the end of each class, and climbed up on the window sills to help me close the windows before leaving. Chin was very petite and always wore tan slacks and some type of polo shirt. Occasionally, Chin's shirt bore the Playboy bunny insignia. One day while passing out papers, I leaned over Sally to give a paper to her classmate, instructing him, "Be sure to give one to Chin. I don't think he has one." Sally whispered in my ear, "Chin's a woman!"

I have told this story many times even though it is incredibly embarrassing. I like to tell it to show fellow teachers that even though we discourage our students in the composition classroom from making assumptions about a text without undergoing research or stating facts without proof, we too are vulnerable to ignorant inferences that leave us blushing.

—Bethany Blankenship

NOTES

TALES 59-63 (pp. 76-77). In the way our comp tales portray students, there is a strong tilt away from anger, disparagement, or condescension toward tolerance, humor, good will, and not a little wonder. Often the feeling is a kind of parental "what next?" This generous but suspended judgment touches on a contradiction concerning students that is different from those teacher/student conflicts, often attributed to writing instruction, expressed in terms of generation gap, cognitive dissonance, clash in culture or class, or difference in empowerment. It is a contradiction involving responsibility. How do we tender our knowledge to the student if we do not know how the student is going to use it? We want to help students become the hero of their own stories, we think of ourselves as fairy godmothers or magic donors, but we do not know how the students will use our gift, what stories they are going to write for themselves. And what are we in our story if they use our gift in ways we would not? (RHH)

TALE 64 (p. 78). The narrative voice grabs me because it plays on two words, "fact" and "abstract." It thus calls attention to the ways in which our knowledge of facts and the desire to abstract mediate how we listen to, tell, and retell a past event. When told by the TA of what had just happened to her, the medieval professor "stared at her abstractly across his desk" as he recounts an historical fact which puts a spin on what could have happened between the TA and her student. As a listener, I am struck by the impersonal reaction of the professor, the way in which his recounting of the 1840 event risks reducing the relation and interaction between this particular TA and this particular student of hers into one between a student and a teacher (at the University of Virginia in 1840) and that between any student and any teacher. And yet, I am also struck by the importance of that sort of "abstraction," of putting the intensely personal drama into the broader social history of the U.S. academy. The narrator refuses to let me resolve the tension created by my two reactions. He tells us that another historical "fact," the recent schoolroom killings, has made him stop telling the event. He thus depicts himself as relating to the event in part as the medieval professor had. At the same time, in admitting to his own confusing of the actual TA with another TA, he also puts a question mark on the ways in which he himself might have "abstracted" the event when telling it to all sorts of teachers in the past. (MZL)

TALES 67–70 (pp. 80–83). For me, these Blakean tales of students lost are very powerful. Carolyn Ericksen Hill remarks that in an effort to keep our inner lives flowing smoothly, writing teachers have a very human way of disregarding the personal stories of others that are inconsistent with our own stories. We relegate them, as she says, into a "bin of neglected others, of untold stories" (1990, p. 80). Hill is saying that students lost have their own stories, which for us are stories lost. It takes courage for teachers to tell "untolds," to risk our own coherence with the stories of J.B., The White Rat, and Carol, and it takes even more courage to use them to re-story our own teaching in an effort to write a new and more embracing coherence.

These tales of students lost may be some of the most disturbing in the book, but *in the telling* they are not pessimistic. We tend to tell stories about what troubles and offends us, and although that may leave under-represented a great bulk of our professional lives and accomplishments, on the other hand the very telling of a disturbing event shows that we are trying to get a handle on it and that we are learning from it. I would say that these tales present teacher *lore* in its most constructive sense, that practitioner's realm of what "worked, seemed to work, or might work" (Stephen North, 1987, p. 24). It doesn't change North's definition to add to it "what didn't work." (RHH)

TALE 69 (p. 82). I am still trying to figure out what I would have said if the anonymous author had decided to tell this story face to face to me. I know my response would impact how I use and retell this story in the future. When writing teachers act on two of our ideals—the concern to listen and take seriously the thoughts and feelings of writing students and the concern to acknowledge the relation between writing and living—we often lead students to see us as someone in whom they can trust, confide in, and seek help from on issues concerning not only writing but life in general. How to walk the fine line between teaching writing, personal counseling and surrogate parenting is a question we must therefore struggle with on a day to day basis. One side of me wants to believe that the student never returned to the class because he had figured out and accepted the fact that a writing teacher cannot, ought not, pretend to be a counselor or a parent and that, at the moment, he needs help from the latter two more urgently than from a writing teacher. Another side of me is nevertheless smitten by guilt. In spite of my conviction that writing teachers could or should never try to counsel or parent their students, there is still a tiny bit of me which remains vulnerable to the temptation. (MZL)

TALE 70 (p. 83). This tale calls into question existing definitions of what counts as "weird" student behavior and who should be sent to the writing centers. The narrator reminds us that our "most challenging students are not basic writers." Tale 70 illustrates the "weirdness" of students who feel so "at home" that they see themselves as having "English in [their] genes." These students are "basic writers" in the sense that they too are having difficulty grasping the discrepancy between their notion and the teacher's notion of good writing. The story makes me wonder how and why we seldom consider the benefit of sending such students to basic writing courses and to writing center tutorials. (MZL)

TALES 74 AND 75 (pp. 88–90). Another reminder that what we say about our students often says less about the students than about us, especially about our habitual reaction to difference and the impact such habits have on how we view our students as well as their writings. What are the standard codes we use to name students as ESL, athletes, older, female, housewives, persons of color, resistant, etc.? What do such codings tell us about our sense of who we are and what we do best? How might we revise these codes when interacting with students who appear to support or challenge the validity of such habits of reading? (MZL)

TALE 75 (p. 90). For me, this anecdote takes on the shape of parable, a gist of what these comp tales tell us about students. What they tell may be more honest than the theory and practice offered by other discourse genres of the field. These tales say that sometimes the theory and the practice work, sometimes they don't. Sometimes individual students succeed beyond expectations, sometimes half the class fails as expected. Sometimes we lose students and sometimes they just get lost. And when they are found, it is one at a time. And we can never take full credit for finding them—they seem to find us. The tales say that teaching writing is not a known science and consequently is full of embarrassment, surprise, and not a little wonder. Just as we get comfortable, someone whispers in our ear, "Chin's a woman!" (RHH)

CHAPTER 7

⌇

The Public

Until recently I'd cry in the morning. I didn't want to get up. I'd dread Fridays because Monday was always looming over me. Another five days ahead of me. There never seemed to be any end to it. Why am I doing this? Yet I dread looking for other jobs. I don't like filling out forms and taking typing tests. I remember putting down on an application, "I'd like to deal with the public." (Laughs).

—Sharon Atkins, receptionist, in
interview, Studs Terkel (1972, p. 31).

The crisis underlying the profession's sense of *the writing* seems to be largely of historical origin, that underlying our sense of *the student* seem to be epistemological, and that underlying our sense of *the public* sociological. A gross simplification, I believe. But the division offers an entry into the vexed issue of what the writing profession conceives of as the public. "The public" is not a body of people who can be historically mapped. It is a psychological, social, and cultural dynamic, a matter of perspective and positioning. The public is whoever we think lies outside our in-group and should be informed about it.

The in-group condition of college composition teachers is complicated by recent changes in its socio-professional footing. When performing arts and communications left English, they became part of our public. The same happened whenever composition folk and literature, linguistics, TESOL folk separated. Sometimes writing center faculty imagine the rest of the composition faculty as their public. Such recent splittings have helped foster a general sense of inferiority along with the pride that comes with a tightening of group. At the same time, encouraged by WAC initiatives, everybody still wants to conceive of themselves as one big family, an academic community.

Comp tales provide an insight into those expanding and contracting circles that describe the degrees of publicness in composition or, alternately, provide insight into the layered way it defines itself as a group. An unspeakable that looks very private, told by one in-group member to another about a third, may still convey a sense of the public because it speaks of the membership of the third as questionable. Tales located a bit further out, with out-group characters, often include the public as audience, if not in the gossipy sense that by telling this tale sooner or later the out-group will hear about it, then in the preacherly sense that they *ought* to hear about it. Even further out, where whole new cultures are being discovered as kin (e.g., banking personnel, the stateside homeless, learners of English for special purposes outside the U.S.), the tale may look back upon itself and discover that private, in-group ways now appear pretty insular. Comp tales are a remarkably sensitive barometer for the contradictions we feel as part of these fluid groupings and regroupings that form the short history of our profession. (RHH)

☞ ☞ ☞

76

One of the most surprising pieces of advice I received when I agreed to direct the writing center on a university campus was that, when collecting demographic data, I should not record the names of the courses or the instructors for which students were coming for writing conferences. When I asked why, my colleague, indeed an English department rhetorician, explained that these numbers could be used against those instructors. "Administrators and other evaluators will think that faculty members aren't doing their jobs well if their students need to use the writing center," he warned me, "so don't keep that information where anyone with clout can get at it." At the time, I could only mumble, "Thanks, I'll think about that." And indeed I have, largely because it reminds me how few of my own beliefs about composition and collaboration are universal.

This story I tell almost every time I teach a course on issues in tutoring writing and often in comp theory or pedagogy courses.

—Carol Peterson Haviland

7 7

Walking down the hall to my office, I was stopped by one of the litera-ture faculty. The previous year he had not been a member of the depart-ment to congratulate me when I made tenure. But this time he had some-thing to say. "Heard you published a book." I had—a research mono-graph. "What is it," he asked, "a textbook?" As usual, I didn't have a clever riposte, but then he didn't wait around for an answer of any kind.

I told this to all my friends in that university, but I've discarded it since I left it. You have to know the man.

—Author's name withheld

7 8

I push the pieces of shrimp, chicken, and scallop around the rim of my plate, which is decorated by a maroon meander. I overhear the sotto voce complaints from the nursing professor to the two administrative assistants and the technology instructor about the quality of writing skills her nursing students possess.

"They don't know how to spell," says the nursing professor, in a now distinct voice as she munches on her eggroll. I stab my shrimp with my chopstick.

"And forget punctuation. Doesn't anyone teach apostrophes?" she queries in my direction. I smash the scallop of my Mark Pi Three Delicacies sampler plate.

"And grammar. I don't feel I should have to teach English. That's not my discipline," adds the nursing professor with some finality and a flourish of her fork into her Mu Shu pork. I bite the chicken piece off my chopsticks, chew it a few times savoring the garlic, swallow hard, and suggest, "Perhaps you should mention your concerns to the director of the English program, Professor X."

"Oh, I talked to her already," she snappily replies as if she had anticipated my suggestion. "She thinks she is teaching thinking or crit-ical writing, expressing, or something."

I repeat this luncheon conversation I had with my inter-disciplinary colleague because I am often deeply pained by the lack of information and, yes, even disrespect, colleagues outside the English department occasionally express about the quality and nature of what teaching English should be. The duties of a teacher of composition and rhetoric are reduced to lower-order editing and spell-checking. Perhaps I have been inordinately exposed to these conversations, if they may be called that, because the unique nature of teaching at a satellite campus of IUPUI puts me into direct and daily contact with colleagues from other disciplines. Most people, inter-disciplinary colleagues, and sometimes intra-disciplinary colleagues in English-related fields have little knowledge of the theoretical and practical underpinnings of the teaching of writing. I truly wish to be more effective as a communicator and colleague; however, these rare moments test my commitment to civil social intercourse. On good days I enjoy my Three Delicacies without indigestion. On some days I utter the plaintive cry of the comedian, Rodney Dangerfield, "I don't get no respect."
—Katherine Tsiopos Wills

7 9

When I first came on campus as a WAC director at a large, state-supported urban university, I made the practice of visiting each of the Schools and Colleges to introduce myself and my staff and to get some sense of various constituencies' take on WAC at the university and within their own areas. I was at the School of Engineering, sitting around a large table with at least 15 to 20 other people. When I had finished a little speech about who we were and what we could do for instructors in engineering, there was a very deep, gruff voice from the far end of the table, "Well, he didn't say the right thing." For an instant, I was sure my new position was in jeopardy. I was able to recover and talk to the professor, who wanted us ultimately to grade his students' writing. I made an appointment to see and talk to him in his office about responding to student writing.

Frank, one of the graduate students in composition who was on the WAC staff, accompanied me to the meeting. During the meeting the engineering professor showed us some student writing. As he and I talked, Frank looked through the writing. At one point Frank said, "There sure is a lot of passive voice here that erases any sort of agency." The engineering professor appeared impressed with Frank's analysis and said something like, "See, that's what I mean. I don't know anything about voice or discursive agency in a text." However, when Frank continued to suggest that "three milliliters of water were poured into a glass beaker" be changed to "I poured three milliliters of water into the glass beaker," the engineering professor actually took the paper out of Frank's hand. It was the last time anyone from the Engineering School ever suggested that we should grade their students' writing.

I think I tend to tell the tale to folks who doubt that disciplinary faculty have pretty strong ideas about the writing their students do. And, to illustrate how limited and arrogant people who work in WAC can be. I find/found interesting (thought about yesterday when I was writing this out—I've always told that tale and never wrote it down) is the nerve that Frank and I had to suggest to an engineering professor that he have his students write in active voice. I think we in comp tend to confuse the knowledge disciplinary faculty have about writing in their areas with their ability to articulate that knowledge in ways we find interesting or relevant.

—Brian Huot

80

Like all of you who work with writing centers and WAC programs, for years now at our college we have been trying to woo faculty across the curriculum to see writing as a skill beyond the sole responsibility of the Writing Lab or the English department. We have a friendly receptive faculty, generally without all the turf hang-ups that might be present on some other campuses. All the same, the changing of minds is a difficult process when most believe the reason they can write well is because an English teacher (a darn good one at that!) somewhere along the line taught them how to diagram sentences.

At our opening faculty workshop this year when we were scrutinizing and dissecting our current general education program, a proposal arose that will bring tears to your WAC ducts. From a corner of the room, Mr. Biology Faculty stood up and suggested, "We think it's time that departments create writing-intensive courses required of their majors. Of course, this would be in addition to the required Comp I class. Unless we all make this a priority, students are not going to write well." It was one of those moments that usually comes in early June, all green and sunnysparks tripping across a lawn smelling of new-mown grass and baby's breath.

Posted on the writing center listserv.

—Katherine Fischer

8 1

One of my committee assignments at the large midwestern university where I taught first-year writing and worked in the writing lab was to be the so-called "Director of Student Affairs." As a committee of one, I was obliged to investigate student or faculty complaints about grades, teaching, harassment, or plagiarism for a program of 5000 students. One of my most startling "cases" was one which turned back on me, so to speak. Two papers written by two different students, one for a lit class, one for a composition class, made their way to my office: a teaching assistant had casually glanced at the top paper on a pile of papers left by another TA to be picked up by students and was startled to recognize a paper which looked remarkably similar to one he had received earlier in his own class; upon examination, the papers turned out to be identical. In the course of the investigation, I turned up even more copies of this paper floating around and traced it to its source. Though no one was very forthcoming at first, the story of "the mother paper" as the dean called it gradually emerged and I began to piece together different students' roles in its distribution. In the teeth of the growing evidence, two of the students whom I happened to have taught earlier in the writing lab came to me, somewhat sheepishly, and admitted their involvement, vowing never to do it again. A third student however, maintained his innocence, supported by his parents, who claimed to have "helped him work on the paper" during the Thanksgiving break, even though the evidence clearly showed that an identical version of the paper was already in existence by that time and had been turned in by another student. The case went on to an appeal, and after a lengthy process of further investigation, interviews and hearings, this third student was found guilty by a panel of students and faculty members and was punished according to university policy, receiving, as had the other students, an F in the course for which the paper had been turned in.

A few months later, just before the fall term was to begin, I was summoned to the dean's office and handed a notarized affidavit written by a student I had worked with over the course of two years both in the writing lab and in the first-year course. The affidavit accused me of having helped him "cheat" by writing his papers for him. It was accompanied by a letter from the parents of the student involved in the plagiarism case, demanding that I be fired, saying that I wasn't a fit person to be teaching young people.

This, of course, was revenge. But though I could draw the original plagiarism case to the dean's attention—indeed, he already knew of it though no mention was made in the letter—and suggest a possible motive for this letter, the investigation still had to proceed. And though I could try to imagine what hold this family might have over my student (he was an athlete and they were well-known boosters of the football team and known for helping out players in non-NCAA sanctioned ways), I could not get over my student's betrayal. By no stretch could the sort of help I gave him in the writing lab and in the class be called cheating. His claim that I had typed papers for him could only refer to the papers we had used "for publication" in our own class or for inclusion in the writing lab publication of student papers. He knew how long and hard I had worked with him and for what purposes.

The case dragged on for two years, investigated first by the arts and sciences dean, then turned over to the dean of the law school (a special prosecutor!), then shifted to a concurrent examination with an NCAA investigator since some students involved were athletes. My colleagues were outraged, feeling that the administration was letting me "twist in the wind" as one said, just because the athletic department was involved. Indeed, I was told I had a "right to counsel" via the university lawyer, but because of the potential damage to the university brought about by an NCAA investigation and possible "conflict of interest," I was advised to find a private lawyer. Finally, I was exonerated, some poor underlings in two deans' offices having had to wade through the volumes of writing in ten of the twenty-two folders from the writing class, not to mention other written evidence from my writing lab teaching as well as taped interviews with students and colleagues and long documents from me explaining my teaching methods and principles.

I told this story at the time to many friends and colleagues, partly to survive while I was in the middle of it. Teaching practices which I valued, which centered on student needs and student learning, and which were highly labor-intensive, involving extensive individual as well as classroom work—these practices had made me vulnerable to the worst betrayal I had ever experienced at the hands of a student. Of course, I knew that just one student was involved—perhaps one who felt cornered or who was simply amoral and took a payoff. Nevertheless, it altered my sense of who I was in the classroom; my assurance that trust and goodwill existed between me and my students disappeared. My teaching had been scrutinized before by tenure committees but never with the searing attention and excruciatingly detailed questions posed by these investigators. I became wary, preparing every document for class, every comment on a student paper with a public and potentially hostile audience in mind.

Why do I tell this story now? Because it provided one of those moments—we all have them in some form or another—when I realized how unstable the teaching relationship is, how irreducible to any single model of "helping" or "facilitating" or "guiding," how dependent teaching practice is on external determinations of "value." The experience dramatized for me at any rate, that all terms within a classroom can be contested—even so seemingly benign a one as "helping." And that all teaching acts are potentially deeply political, embedded as they are within institutions which have competing political agendas and constituencies. In the aftermath of the investigation, I attempted to find out from someone in the administration what effect this case might have on my tenure decision. "Well," said one (joking I suppose), "it's not something you'd want on your activity record." No. But I wonder what would happen if tenure committees looked at teaching practices as seriously as that investigative committee did—and not for purposes of indictment.

—Elizabeth Robertson

8 2

It was obvious that the star basketball player was very bright by the comments he made in class; however, he never turned in his work on time, and what was turned in was only half done, often with much of the assignment missing. One Tuesday morning on the way to class, I picked up a copy of the student newspaper, and found my student's full length picture all the way down the side of the front page. I carefully folded the paper so the headlines proclaiming his scoring ability and the upper part of the picture were visible. I walked into the classroom with the folded paper and laid it on the basketball star's desk with the words, "There will not be any of these headlines next year if you do not pass this class." I walked away and began the class.

After class, I was afraid that I had acted too impulsively and had engendered not only the wrath of the athletic world in general but of our fledgling athletic department in particular. I picked up the phone and dialed Coach X and explained in detail what had been said and why. He thanked me for the call, said he would speak to the student, and asked me to call him back and let him know if the student passed or failed.

At the next class meeting, it was evident that the student was different. His work was prepared; it was well done, and he participated enthusiastically in group discussion. He had truly had a conversion experience! It was not until the last day of class when the portfolios were turned in that this student came up to me and asked, "Well, how did I do?" I praised him effusively, and assured him that if the quality of work I had lately observed was in his portfolio, he would surely get a very good grade.

He looked at me pleadingly and said, "Would you please call Coach X and tell him? I have had to run laps every morning since you called him the first time. He said that would stop only when you called again!"

One of the stories I frequently tell to people both inside and outside the university when they question our policy of admitting students who have a less than stellar academic record.

—Betty J. Anderson

8 3

Recently, at a friend's wedding, I was asked the inevitable question of what I did for a living. My patented response is to reply that I am a writer and a teacher of composition. This short but succinct answer elicits two different responses. The first is overwhelming fear. A fear that I will critique each word that they utter for the rest of the evening. The second is a very terse and self-important, "It must be so easy to teach writing. You must have a lot of free time!" Which is exactly the response I got on this occasion. To this I usually respond by asking, "How easy do you think it is to teach someone else how to think, and express their thoughts in a cohesive manner on a page?" This usually sends them back to the buffet line cursing me for being so flippant, but then I often think that their shortsighted opinion is the result of simply not caring to think at all.

This incident, and others like it, reaffirm my belief that most (and many students) see composition simply as a collection of words on a page without ever considering the communicative power of writing. That power is something that I try to impress upon my students throughout the semester.

—Michael A. Lubarsky

8 4

When I am introduced to people and they learn that I teach college-level English, they then ask, "What do you teach?" Before I can answer I can already see signs of anticipation lighting up their eyes, as if I am going to mention something about literature they hadn't heard before, some juicy tidbit that they can add to their collection of cultural artifacts. Perhaps I will introduce them to a book they hadn't considered, or mention something rare about a famous writer. Often I will see my questioner waiting for my answer with something like baited breath. I often will hesitate in response, not because I am about to announce something momentous, but rather because I will often debate with myself whether this will be the ripe moment to finally be able to say, "Composition." Having answered this way in the past, I have found myself facing a blank in response. Given this previous experience, I have developed the alternative answer, "College writing," which seems to me to have a less hollow ring. However, this answer too is often met with dimmed eyes. Because I have said nothing about literature, my questioner will then nod. A moment of embarrassed silence will then follow for both of us as we each search for a another possibility of common ground.

I tell this story because it highlights the fact that most find composition a dull subject. Apparently, they have unremarkable memories of composition, in contrast to literature. As a result, you will not hear people say that they are going to cozy up with a good pen and paper as they will with a good book. This situation raises a challenge for those of us teaching composition: how to make our writing courses as interesting or even as appealing as composition's more attractive relative, literature. (Told at the same orientation workshop as Tale 76.)

—Scott Weeden

8 5

When I attended the 1993 meeting of NCTE in Pittsburgh, I rode the shuttle buses from one of the outlying hotels to the main conference hotel each morning and evening. Because I was the only passenger on one shuttle bus, the bus driver and I conversed during most of the trip. At one point in the conversation, he asked me about my occupation. I told him, "I direct the Writing Program at Syracuse University." Without a moment's pause he responded, "Do you use the Palmer Method?"

The Palmer Method was for many decades a common program for teaching handwriting in elementary schools and even in Palmer's school for secretaries. It was the method used in my elementary school in the 1950s, for example. I sometimes tell this story to colleagues to illustrate how we need to do a better job of explaining our work to the general public.

—Duane Roen

8 6

On my way to the CCCC in Seattle some years back, I was seated next to a man on the airplane who looked to be in his mid-forties and was obviously on his way to a sales meeting or seminar. He had a large notebook spread out before him filled with pages of text and flowcharts about "reaching potential," "surpassing quotas," "dealing with management," etc. When he saw me perusing my conference program, he asked what I did and where I was headed. When I told him I taught college writing and was on my way to a conference about the same, his eyes lit up, his voice grew animated, and he said he thought that was "wonderful, just wonderful," that writing was one of the most important things one could learn and teach. He continued in this vein for some time, propounding on the importance of good writing skills in today's world and lamenting their lack. Then he told me that he had got hold of a book about eight years ago and it had changed his life. He had read it dozens of times, shared it with scores of men and women he worked with, and carried it with him wherever he went—"like a Bible." He said, "It was written by someone who does what you do. Maybe you've even heard of him." Then he said, "Well, I've got it right here." And he reached down into a pocket of a black leather sales/display case and pulled out a worn and yellowed and dog-eared copy of Peter Elbow's *Writing Without Teachers*.

—Patricia A. Sullivan

8 7

The tale is set in China, where I taught in 1988–89. I was teaching writing, and students were engaged in an activity except for one young man in the back row, copying something furiously. I asked him what it was. (I was obviously not pleased, but also curious.) It was, he said, for his political studies class (which I knew met every Friday). "Ah," I said, "somebody's notes from the last session?" "No," he replied, "it is the final examination." I was puzzled. "You mean the questions?" "No," he shook his head. "The answers. You see, our examination is on Friday, and the teachers know that if everyone writes a good answer—the same answer—that their work as teachers will have been successful. They will look good, we will look good, and the party leaders will be pleased."

I tell this story in graduate courses, TA training sessions, and workshops on pedagogy by way of stimulating discussion on the relationship between teaching and learning. Its setting makes it a good fit for currently fashionable modes of ideological analysis, but it provides useful leverage in other contexts as well.

—Steve North

8 8

When I started teaching in southern Texas, I had lots of "non-traditional" women students in my classes, students who had clawed their way through the local community college, got their sixty hours, and got here on their way to a career. Many of them had experienced major problems in their lives, and for some, these problems would eventually surface in one of my writing classes. I'd inevitably end up knowing things I didn't really want to know. We didn't have much of a counseling center in those days, so I kept business cards from local female counselors whom I had met while teaching journal writing in a local psychiatric hospital. Eventually, a therapist at the hospital and I worked out a deal: she'd invite some of her "clients" who like to write, and I'd invite some of my students who like to write and couldn't afford therapy, and we'd have a creative writing workshop each week in the mental hospital. This was eight or nine years ago.

That's where I met "Shirley." Shirley is this wonderful, brilliant, intuitive storyteller who comes from an East Texas, black sharecropping tradition. She had some bad family experiences growing up, chopped cotton, finished fourth grade. We hit it off fine, and she told me that she wanted to work on a GED some day. She wanted to write a book about her life experiences, so she'd write the draft, and I'd type a corrected version into the computer for her. She'd practice her reading on the printout, and then make revisions. Eight years later, she and I are meeting in my office, still working on her book. By now she's got a sheaf of poems and a manuscript of a novel. Lately I've been teaching writing at a local therapeutic children's home, to a group of adolescent girls sheltered there from abusive situations at home. The girls heard me talk about Shirley, so they wanted to meet her. I asked Shirley if she wanted to come meet the girls some evening. She did, and she gave a wonderful testimony about her life experiences, and about how much writing had helped her heal. She even showed them her journal and handed out copies of her poems. She finished her talk by saying, "Take advantage of what's on offer here and learn. Don't wait, like me, until you're fifty-six years old." When she finished, the girls clapped and cheered, and then they spontaneously formed a line to talk to her. Many of the girls wanted her to autograph the copy of the poem she had given them to read. Later, when we had cleared the girls' living quarters, Shirley collapsed into my arms and started to cry. She told me she was overcome by the girls' responses, that they even wanted her autograph. "That's just about the best thing that's ever happened to me in my life."

And she's taking GED classes now, too.

I've never told this story to anyone, although I have talked about Shirley with folks, especially women, in sheltered environments. My habit is to keep this kind of information confidential. Also I think I have not told this story about Shirley because I would be afraid listeners might think I was trying to take some credit for her achievement. I can tell it here because I can make it clear that it is Shirley who gets all the credit.

—Robb Jackson

8 9

When I teach my students the importance of using non-sexist language, they sometimes do not understand why it's exclusionary to say policeman, fireman, or postman instead of police officer, fire fighter or postal carrier. But when I tell them a story about my seventy-five-year-old father, who I have a very close relationship with, the point always becomes clear. Dad has a favorite saying that goes, "Time waits for no man." For two years every time my father said "Time waits for no man," I would say, "or woman!" Then, I would explain to Dad that he was excluding Mom, my sister and I when he referred to the human race in this way. The last time I was home for a visit, my father was speaking to one of his grandchildren about getting a job with a new company. During the course of the conversation he said to his nineteen-year-old grandson, "Time waits for no man—or woman." He then paused a moment and rephrased his expression yet again, and as he turned to me and smiled he said, "Time waits for no one."

One of my favorite stories. I tell it to my students every semester!

—Tammy Winner-White

9 0

There are two versions of this story, plus a coda. The first is the story I tell colleagues whenever the subject of plagiarism—usually accompanied by laments about "students today" or breathless accounts of library and Internet detective work—comes up. The second is a related story my family often tells. As for the coda: If you read it and think, "Ahhh . . . justice is served," then I haven't told these stories well.

VERSION 1: I come from a family of plagiarizers, a family that has never defined plagiarism as bound up with morality. My parents view school systems as just that—a system, something to get through, out-smart, and hopefully emerge from, fully credentialed, relatively unscathed. The system is inflexible, remote, menacing. Plagiarism is an act of survival. Or maybe it would be more accurate to say plagia-rism was how we hoodwinked the system. It gave us a little power, a good laugh, and since none of us ever got caught, we got our diplomas too. Does this sound immoral? I suppose it should to me today, but I'm still not convinced. Literacy, gender, class, power: These speak to me more than statements about what's right and what's wrong.

For instance: When I was fourteen, I was deemed by my high school "non-collegebound" and was enrolled in the county vocational center. I deliberately wrote that last sentence in passive voice because I still can't figure out who it is—the system?—that's responsible for this. My par-ents weren't troubled. They figured I could be certified for secretarial work via the vo-tech school plus a year at Katharine Gibbs. (My father, by the way, still has my final grade report from Katharine Gibbs that records my twenty-eight absences. He thinks it's hysterical that I man-aged to graduate with "merit," that I really had my way with the system that time.) Even though I was a student at the vocation center, which offered no classes in English, I considered myself a writer. My father considered himself a writer too. I guess we didn't believe, not at that time, that the system really had the power to determine these things for us. When my brother needed a paper for a senior honors English class, I wrote it for him. Actually, my father and I both wrote it for him, bat-tling back and forth over who would hold the pen, and my father is responsible for the paper's wretched last sentence: "Thus it is evident that Richard Nixon is truly a paradox within an enigma." My mother was assigned the task of typing the whole mess up. That's always the job she was assigned as she was known to be neat and careful about gram-mar, while my father and I—we were the ones with *vision* and *ideas*. My brother didn't help with the paper at all. He didn't need to know how to write (the family logic went) because he was good at math.

So the vo-tech student wrote the senior honors paper. We all had a good laugh about that, though I can also remember a pushy impulse to put my name on that paper along with a great big SO THERE! Even today I feel like yelling SO THERE! whenever I drive by the Lorain County Vocational Center, though I never do because I know it's neither satisfying nor meaningful to shout at a gray, low, windowless building. The paper was turned in under my brother's name and it came back with an A+ and a request from the English teacher to keep it as a model for future classes. Winkwink. Laughlaugh. My parents like to tell this story still.

There's a punch line that they always like to add: Some years later the English teacher showed up at my parents' door. She was agitated, upset, and very apologetic because, it turned out, someone had stolen that model paper on "Richard Nixon: A Paradox within an Enigma" and submitted it for another class. My parents expressed horror. They promised to relay to my brother the message that she'd done her best to protect his words. Winkwink. Laughlaugh. When they tell this story, I think my parents aren't just amused but proud. Sometimes I think that I'm proud too. Mostly, though, I feel strange, now that I'm an English teacher too.

VERSION 2: When I was in second grade my mother signed up for classes at a local college, thinking she might become an elementary school teacher. Her try at college didn't last long, and all I know about her experience (because I've never asked, not once) is the story of how my father wrote all her papers for freshman comp. Mom would protest—this is what she says today, whenever the story comes up— and try to write them herself. But then my father would appear. This was in the kitchen, my mother working at the table by the window. He would look over her shoulder and say, "No, no, not that. Here, move over. Let me do this." My mother got all A's on those papers he wrote. That's a part of what makes this a story they like to tell. "See," my father says, some thirty years later. "I told you I could write them better, and I could!"

For this story too there's a punch line: At the semester's end, the professor asked my mother if he could quote her essays in an article he was writing about how to teach writing.

Coda: Years later when my brother was in the Persian Gulf, my mother asked me if I could write a letter for her, one she could edit and punctuate, to send to his ship. Instead I gave her a copy of Peter Elbow's *Writing with Power*. (One year into a master's program, and I was already so much a part of the system, I couldn't even see it. I thought I was being benevolent, helpful, kind.) Sometime after that, when I asked her if she'd read Elbow's book and if she'd written to Jim, she showed me the book. Yes, she'd read it. She'd marked one or two sentences on almost every page with a yellow highlighter. She had highlighted the instructions for and benefits of freewriting, made note of the difference between criterion-and reader-based feedback. But as for the letter, no, she never wrote one, and my father, struggling, depressed as 1980s downsizing bounced him from one job to the next, didn't feel like writing anymore. My mom sent my brother a videotape of a family gathering instead.

No one in my family tells this story because there isn't a good laugh here, nothing to make us say, "Yeah, we really got 'em there."

—*Nancy Welch*

🖙   🖙   🖙

NOTES

TALES 76 (p. 96) AND 77 (p. 97). It is a standard finding of the sociology of groups that feelings of enmity are strongest between groups contingent to each another (think of cross-town athletic rivalries). As a group, people who work in writing centers—aptly named—sometimes seem the most encircled and conflicted. They may sense everyone else, including other composition specialists, as both friend and foe, us and public (see Tale 134). Composition generalists sometimes have the same kind of love-hate relationship with the literature "side." In comp lore, traditionally the other two hometown out-groups are athletes and the Greek system, a conflict that can be heard in comp tales scattered throughout this book. But how much of the enmity is rivalry? And if we tend to feel these other groups as rivals, what are we competing for, and how are we matched? (RHH)

TALES 79 (p. 98) AND 80 (p. 99). With the writing-across-the-curriculum movement, faculty outside English no longer appear so purely as public. I've pretty much stopped telling of a teacher I once knew in the journalism school who informed his students that a sentence could never have more than one comma, and I certainly don't tell it to WAC listeners. My sense of the comp public has changed. As everybody involved with WAC knows, and as Tale 80 relates, the in-group turns out larger than the composition profession used to think. (RHH)

TALES 83–90 (pp. 103–108). It seems that the more we move out beyond the walls of the university, the more diffuse and scattered are the comp tales. We received few tales, such as Tale 88, from areas that composition is just beginning to occupy—community service, computer technology, business and industry, distance learning, family literacy. And not many of the few we got have the sharp, familiar plots, for instance, of the comp/athletics or comp/literature tales. The voice of the public, heard at times as antagonistic and at times as friendly, is a voice we are not very sure of. It's as though the tales are exploring their own potential as the profession explores the new territory. (RHH)

TALE 88 (p. 106). A rare story of collaborative teaching with people outside the academy: first with a therapist in a mental hospital and then with a psychiatric hospital "client" turned writer at a local therapeutic children's home. I can't help thinking the narrator has to take some credit for his willingness to work with such a broad range of collaborators and students. The narrator's reflection points to the role of the audience in the life of the story. His concern over confidentiality suggests that he does not believe writing teachers would hear and retell the story in the same way as "women, in sheltered environments" would. I also find interesting the narrator's conviction that writing allows him more control over how the audience hears his intent for telling the story than oral storytelling. (MZL)

TALE 90 (p. 108). Welch wrote to us, "the story is about my family, and the connection to schooling, to comp, to me as a teacher/storyteller today might be too tenuous." Tenuous in today's world of composition, perhaps, but not necessarily in tomorrow's. (RHH)

TALE 90 (p. 108). There are so many stories about the teaching and learning of writing folded within each version of the "plagiarism" stories that, as my students like to say, "it makes my brain hurt." Just to mention a few: This tale points to several possible hidden scripts to student plagiarism. The narrator's family wrote papers for one another "to hoodwink the system." And they did so by pooling the individual strengths of the family team—to get the best work done in the most efficient way, which, ironically, is a common workplace literacy skill observed by various studies. The story also indicates that the ability and desire to write is related to the person's ability to retain a sense of her or his self as a writer in spite of the tracking of educational systems. Depressed over his job situation, the narrator's father "didn't feel like writing anymore" (probably because it had become harder for him to believe that the system really does not have the power to determine "for" him who is or who is not a writer). By recounting the request of her mother's professor to cite the essay her father had written, the narrator calls into question the validity of composition scholarship that relies on student writing. (MZL)

CHAPTER 8

⟿

Professionalism

For philosopher Alasdair MacIntyre, morality consists not in the following of rules but in the exercising of the virtues. MacIntyre would argue that in the teaching of composition, as in any professional practice, right action will be better expressed in stories than in a code of ethics. I hasten to say that MacIntyre does not believe that morality is purely situational—quite the opposite. For MacIntyre the virtues are kept stable because, when exercised, they achieve the goods internal to professional practices and they achieve the personal development and social integration necessary for a satisfying individual life. He says they also sustain the cultural traditions in which practices are embedded and from which individuals acquire their sense of identity. MacIntyre is speaking of virtues such as courage, truthfulness, constancy, integrity, justice. Without them, he is saying, our *beginnings* never acquire the satisfaction and wholeness of a *career*, our *colleagues* never transform into ideal *imagoes*, and our *classroom* practices never convert to *professionalism*.

If this all seems a little cloudy and more than a little abstract, note the hard fact that the field of composition does not have a professional code but does have a working set of tales. In maintaining the kind of virtuous acts that add up to what we call professionalism, stories serve because they illustrate people making choices rather than applying rules. Virtue manifests itself, says MacIntyre, "in the kind of capacity for judgment which the agent possesses in knowing how to select among the relevant stack of maxims and how to apply them in particular situations" (1984, p. 223). What is professionalism, then, as narrated by comp tales? It is comp teachers making commitments to ethical positions through choices that can be called virtuous because they support the goods of the practice, the traditions of the community, and the growth of the teacher, commitments made with the awareness that the choices cannot be fully defended, that other options are defensible. Acts of professionalism appear wherever there is a need for contested choice, that is, a need within sites shaped by the deep ambivalences of the writing, the student, and the public, and always within the self. For its expression, comp professionalism finds in comp tales a natural vehicle. (RHH)

⌐ ⌐ ⌐

9 1

Last semester, one of my Advanced Exposition students began addressing me by various nicknames whenever he ran into me outside of class. His favorite nickname was "Easter Bunny." I don't know why he picked "Easter Bunny," but clearly the point was to test me—to see if he could get away with insolence, or to see if he could get me to lose my temper. So I tried to laugh off his name-calling: I asked if he had forgotten my name or if I should spell "Deb" for him. But when he decided to call me "Easter Bunny" in front of the class, I knew I had to respond more sternly. Knowing he came to Advanced Exposition immediately after History of the English Language, I asked him if he ever called Dr. Brosnahan "Easter Bunny." He said of course not, he always addressed Dr. Brosnahan by title. I told him that I deserved as much respect as his other (male) professors, so he should begin calling me Dr. Knutson. Apparently, he liked this show of authority: he responded by asking me out for a beer. Immediately, several of his classmates jumped in. They told him he couldn't ask me that. And while he had talked back to me when I had called him on his behavior, he promptly retreated when his classmates spoke up.

Students who test the boundaries with me are bothersome, but not nearly as troubling as those who test the boundaries with other students. I am a lot tougher than the students realize, and I won't hesitate to stand up for myself. But in parallel situations, many female undergraduates accept bullying behavior from their male classmates. In fact, many don't recognize that they are being tested, and others even seem to enjoy letting male students assert power.

This semester, for example, I have two students from the baseball team in one developmental writing class. In one early paper, they each wrote about how "everyone" looks up to them because they are athletes. When I read their papers, I thought them terribly naïve. I had already had to kick them both out of class for being disruptive and unprepared. Who would look up to them? Yet one day this week, when I assigned a group project, two of my more serious female students rushed to join the baseball players' group. The players were very glad to have these women in their group: the women did all of the work while the men talked sports and parties. Perhaps the women would have preferred to have the men help, but they were willing to work unaided if it meant they'd have an opportunity to be close to the players. Dealing with the players is actually the easy part of this situation. Naturally, the next time I assign a small group task, I'll assign students to groups to see if other peers will force the players to work. But I don't know how to make these women understand that they shouldn't have to put up with such behavior.

Back when I first started teaching, I used this story whenever I had any type of discipline problem in the classroom, I would become practically obsessed with how student behavior affected ME. But as I've come to realize that I will always have some underprepared students who have little idea how to behave in a college classroom, I've also come to realize that their behavior doesn't have a great effect on me—but it can, unfortunately, affect my other students. Therefore, I use this story when talking to new teachers about various ways to deal with discipline problems in the classroom. And I also use such stories in undergraduate classes (with some modifications so no one will recognize a friend or roommate) to illustrate why I have a participation grade (rather than an attendance grade) and to explain what kind of classroom behavior I expect.

—Debra S. Knutson

9 2

My first semester as an assistant professor, I found myself required to observe the teaching of a GTA. I arranged to visit his classroom about the eighth week of the semester. Novice that I was, I still knew something major was wrong even before the teacher came in. The students were glum and sullen, isolated, staring at the floor. The teacher marched into the room, radiating ill will. He gave a twenty-minute talk over coherence, full of mistakes and illustrations sounding like they had been taken from a sixth-grade primer. He then handed out a page of "transition words" and told the students that they had to have them memorized by next period. He spent the rest of the hour quizzing the students over usage conundrums: *shall* and *will*, *between* and *among*, *like* and *as*. No one volunteered, and when he called on someone, he often cut the answer off in mid-sentence. Correct responses were rewarded with sarcasm: "Good guess, or did your little sister teach you that?" I had never even imagined a classroom in which students and teacher had come to hate each other so palpably.

The next Monday the GTA came to my office, late in the afternoon. He asked me to write him a letter of recommendation. Inner panic. I had been trying to think of positive things to say in the classroom observation report I would have to send to my chair. How could I recommend him in a letter? But I was too green to say no. I told him, sure, I would be willing to write him a letter. He said, no, that he needed it right now. "This week?" "No," he said, "Right now. Just a paragraph, that's all I need." I swear—it seems impossible, looking back on it now—but I swear that I was within an inch of saying OK. But then a gear inside me turned a notch, like some kind of clock mechanism, and I looked at him and said, "I can't do that." He got up and left my office without a word.

A few days later the department discovered that he had packed his bags that evening and left town, without notifying his landlord, the chair, or anybody. I thought to myself, thank God that inner gear turned, and I felt (not for the last time in my career) that I had finally come of age.

I told this around at the time but only rarely since, usually to younger colleagues when the subject of letters of rec comes up.

—Author's name withheld

9 3

In the semester before I became director of the composition program, I made an effort to bridge the gap between tenure-track and part-time faculty; I planned a composition reception at my house, inviting the current director, a male literature faculty member who is still at State

U, and all other instructors of composition, faculty, TAs and adjuncts. A week or so after sending out invitations, my husband received a phone call from one of the male faculty inviting him to "a department poker game" scheduled at the same time as the composition reception. Knowing that the director is a poker player, I asked him if he was planning to attend the reception. No. He's going to the game. So are most of the male faculty in the department. Neither myself, nor any other female in the department is invited, nor are any part-time faculty. Feeling a bit put out both by the timing of this game and the fact that my husband was invited while I was not, I asked the previous director why I had been overlooked. Was it the scheduling? Did they, in other words, plan to have their game conflict? No, he said, he hadn't realized they were at the same time. Then why wasn't I invited? I happen to be a fair poker player and enjoy a friendly game. Getting only "umms" and "wells . . ." I asked if it had anything to do with the fact that I wasn't a man. For that, I got a grin. No, we just didn't think you'd want to. Oh, I see. So it was a penis thing after all. I had another conversation about this same poker game with a younger male faculty member. I expressed my dismay at having my husband invited to department get-togethers while I was excluded. (I should mention too that this little situation put a strain on my personal relationship as well. Because I was vocal about feeling excluded on the basis of sex, my husband was not invited to any other "male" functions including departmental golf outings, in which he had participated a number of times. It seems he was ostracized because he couldn't control his "mouthy wife.") I mentioned my frustration at this situation to these two men not be confrontational, but to make a point about gender discrimination. And make it I did, for the next day I found a note in my office mailbox that contained the following "joke":

Top Ten Reasons Why the English Department Pokerplayin' Boys Won't Invite Their Female Colleagues to the Table

10. Too many important university decisions to be made
 9. Playmates of Sweden playing cards
 8. Desire to play more than four hands per hour
 7. Averse to cat fights
 6. Would upset the yin-yang of post-game orgy
 5. Averse to Cindy Lauper background music
 4. Long-standing castration complexes
 3. Played cards with domineering mother as a child

2. Would have to place moratorium on tampon jokes
1. Girls just don't know how to lay 'em down

Upon reading this mistake of a joke, I went to my office and printed out a copy of the legal definition of sexual harassment from the Internet. Highlighting appropriate passages (especially the passage which defines gender harassment as "Generalized sexist statements and behavior that convey insulting or degrading attitudes about women. Examples include insulting remarks, offensive graffiti, obscene jokes or humor about sex or women in general"), I stapled this definition to a copy of the "joke" and left it in the department chair's box. I watched him from my office door as he retrieved the papers, reading first the "joke," which was on top. He laughed out loud. Upon turning the page, however, his face went white. It was then that I approached him and explained the inappropriateness of such a document. Two days later I received a detailed apology from the sender of the "joke." Matter closed. I had requested a public discussion of this event in order to raise consciousness about sexual harassment in our department, but the issue was not mentioned again.

—Author's name withheld

9 4

I once wrote an article about three of Hemingway's Nick Adams stories. My thesis was that the three stories had to be read as a group because the later two gave clues about how the first was to be interpreted. I also argued that the first one had been seriously misread by most of the critics. The manuscript was far too long, but I figured that if it was of good quality, *Studies in Short Fiction* would probably want it and would give me advice about how to cut it.

I was somewhat taken aback when the editor's response arrived. It said that they liked my reading of the first story, but didn't find the second half of the article sufficiently useful to warrant publication. Would I, they asked, be willing to chop it in half and publish simply an interpretation of the first story?

Now since my point had been about the necessary connections among the three stories, the ethical thing to do would have been to say no. But who wants to be that bullheaded when it comes to having a publication accepted in a major journal? So I threw away my thesis and the discussion of the later stories.

The piece was published, and has been reprinted in two anthologies since then. I say, learn to trust editors!

I tell this one in advanced and graduate courses to illustrate both the pragmatics of getting published and also what global revision can involve. There is more than a trace of irony at my own expense, as well as implied critique of a system in which "getting into print" is more important than what you wish to say.

—Richard Fulkerson

9 5

Last spring I designed the curriculum of my first-year, research writing course around issues of the Vietnam War. One of the students to express keen interest was a young man named Don. Within a few days, the reason for his interest became obvious. "My father was a part of this war," he wrote in his learning log, "and it really screwed him up. The war is why my father left my mother." I learned later that Don and his two brothers rarely saw their father as they were growing up, and Don himself had only recently pursued regular contact with his father.

I handed out all four paper assignments early on, and Don immediately knew how he wanted to orchestrate his choice of options. First, he would research the Green Berets. His father had been a Green Beret medic. Then he would dedicate his "hero" paper to his father, who had been awarded the Congressional Medal of Honor for saving a buddy's life. Finally, he would research Post Traumatic Stress Disorder (PTSD), which had plagued his father and ruined his parents' marriage.

In Don's paper on the Green Berets, he reconstructed what he knew about his father's war experience. The story goes that as a medic, his father had shown extraordinary bravery in rescuing the life of his best friend and had been awarded the Medal of Honor (this country's most distinguished combat award). Later, that friend would die in battle, and his father placed the medal on his friend's coffin in tribute to him. After reading Don's rough draft, I tried to look up his father's name on the Vietnam Veterans Home Page, which lists Medal of Honor winners. His name was not there. Could it be that Don's last name was different than his father's? Or perhaps the mission had been covert and therefore classified? Or had Don misunderstood, or been misinformed? Should I warn him? What about the personal cost to him when he finds out? In the end, I decided to say nothing. This was

Don's battle, a very personal one, and I already knew that given his sequence of research projects, he would soon find out for himself.

How and when, I'll never know, but in the next rough draft for the "hero" essay, I learned that Don had indeed made the same discovery. His reaction? He called his father and asked him, "Why did you lie to me about this medal?" The essay relates the amended version of his father's story; Don kept faith with his belief that his father was (still) a hero. By his final paper, analyzing the causes of PTSD in Vietnam veterans, Don could relate several stories his father had told him, stories that explained the years of alcoholism, isolation, and suicide attempts.

In Don's final assessment of the course, he wrote: "The papers I have presented throughout the semester are dedicated to my father, a Vietnam veteran and PTSD sufferer. He will never gain his sense of direction back, and will keep living his life in the past. . . ." What stands out for me is Don's personal journey, the hard truth he faced with courage, the relationship he understood more clearly and valued more highly because of his expanded awareness. I don't think he ever worried about the "cost." He experienced something far more important: "my assignments have helped me gain a sense of accomplishment, understanding, and peace."

I've told this only to a very few people, one a friend and colleague at another university who is interested in the ethical complications of teacher and writing-student relationships.

—Jan Haswell

9 6

This year, I found a site prepared by a *professor* who had lifted the entire RSCC online writing lab and placed it on his site!

As writing and design become more integrated, I think we're going to have to worry about design plagiarism, too.

Appeared on the writing center listserv.

—Jennifer Jordan-Henley

9 7

Whenever I hear teachers complaining about students plagiarizing in their papers, I think about the problems of figuring out exactly what constitutes fair use and when that slips off the edge into stealing. For those of us in writing centers who've ventured into setting up OWLs (Online Writing Labs) that include instructional materials on our Web sites, this is a perplexing problem that won't go away.

How do we define the parameters of sharing vs. violating fair use standards on the Web when the Internet invites such easy exchange? That wasn't on anyone's mind one afternoon in our writing lab when one of the grad tutors sat at a computer near where I was talking with some other tutors. (It was a slow day in our lab.) As this tutor surfed some Web sites with interests similar to hers, she remarked to us that she found someone whose OWL had instructional materials on the topic for which she had written handouts for our OWL. As she read one of the handouts on this other site, we heard her say, "WOW, this guy thinks about this stuff too . . . ummmm . . . this sounds familiar . . . this is awfully familiar . . . HEY . . . I wrote that."

We raced over to join her at her computer monitor as she explored the site. Slowly we realized that what this person had done was to download many of our instructional materials and put them up on his site, stripped of any shred of our identification or our copyright notice. She sent an e-mail message to him to let him know we had seen his site and thought that he either had to acknowledge his source or take down the site. It took several messages from her before he eventually deleted the site, grumbling that all he had wanted to do was to show others on his campus what an OWL should look like. He never did explain why that necessitated deleting our name, our copyright notice, and any identifying link back to our site.

When I tell this story, I tend to add that I wonder what this guy does when he suspects one of his students has plagiarized some material. I also tell this story to counter the one-sided view that only students (the eternal "they") plagiarize while teachers (the eternal "we") are above that sort of mortal sin. We need to remember that we too are prone to shortcuts and to thinking that our excuses are valid even though students' reasons aren't. I've also told this story when I hear people talking about the glorious freedom of the Internet that permits us to share, as if any curbs or definitions of fair use inhibit the free exchange of ideas that academics revel in. As academics we need to remember that we are not above making unfair use of the work of others.

—*Muriel Harris*

98

I had just moved to a new university, a large state university in a rural area. I was teaching basic writing, and had asked my students to write about a "subculture" to which they belonged or knew something about. Three African American students wrote first drafts about city gangs. I returned all three papers with suggestions for drawing more on personal experience or introducing some research, as all three lacked much detail.

One of the students, a football player from California on a full-ride athletic scholarship, brought his revision to me at the next class to look over before he shared it with his group. The personal experience he had added was about being the driver in a van for a drive-by shooting, one that resulted in the death of an elderly man and the wounding of his grandson, a rival gang member. I did not know what to do. I certainly didn't want the student to share this with his group. I gave the class a quick writing assignment and headed for the nearest phone to talk to my department chair. He advised me to find a reason to keep the paper and come to his office immediately after class.

When I arrived at his office, he had already notified the police. A copy of the paper was quickly faxed to police in the student's hometown. For the next couple of weeks, university attorneys coerced me into playing for time with the student, asking for a new assignment, not telling him what had happened. I was scared for him, and for myself—as I was not told what kind of investigation was taking place, whether the student had been questioned—no details. It occurred to me that I might even become a target for a revenge shooting.

Then the student disappeared. I inquired through my chair whether the student had been arrested. Again, no one would tell me (or my chair) what was happening. I was told, however, that if I did not give the original paper to the police, I could be an "accessory after the fact." I had some doubts about the veracity of the details (I knew from years of teaching that students, like other good writers, often enhance their personal experiences to make better stories). I knew that this student, who had shown strong talent as a writer, had escaped from the 'hood on a scholarship—and that my inquiry as to what to do with his paper may have taken him straight back and to jail. I never did find out what happened to him, and to this day I ask myself whether I did the right thing.

I now warn students that my confidentiality as a teacher is not privileged, and to be thoughtful about what they share.

I've told this to a few close friends.

—Author's name withheld

9 9

Last year in freshman composition I had a student I'll call Brian. He was a big, fun, friendly guy. To say that he didn't perceive himself as intellectual would be an understatement, but he worked hard in a setting in which he obviously was not comfortable. His grades hovered at around the C level even with a fair application of effort.

Toward the end of the semester I always have my students engage in a collaborative, multi-genre project. It is self-directed and creative, and the writing responsibilities are shared across the group, so usually enthusiasm and creativity run high, and most students do well on it. Brian's group was no exception, and they ended the semester with an A on the project.

As I calculated grades for the semester, I made an error on Brian's. Even with the final A, he should have been somewhere in the B- to C+ range, but I miscalculated and gave him an A. I never would have known, except that some of his group members came to see me at the beginning of the next semester, wondering why Brian received a higher course grade than they did, when they had higher grades going into the final project than he did. I mumbled something about how they probably didn't know all of the factors that went into the grading, then I went to my grade book and checked on it. Sure enough—his grade was wrong. I struggled with what to do. It's one thing to call a student with the news that I had miscalculated and that the grade would be raised, but I felt very uncomfortable about taking something away once I had given it. I struggled over what to do for a couple of weeks.

In the meantime, Brian had enrolled in my section for the second semester of the comp sequence. He came in the first day and claimed a prominent seat, engaged with me and the material immediately, took students new to the course under his wing, and generally kept his level of enthusiasm and excitement high. His answers were smart, and his enthusiasm was contagious. Needless to say, I did not change the grade, and Brian's behavior remained consistent through the last day of the course. He earned his A this time.

While this took place just last year, I have told this story many times—to university colleagues while talking comp, to high school teachers during staff development workshops, and to education students in classes I've taught on both the graduate and undergraduate levels. It illustrates the fundamental dangers and impossibilities of the grading system we use. Low grades, even if they are fair, serve more as an inhibitor to improved performance than a motivator. But even more frustrating to me is the fact that this story does not furnish us with a method of providing for all students what I inadvertently provided for Brian—not in the context of the grading system we use. To raise grades on purpose across the board renders them meaningless. It is only because Brian believed that I saw true ability in him that it "worked."

—Cindy Sabik

100

In my third year as Director of Writing Programs, I got an angry phone call from a computer sciences professor at my school. His daughter had gotten an F in English 101, and he was sure she'd been treated unfairly. I told him that I would talk to his daughter, not him. He put her on the phone. We made an appointment. In the meantime, I called the instructor, who explained that the girl had missed seventeen class meetings and had not turned in an equivalent amount of writing. I got a copy of the grade book. Clearly the F was warranted.

The girl showed up at my office and I asked her about the absences. She immediately agreed that she'd missed that much class and that the F was deserved. The only reason she'd come in was because her father had made her. The rub was that the father didn't know about the absences. She had missed that much class because she had taken a job, against her father's wishes, and he couldn't know about the job. She was telling me this in confidence, and would I please not say anything to the father. I agreed but noted the position this put me in. She was embarrassed by the whole deal but also didn't want to get in trouble with dad; she told me I could tell him she failed because she missed class but I couldn't say why and she wouldn't confirm for him what she was willing to confirm for me.

A few days later the father shows up at my office, and he's pissed. The girl is with him. She's told him that the grade stands. I tell the father she failed because she missed seventeen classes. The father calls me a liar and the teacher a liar. "I bring my daughter to campus every day, including the days you say she missed class. She walks in the building with me." What the father does not know is that the girl walks in the back door of the building with him and then out the front door by herself, to catch the bus to the mall, where she works at Target. I stand by the teacher. The father yells at me. The girl looks at the floor, silent. That was eight years ago. The professor/father has not spoken to me since then.

I tell this story to show the complicated roles that writing program administrators find themselves in, to show the need to keep confidences and the terrible costs sometimes of doing so.

—Doug Hesse

NOTES

TALE 92 (p. 115). A first-time teaching tale to be read and retold alongside Tale 6 (p. 14). Both teachers face the dilemma of having to lie in order to carry out the professional dictum of finding-something-positive-to-say-about-the-performance-of-students, undergraduate or GTA. In both cases, it was the student, his ability (or refusal) to grasp and acknowledge the teacher's unspoken critique of his performance, which ultimately shaped the contour of the teacher's professional journey. (MZL)

TALE 93 (p. 116). Another tale pointing to the relation between our understanding of collegiality and our sense of professionalism. Three aspects of this story stand out when I put it beside Tales 20, 21, and 22. 1) Would the "Pokerplayin' Boys" invite the male TAs and adjuncts to their game? 2) U.S. culture tends to personalize social relations when dealing with asymmetrical power relations along lines of gender, race, and class. The narrator's request for a public discussion of the event was ignored. On one hand, a "personal" apology from the sender of the "joke" to the narrator (but not from all the pokerplayin' boys to all female colleagues) is all that it takes to "handle—dissolve" a critical inquiry into the issues involved. On the other, efforts to preserve the status quo are localized into punishment of the husband for failing to micro-manage the "family" relation. 3) To what extent are some of our reservations towards hiring couples related to the potential disruption such hiring might bring to conventional "collegiality" inter and intra the sexes rather than related to the fear of creating voting blocks? (MZL)

TALE 94 (p. 118). This tale reminds us that irony is often deployed by the narrators of comp tales not only because of its standing as one of the dominant dispositions of the English profession but also because it enables both the teller and the listener to criticize the "system" without losing sight of the agency of individual members—that is, one another's responsibility to imagine and work for alternatives to those credible options allowed for by the system at a given time and place. It also raises the question: if "getting into print" is so central to the making and breaking of writing teachers' careers, how and why do we have so few stories concerning this aspect of our work in the collection? (MZL)

TALE 95 (p. 119). Works well with tales similar to 38 (p. 46) and 69 (p. 82). (MZL)

TALES 96 AND 97 (p. 120). Jordan-Henley's startling two-sentence narrative of what happened to her community-college online writing lab was immediately supported on the listserv by Harris's tale. How often one tale is prompted by another as an act of community cohesion! This tale by Harris illustrates another important function of comp tales. Although sometimes they can serve as moralia, perpetuating stock virtues of the profession, other times they serve as more speculative exempla, explorative of new territory where the traditional maxims may or may not apply. (RHH)

TALE 97 (p. 120). Another example of the connection between "professionalism" and the profession's official representations of "students" and their "writings." It suggests the need to experiment with and the possibilities of telling and retelling some of the stories in Chapters 4, 5, 6, alongside stories of "professionalism" similar to this one. The narrator reminds us to review the actions we take towards students' violation of our sense of professional ethics in the context of how we practice such ethics in our professional activities. (MZL)

TALE 98 (p. 122). When I read this tale beside Tale 81 (p. 100), I am reminded of the ways in which legal institutions and extracurricular relations mediate our teaching. Decisions on what kind of writing we solicit from students as well as what to do with their writings are never purely academic. When I read this tale alongside Tale 100 (p. 124), I am reminded also of Tale 90 (p. 108). Decisions on what we tell and do not tell our colleagues about what we know about our students cannot be separated from our sense of the differences in how each of us and the individual colleague might respond to the words of the students. And those decisions depend on our sense of how that colleague might deploy the power he or she enjoys over us and/or the students in reaction to the revelation. (MZL)

TALES 98–100 (pp. 122–124). Professionalism shows best on new ground. Tale 98: What do you do when the law asks you to break student-teacher confidentiality? Tale 99: What do you do when student-teacher confidentiality asks you to keep quiet about your own mistake? Tale 100: What do you do when student-teacher confidentiality asks you to lie in public? At some level every comp tale is a tale of professionalism, a tale of an event, actual or virtual, that tests the way all of us in the field should behave. But these last three tales of the chapter record comp life at its most complicated and conflicted. What other discourse mode could convey as fully the hard-earned virtues of experience? (RHH)

CHAPTER 9

⇆

Imagoes

*Well, I do not get answers, but the memory of similar
situations, that is the answer. That I spontaneously
remember how he reacted when the chaos happened
with the car. That somebody had crashed right into my
car which I had parked in front of the house. And it was
the day we came from the celebration of the final school
exams of my daughter. And then the smashed car in
front of the house. That he said: "We wanted to drink
coffee now, and so we will do it." And we did exactly
that. This calmness, this only comes when I am in a
panic, when I am standing in the cemetery and say,
"Well, I have lived through something very bad," and
then I hear that. And then I get also quieter.*

—Woman informant,
who goes to her husband's grave to talk,
recorded by Ingrid E. Josehs (1997, p. 365).

To the degree that comp tales are personal anecdotes, stories in which
the teller is the protagonist, they contain not heroes but *imagoes*. An
imago is the way we personify our self or our selves. It is the kind of person or persons we imagine ourselves, ideally, to be. An imago is not the
central personality construct or archetype that a trained psychologist
might realize is controlling our lives (martyr, orphan, fighter, etc.). More
restricted, more transient, imagoes are the current main characters of
our lifestory. Dan P. McAdams calls them "capsule self-definitions" (1996,
p. 141). Tough-love-teacher. Taker-of-the-student's-side. Grammar-witch.
Lone-cutting-edge-explorer-of-technology-in-the-department.

Just as every comp tale projects a professional act, every comp tale projects an imago. In Tale 100, for example, Hesse comes across as the caught-in-the-crossfire-but-honorer-of-his-word-WPA. The imagoes illustrated in this chapter, however, are one step more complicated. They project the teller's identity through a person that stands outside them. These imagoes run the risk of looking like fictional heroes, characters that take on the shape of role model or *beau ideal* or figurehead. But they are more complex than that. As McAdams points out, the imagoes of one's lifestory emerge from conflict and convey that conflict. Commonly people maintain two central but contradictory imagoes at a time, sometimes more (1993, p. 122). And people constantly create, modify, and reject imagoes as the story of their life keeps changing (Maruna, 1997). Comp imagoes reveal, then, the way comp folk have coped with the contradictions of their lives, but they do not have to gloss over the contradictions. (RHH)

⏳ ⏳ ⏳

1 0 1

I was first tossed into the tumultuous waves of composition teaching in the fall of 1973, as a first-semester graduate student in the comparative literature program (focusing in English, of course) at the University of Illinois at Urbana-Champaign. I felt completely disoriented, uncertain, and, well, plain afraid. I was assigned to teach Rhetoric 105, the freshman composition course. I felt somewhat hypocritical, as it was a course I had not been required to take as an undergraduate. Now I would be teaching not only Rhetoric 105, but a section specifically for engineering majors. The all-male class, as I would later learn, boasted a population of students at most three years younger than I was at the time. The word "fear" understates what I felt at the time.

The texts for Rhetoric 105? I see them now from my computer, the books for my first class—time-honored, revered texts that I will not give or throw away: the black-and-red covered *Writing With a Purpose* (which we grad students quickly renamed "Writhing With a Porpoise") and *The Norton Reader*. Because of McCrimmon, I still hold in my heart of hearts the probably incorrect maxim that paragraphs are indeed "compositions in miniature."

I also keep on my shelf my yellowing, mimeographed copy of the "Handbook for Instructors of Rhetoric 105 and 106—1973–1974." The woman distributing the copy to me back then was Mary Lou

Sparbel, the more experienced TA selected to supervise our group of fledglings. If I remember correctly, she was writing a dissertation on Dickens and lived with her mother in a trailer in Mahomet, Illinois. She was serious, smart, no-nonsense, and extremely helpful.

She was available to us newbies, teaching the nuts-and-bolts of what would become an occasionally hypertheorized discipline: What, indeed, would we do on Monday (or Tuesday) morning? I was able to infer from Sparbel that the best composition teachers—or any teachers, for that matter—learn to punt early on. While syllabi are part of a necessary genre of accountability, the best teachers of writing learn to go with the needs of the class (in orderly, logical fashion, of course).

But Sparbel wasn't perfect by any means. Indeed, one of her first comments about my teaching after she observed my class was that I shouldn't raise my arm up too high on the board when I was wearing a short skirt. I decided to take that as praise, however, since she had nothing bad to say about the way I had conducted the class. As far as I was concerned, I was grateful for her input; she was the wise older sister I'd never had.

I don't know what became of Mary Lou Sparbel. I remember her fondly, gratefully, among my first real teachers in graduate school— probably the first. Sparbel was my first peer mentor, to a good extent responsible for my turning to composition studies as one of the many of my generation to embrace it along with literary studies. I think I neglected to thank her at the time, but it would also be years before I understood exactly how much she had done.

When I tell this story (and I haven't that often) it's usually to graduate students in my Pro-Seminar for Teachers of Writing. Students appreciate knowing that most of their professor/mentors didn't come to them ready-made. I've told it to my children, too, if only to confirm their notions that I'm not perfect (oh, realllllly????) and that we all learn from one another. I also hope to suggest the importance of letting people know sooner rather than later how much their assistance has meant.

—Deborah H. Holdstein

1 0 2

As is the custom near the end of the semester, my supervisor arranged to observe one of my composition classes so that she could write my bi-annual evaluation. I had been a teaching associate for nearly two years and was confident that my evaluation would be positive. I knew how to plan each class so carefully and thoroughly that nothing would take me by surprise. And since I was to be observed, I planned this particular class with even greater care than usual. After reading through the essay I had assigned, I outlined the points that would demonstrate the ways in which this professional essay was constructed much like those the students themselves would be writing. I had even color-coded the points in my outline to correspond with lines and paragraphs in the essay. Finally, to be sure that I wouldn't run out of time, I inserted into the outline the number of minutes I would spend talking about each topic.

In the classroom the next day, moving gracefully from my notes to the text to the chalkboard, I guided the students through my outline, showing them, with flawless logic, how this assigned essay could help them with their own. Occasionally, I would pause to take a breath. And during one such pause, two-thirds of the way through my presentation, a young man raised his hand to ask me a question about the essay and to make an observation about how one portion could be read and used to extend my explanation in a different direction. Politely, I agreed with him, thanked him, and turned back to my notes.

But before I could find my color-coded position, I found my supervisor standing at my side, asking for the chalk. Now, anyone who has been teaching for any amount of time knows the Rule of Observation: The observer is to sit quietly at the back of the room and take notes. Any behavior to the contrary, particularly behavior that includes speaking or engaging the class in any way, is a sure sign that the teacher being observed has lost control of herself or her students.

Aware of this rule, I handed over the chalk and stepped to the side of the room, watching in a silent stupor as my supervisor wrote on the board some of the words that the young man had identified and built a new and extended example around them. I was thankful that the students were watching her, not noticing me melt through the windows and out to the lawn. I was also thankful that the class period ended quickly, that I had enough saliva left to give an assignment, and that my supervisor had to run off to observe another class. In fact, she had to run off to several other classes, and it was days later before I found the courage to ask her about my class. Bracing myself for the words of criticism, I was silenced once again when she smiled and said, "The class was great! The comment your student made about the essay really opened things up and took the discussion in an interesting direction. I really enjoyed it."

Though it was some time before I could share this experience with others, let alone learn something from my own response, it has since become a reminder of the importance of being in the classes we are teaching, of listening—honestly listening—to students. I still outline my class plans, and once in a while I use color-coding, but it's not so scary for me any more to let something completely unexpected intersect with that plan and lead in a direction that surprises me and the class.

I tell this tale to new or newish teachers and tutors who have told me about classes seeming to go bad or to move in a direction that they felt they couldn't "control." I've also used it after I've observed new teachers teaching, and I'm wanting to help them understand what it means to listen to students.

—Sheryl I. Fontaine

1 0 3

On a visit to my class, Dan Fader got involved in the group discussion of a paper. The student writer had a rather long paragraph on one page and some students suggested that the writer break up the paragraph; others disagreed. "How many paragraphs should there be, Susanmarie?" someone asked. I launched into an extended discussion of the rhetorical situation, of the need to focus on the purpose of a paragraph, on the impossibility of constructing strict rules about how many paragraphs an essay should have, and other principled points. Students looked at me, somewhat bemused, wondering, no doubt, why I could never give a straight answer to such a clear question. Then someone turned to Dan. "How many paragraphs on a page?" "Two and a half," was his quick response. The class burst into laughter, both at the contrast of his answer to mine and at its precision. 2.5 paragraphs per page? How odd. But then Dan explained how paragraphs functioned visually as well as rhetorically, and how they served on the page to chunk information for readers, and that in his view 2.5 paragraphs on a page was a good size limit, one that helped readers move along without getting overwhelmed.

I tell the story because it illustrates that I was right and that Dan was right. It's hard to make rules about writing, but it's possible to illustrate rhetorical principles, and sometimes it's even possible to offer quantitative responses to rhetorical questions. I think Dan's discussion helped students understand the rhetoric of paragraphs more effectively than my philosophical musings.

—Susanmarie Harrington

1 0 4

Having begun graduate school in the late '80s with courses in both composition and computer programming, I was unsure of the direction my studies would take, feeling confident with computers, yet curious about composition theory. While programming a database offered little stimulation, I was intrigued by the "other" work I'd been exploring—Flower and Hayes, Kinneavy, North, Hairston, Cooper and Odell, White, Elbow—the whole gang. Fortunately, computers and composition serendipitously became a thriving subfield just as I decided to complete my degree in rhetoric and composition after all. So when the Web, the composition listservs, and the online organizations like Alliance for Computers and Writing arose, I quickly became a member of the community, working especially actively with Trent Batson on the Epiphany Project.

At one of their Faculty Development Institutes, I was helping Paul Leblanc in a workshop for "newbies" learning CommonSpace software. As an assistant in that room, I spent all of my time behind the participants, looking over shoulders and helping folks to position the mouse or to click the right box. One gentleman in particular was having no end of trouble negotiating both the hardware and the software, and I constantly found myself returning to stand behind his tall frame as he hunched down in his chair to see the screen, reassuring him and praising him for the smallest improvements in his struggle with the tricky software. I could feel the genuine desire he had to succeed, and the look of triumph in his eyes when he mastered something was as rewarding as teaching has ever been for me. When the workshop finally ended, he stood and shook my hand warmly, turning to face me for the first time.

That's when I saw his nametag: the "newbie" I'd been nurturing was Lee Odell!

I normally tell this story to other colleagues and graduate students in computers and composition, illustrating that we all have our strengths and challenges, regardless of our age or level of experience. I especially like to tell it because of the irony—had it not been for Odell and dedicated, inquisitive theorists like him, I'd never have found myself in this field, so meeting him in that workshop was coming full circle for me professionally and personally.
—Claudine Keenan

105

At 4Cs in Nashville, 1994, I sat across a large table while my friend Sue Yin Hum, then a graduate student at Texas Christian University on the market for the first time, and Winifred Bryan Horner discussed a potential job and contract that had been offered to Sue. I was just hanging out, waiting for them to finish so that Sue and I could go to lunch and catch up on our respective first employment quests. As I caught fragments of their conversation, I began to become much more intrigued by it than by the materials from several sessions that I was trying to organize and annotate for future reference. It was not so much what they were saying as just what it was like. I had never met or seen Win Horner before, though of course I had heard of her. And while on other occasions I have had the chance to talk to her at more length, that day my only direct impressions were from a brief introduction and handshake. As I sat there, though, I soaked up the unmistakable impression of a great soul. She had not been Sue's dissertation advisor, and was not acting out of any special sense of obligation. But as they sat, exchanging stories, theories and contractual details in what seemed from the fragments I heard to be one grand unified conversation, it was clear that Horner's care for Sue blended the meticulous attention of a corporate lawyer with the warmth of a favorite grandmother—all from within, of course, a scholar's erudition. Eventually, I just quit trying to pretend otherwise and watched them. I should have taken notes. I have no details left in memory, only the impression of an extravagant generosity, patience and care, of a very serious person taking herself so lightly that it could only have been the result of a sincere and consistent attitude. I'm not a person who is easily impressed by celebrity, and if anything I have used an anti-authoritarian, challenging mode in most of my dealings with the major figures in composition. But I'm afraid I went completely gaga over Win Horner, and remain that way to this day.

I tell this story when conversation—or inner musing—turns toward becoming altogether too jaded with the comp/rhet "star system." Some stars are worth it all.

—Keith Rhodes

106

I know that working conditions at the University of Cincinnati were instrumental in my decision to pursue the doctorate. In about 1984, a few adjuncts decided that there should be a union to negotiate for better working conditions—or better yet, that we should be allowed to join the AAUP, which represented the full-time faculty. The immediate response from the department was to call a meeting of all the adjuncts with Jim Berlin and the department head at that time. The meeting consisted of Jim getting red in the face and yelling at us, telling us that if we wanted to keep our jobs, we should just accept things as they were, because if the working environment would improve, the department would do a national search, and none of us would be hired into those "newly created" positions. I loved teaching, and I knew that I did not want to feel like the permanent underclass, so I plunged into graduate study, and I have never regretted that. However, I do not feel that Jim rose to the occasion that day.

Posted on the WPA-L in response to the question of Berlin's support of unionization of TAs today—the only time I have told it in public, I think. But I told it to myself many times, and it was strong motivation for me to complete my doctorate.

—Elizabeth H. Campbell

1 0 7

In the fall of 1982, I was hired as an adjunct instructor of composition by Jim Berlin when he was Director of Composition at The University of Cincinnati. During my first term there, I had a female student whose father was a very well-known, but controversial, politician. When I called her name, which was very unusual, on the first day of class, I asked her if she was related to the man. When she said yes, I said: "That's okay. We'll like you anyway." For the rest of the term, she never really trusted me.

Near the end of the term, she complained about me to her academic advisor, and that person called Jim. He called me in and said, "Give her the grade she deserves. I don't care whose daughter she is." Since there was no question of her failing, I never thought much more about it.

The first-year composition sequence consisted of three courses, and when she did not enroll for one of my sections in the second term, I took no notice because there were very few students who followed instructors from one course to the next anyway. The third term, however, she enrolled in my class again along with her boyfriend and three other friends. I often wondered what happened in the second term to redeem me, but the most amazing thing happened when Jim came to observe my teaching late in that term. She and her friends (who had known for about a week that we would be observed that day) performed brilliantly. They were not only prepared, they had done extra readings and generated discussions that sounded worthy of a graduate seminar. I smiled in amazement, and after they left, I told Jim that she was the student who had complained about me the first term I was there. He said: "She's too nice. She must not be her father's daughter."

Having Jim for a supervisor taught me a lot about trusting teachers to do the right thing.

I used to be a National Writing Project Director, and I'm sure that I used the story with those teachers as well as composition teachers whom I supervised when I was a composition director.

—Elizabeth H. Campbell

☞ ☞ ☞

NOTES

TALE 101 (p. 130). I am intrigued by the narrator's speculation that she did not thank her TA mentor at the time because it would take her years to understand exactly what that mentor had done. This offers a counter-story to the academy's reliance on end-of-term student evaluations and peer observation/recommendations to assess our teaching. The statement suggests that the work of teaching (or mentoring) extends far beyond the duration and immediacy of face to face contacts. That work is often also a result of the learner's changing understanding of these contacts in relation to the changing material conditions of the learner's life and the learner's changing experience as a teacher and learner. (MZL)

TALE 101 (p. 130). Holdstein titled her tale "The Unsung Mentor." Notice how this celebration of her first helpful colleague retains the sense of composition teaching as a fast-flowing discipline, into which new teachers step sometimes unaware that the best advice they will get likely will change very soon. Also in jest, my TA buddies and I called McCrimmon "Writing from a Pulpit," but it never seriously occurred to us that the book was anything other than holy writ. Would we have had the nerve to start teaching had we not? (RHH)

TALE 102 (p. 131). The mentor contains that ever-present contradiction lived by classroom teachers who must always choose between letting themselves or their students take over. I like the irony of the observer who has to take control to teach the teacher that she should give it up occasionally. This tale belongs in the book, yet to be written, on the techniques of not-teaching and un-teaching. (RHH)

TALE 103 (p. 133). Harrington tells another story she heard about Fader, how he once dozed off in the back row of a class he was observing. The next time he visited the class, he noticed that the class log mentioned a student who had suffered from "faderitis" the period before. I am attracted to this tale in part because it reminds me of my father, who said he once fell asleep in his *own* class while listening to student reports, in part because it is the only example in this volume of a story achieving eponymic status, but mainly because it draws attention to student storytelling. It was the students who converted the story into an eponym. Harrington, who writes that Fader "was a mentor to me, and arguably even a hero," comments about the "faderitis" story: "I would hate for anyone to read this story and think that Dan's dozing off in class was typical of him as a colleague, mentor, or teacher. Perhaps you'll have to think of that part of the Fader tale as the 'underlife' of comp tales—tales people told you that they don't want you to tell in public (or am I the only person who looked at a story and said, 'Gee, maybe that one wasn't such a good idea anymore'?)." She wasn't, of course. But her reference to "underlife" (see Brooke, 1987) makes me think that the next volume of *Comp Tales* should collect student stories. For comp teachers that would provide a novel and insightful "bin of neglected others, of untold stories" (Hill, 1990, p. 80). (RHH)

TALE 106 (p. 135). I wonder if we can also read the tale as pointing to yet another potential conflict in the work of program directors and writing teachers charged to both offer career advice and evaluate/mentor the teaching or writing of students and teachers. The doctorate (or BA, MA) program is as much a certification mechanism as a place of learning. How do we advise those (undergraduate and graduate) students, GTAs, and adjuncts whom we feel might only benefit from those programs in the sense that these programs might secure them a career in doing what they like to do and do well but not in the sense of really helping them to develop as writers and teachers? I experience the conflict most intensely when dealing with persons whose financial and familial conditions confine where they might go for those certifications. (MZL)

CHAPTER 10

⤺

Careers

When I was 15, I worked on a ranch in Montana for the summer. I told a cowboy that I had never been thrown all summer. The hand replied, "I guess you haven't ridden yet."

—Barry Lopez, in conversation, 1985

"Our lives are ceaselessly intertwined with narratives," writes Donald E. Polkinghorne, "with the stories that we tell and hear told, with the stories that we dream or imagine or would like to tell. All these stories are reworked in the story of our own lives" (1988, p. 160). So it cuts both ways. Remembered from the past but reshaped for the present, a personal anecdote, more than just an isolated moment of entertainment, helps narrate a life. And our life, which we keep shaped in the form of a lifestory, selects anecdotes that will add up to our newest history of our self. Tell enough comp tales and you have the comp career.

Well, not *the* comp career, since there are only comp careers. Still, there are plenty of comp tales that center on career issues, and when they are strung together in a rough career chronology, they fashion a kind of career myth. And that career myth—as all narratives—exercises a moral pull. Just as our working contradictions are resolved or contained through a sense of professionalism and a projection of imago, so are they transmuted into a folktale of career. If there can be "story types or genres" in the comp world (see Tale 133), they are most easily detected in these career stories: The First Step, The Indoctrination, The Heroic Work Load, The Resort to the Past, Finding Your Own Way, Fighting Your Own Battles, Changing Camps, Facing the Forking Paths, Living With Your Choices, The Rewards of Longevity. (RHH)

$\bowtie$ $\bowtie$ $\bowtie$

1 0 8

"The first day of the rest of my life." This is what I had written in my file-o-fax the day I chose to sit down and officially begin a dissertation in composition and rhetoric. The phone rang before I began what was (what is) to be the first chapter.

It was an acquaintance, someone who had finished the master's where I got my undergraduate degree years back, when I used to have literary theory talks on the campus steps. He was applying to Ph.D. programs in English and asked me if I knew the most intelligent way to bill himself in his application, "as an Americanist-Post-Colonialist interested in Nineteenth Century Writings or as a Victorian-Post-Colonialist interested in the marginalized Americas." I didn't know. "I've been working on this question of appropriate placement methods for first-year composition," (I looked down at my stack of unread freshman essays, at the journals with Post-it notes in them, at my schedule for that week's mentoring meetings), "on literacy and contemporary theoretical conceptions of post-print age thought and on rhetorical configurations of educational systems," I went on to say about my own "academic journeys," as he called them. I wasn't lying, yet felt like I was hiding something, something that couldn't address his question, let alone give him the answers he thought I had.

"Oh. So you're into practice now," he says and adds a "good luck" to "my program."

I tell this story on the first day that my mentor group meets. We are made up of graduate students in English whose academic journeys have taken us to sites—classrooms, writing labs, literacy centers—which are hard to describe in the academy's terms. It usually stimulates a discussion about real and worthy subjects of study in the changing discipline of composition and rhetoric and reminds us that the question of what to write about is never merely academic.
—Jessica Yood

1 0 9

When I came to Chicago thirty-three years ago this coming September (I thought it would be a good address to leave—I was right; I'll be leaving in a year, with nothing but good memories. Well, mostly good memories), every assistant professor in the humanities was put onto a staff to teach first-year humanities. My staff consisted of people like Wayne Booth, Richard McKeon, Elder Olson, etc. It was an amazing experience. One day Richard McKeon came in to brief us on *Matter and Motion* by (damn, who wrote it—Clark-Maxwell?). Why we were teaching that in a first-year humanities course is a long story. (We were also teaching Euclid's *Geometry*, which baffled me no less.) Anyway, he came in and said rather than just talk about it, he would teach it. And he asked, "Well, now, tell me what this first sentence means." I looked around the room and everyone was terrified. Wayne Booth was looking down at his notes, and slowly sliding down in his chair, hoping he wouldn't be called on. McKeon finally called on one of his own students; I think his name was Bill Swanson or Swenson. Very smart guy, but his face turned as red as any face I have ever seen and flop sweat popped out all over his forehead. He stammered a few sentences, at which point McKeon said, "Oh, come on, Bill, you can do better than that!" McKeon was brutal. You may recall that he was the model for xxxx in *Zen and the Art of Motorcycle Maintenance*. Despite the feeling of abject terror that I would be called on next, it was a good experience. In any event, thereafter, that particular "class" turned into what one would expect: he lectured and I sat there stunned and terrified. And I did not understand a word he said. In fact, I almost never understood anything he said. I had lunch with him once in which he talked nonstop for two hours, at the end of which I could not remember anything that he talked about. Fortunately, the staff discussions became a lot more humane thereafter. We all got indoctrinated in a way that I don't regret at all. In fact, I have always said that I learned more in those weekly staff meetings about how to think, how to read, and how to talk about thinking and reading than I ever learned in my graduate work.

—*Joe Williams*

110

I couldn't decide what I wanted to do. After earning a master's in English lit, pursuing literary scholarship did not appeal to me, but neither did working in the private sector which I also tried for several years. So I enrolled in a Ph.D. program in rhet/comp at a prestigious university. While working on my master's, I discovered I liked teaching composition. I figured if I was going to teach writing full time, I had better know what I was doing. The first day of the fall semester the chair of the English department, a well-known literary scholar, pulled me into his office and in confidence told me that I would greatly increase my chances of "success" if I got to know one faculty member really well. Although I think the chair meant to be helpful, somehow I felt I was being let in on a dirty little secret. His advice made me feel cheap. I felt sorry for the lit majors. The little I had previously read in the composition literature about nurturing students' voices, about setting up student-centered classes, about collaborative learning, convinced me that a democratic spirit and ethic of care permeated the new field. I believed I had made the right choice.

* * *

In my first semester in the introductory composition course taught by the nationally renowned master, I struggled mightily. Theory, theory, theory . . . "linguistics," "discourse," "transactions," more strange fields of study and terms than my feeble mind could grasp, let alone value. Each weekly paper we turned in was graded. On one I received a C. I was crushed. Insecurity set in. I saw my fellow classmates as competitors who were obviously much better trained than I. Instead of opening up to them, I shut down. I struggled with thoughts of quitting and dropping out of school. I worked harder, though, determined to do better, and my weekly grades gradually rose. Maybe the great prof was just testing us. All the grad students had heard the rumors of this course being a "boot camp" where only the tough survive. I earned an A on the final exam and an A on my research project accompanied with a note telling me the paper was potentially publishable. Just what I needed. A week later I received in the mail a personalized grade report from the master. Instead of the A I was expecting because of the progress I had made, I received a B+ and this comment: "When I calculated your final grade you just missed an A- by .005%."

* * *

I remained in school, now motivated to prove I was as good as the rest of the students. A couple of us who tutored in the writing center talked about the lit students and how reluctant they were to share ideas. Some we knew were desperate to publish while still in grad school. Their drafts of seminar papers were private property, closely-guarded secrets. One of my fellow classmates and I teamed up on a research project. We were going to try to find out the effects of my written comments on my comp students' essays. My partner would interview the selected students regularly throughout the semester and note changes in their subsequent drafts. One day late in the semester, one of my students involved in our study became visibly upset when I handed back the class's graded essays. I suggested we talk after class. With some prompting on my part, she finally opened up and told me how confused she was by my comments and by what my colleague was telling her to do. Now I was confused. He was not supposed to be telling her anything about her writing but instead just listening to how she interpreted my comments. I talked to the other students in the study. Same result. I confronted my partner. It became clear to me that he was trying to influence my students' writing with his advice. I retaliated by telling them to ignore what he said and to just follow my instructions. Our research project was becoming a competition to prove who was the more effective writing teacher. The students, caught in the middle, were confused and frustrated.

* * *

A final scene: We are in the delivery room just before Thanksgiving. I am taking one of my last courses in the Ph.D. program. Because our baby is way overdue, my wife's obstetrician decides to induce labor. We have a pretty good idea how long the labor will take. I am also worried about getting my seminar paper finished on time. It is on Bakhtin. I am sitting by my wife's bed. I read a few pages of *The Dialogic Imagination*, then glance at my wife and check the time of the interval between contractions. Still plenty of time, I conclude, and resume my reading.

I use my tales in two contexts, both involving MA students who are thinking about pursuing a Ph.D. The first situation is more typical. These grad students have this sort of "pie in the sky" look in their eyes as they dream about becoming a "doctor." They idealize the academic life (as I did) and believe being accepted into a Ph.D. program will solve all of their problems. In the second instance, more rare, students are thinking about pursuing a Ph.D. too, but are having some misgivings. I simply try to confirm their misgivings, that they are right to consider the personal costs that might ensue, and they need to think very carefully about why they want to pursue the degree and what they are willing to risk.

—Mark Wiley

1 1 1

I was in my third or fourth year as a teaching assistant at a large research institution where I received my Ph.D. As part of my assistantship, I was responsible for mentoring several new TAs, which meant I observed their teaching, they observed mine, and we talked about all this teaching frequently. One TA had a particularly difficult transition into the classroom. He resented the time he had to spend to prepare for class and to grade papers, and he especially resented the time he had to spend talking about his class with me. One day he exploded, "All this teaching is getting in the way of my real work!"

I ask the graduate students I work with now how they think I should have responded, and we discuss their suggestions. I tell the story to make the point that, no matter what their specialization, teaching will be their "real work" along with their research, and time spent on their teaching now in a place where they don't have to worry about keeping their jobs as they do it, can only pay off for them later.

—Donna Dunbar-Odom

112

I remember the first time another student responded to a paper of mine in a writing class. We worked in pairs that day, so he was my only reader. He wrote his comments directly on my paper. When I got my paper back and read his comments, I agreed with him on several items that needed improvement, for instance, more detailed explanation of a particular point I was trying to make when comparing two characters. However, I could not agree with some of his suggestions; I followed them anyway. Neither my teacher nor I were totally pleased with the revision. The result was not my voice; it had become my classmate's—the way he would have written it. With more experience, I learned to accept comments from readers that made sense to me—after thinking about them for awhile. I found responding to the work of others works best in groups of four or five when comments are written on separate sheets of paper instead of directly on my work. When two or three students make similar responses to a paper when they have not seen what other respondents have written and can't piggyback on each others' comments by only saying, for instance, "I agree with Susan," I have to heed their suggestions for improvement. I can't ignore them as if I were a mule with blinders on. I learned that the first words I write are not too sacred to change.

This is a story I tell my students before they respond to each other's writing for the first time. I often share my own writing experiences with my students.

—Geneva Ballard

113

Graduate students come into my office and say: I want to be just like you. Now I know they don't want to be just like me for that would include being of a certain age with certain habits and with two teenagers and a single-parent household to support and with some days a crotchety take on the world and others a fairly bucolic take on the same world and a dog and a cat and so on. What they mean, usually, is they (1) want to be a college writing professor and/or (2) they want to do interdisciplinary work—often in composition and creative writing—and do it in English literature departments. My response is—"Don't be so sure" (remember the dog the cat the lawn that needs mowing, the kids who drink gallons of milk and have a gazillion soccer practices). And "It's not that easy." Because I also know that I ended up a tenure-track writing professor by what sometimes seems to me sheer accident, I try to explain that English department members have not always in my view been as honest as they should be about explaining that they will not become our mentors or professors.

I started out in creative writing, I explain, and found it a difficult field. But I did love to teach when I learned that someone would let me, train me, and pay me—however little as an adjunct—to do so. I wanted to go on for a terminal degree (like my grad students, I wanted to be my professors before me) but I didn't see my way into an English lit program— though I tried I failed some of my preliminary exams. I didn't know or really like the discourse—I liked to read but I'd always prefer my writing to be about things other than other people's writing. I liked to write but liking wasn't enough in the competitive field of creative writing. Someone told me about rhetoric composition degrees, I tried one, it suited wonderfully, I throve, I moved into the very spot where the graduate students now found me. But, in so doing, I had spent at least fifteen years and the education was continuing. I had become competent-to-fluent in the three languages of English: literature/theory, creating through writing, examining processes of learning to write (literature, creative writing and composition). The reason I could do interdisciplinary work was that I had learned my three languages and found that learning was nurturing (though the messages the strands send to each other can be very conflictual and confusing). What I also found is that I was sometimes more tired or worn out than I'd like to be in "trying to keep up" in several fields; and that others sometimes—often—didn't speak my favorite language. That of composition and rhetoric. And that causes me the most dismay in my professional life. I've found that for many literature learning seems to stop at the border of literature. That creative writers learn to speak in the language of the field they'd like to be valued in as makers of literature, but that neither of those fields feel they need the deeper understanding of composition—it is not and probably never will be, except in large GTA/adjunct-run teaching programs, the lingua franca.

So the graduate student who sees me doing intradiscipinary work needs to learn the life-luck choices that led me there and the degree to which he or she will need to sort out dialects, affiliations, connections. They need to learn it's not a career move as much as it's a way of life, a way of living within the complicated confines of the construct we call English department. For all the hard work, I think it's the most rewarding if the student of things English cares about learning—by learning in the new best way to be a generalist. But it's not a matter of enrollment, electing, filing papers in, as much as it is joining a number of conversations.

Over the last few years, I've found myself returning to versions of this story. If I can tell this story just right—I sometimes think—I can help those who are searching for a well-tailored attitude toward English. I can also help those who have strong (but maybe at this point tacit or under-explored) single-strand values from moving themselves into a strand that won't nurture them or their interests.

—Wendy Bishop

1 1 4

Tears ran silently down his face as he sat at the computer writing. His tears had been falling for more than an hour. Bryan was a football player. He was not terribly large, but he was wiry. Bryan had been a student in my developmental writing class two semesters before, and now here he was, sitting in my office, writing and crying.

Bryan did not pass the required exit exam from developmental studies writing during the quarter he spent in my class, although I thought he should have, for his writing was warm, he had a strong voice, and he used examples well. When told stories of his life that he connected with the readings for the class, his words often brought tears to my eyes. The warm and caring human being that he was, a young man who could speak about being loved and loving, a man who used touching examples to do so, came through clearly in his writing. While he was in my class, I learned that Bryan could edit his writing well, too. However, he did not have a chance to edit the timed essay that he had to write to exit the English section of the developmental studies program, an essay read and scored for errors, not strengths, by three writing teachers.

Bryan had appeared in my doorway, asking for help. He told me that he did not know what his writing teacher wanted: that he hadn't had a passing essay for the entire quarter, and that if he didn't write passing essays soon, he would not be allowed to take the exit exam. Both he and I knew that this meant that he would not exit from the program, and that he would be excluded from school for three years. The hope and promise Bryan had brought to his family would die.

As I looked over the draft he handed me, an essay about a meeting with the father whom he had not seen since he was a child, I looked up in amazement. "Bryan," I said, "where are the wonderful examples you used in my class? Where did your wonderful writing go?" At that point, the tears started to flow. Once started, there was no stemming them. Bryan told me that he was doing well in all of his other classes. "It's only English," he mourned. "I can't seem to do it." And so Bryan sat in my office at my computer writing while I asked questions to help him find examples to flesh out his writing.

When Bryan left my office, a revised draft in his hand, I mourned, and I thought back to my own use of words in speech and writing. I thought about the third-grade teacher who told us, rural working poor kids, that we would be judged by how we spoke and wrote. I thought about the words that I used that she condemned, and how diligently I worked to purge expressions and pronunciations from my speech, expressions and errors from my writing. I thought about the emotional split that my eventual language use had had on my relations with my family—of being a child who had "gotten above her raising." Correcting my mother's verb tenses and subject-verb agreement, criticizing who she was because of the way she wrote and talked, wounds were created that never healed. No one had told me the importance of purpose and audience for writing and speaking. No one had told me that I didn't have to be ashamed of who my speech showed me to be, that I didn't have to be ashamed of my family.

In the era of the "revolving door" in colleges, when students had to flunk out to make room for other students, I saw clearly how words, how language was used as a weapon as I saw friends failing English, one of the notorious "flunk-out" courses. I knew they could use language as well as I, but that I had "lucked out" by placing into advanced English: the result of being able to write timed essays with facility.

During the next class period, as my students were writing, I wrote an essay about my own experience with words that wound that I have shared with every writing class since. I also tell Bryan's story, and my story from that university: of being fired for protesting the institutional racism and classism in the English department and throughout that university. My story is a story that the rural and inner-city Georgia students that I taught and the Appalachian students that I teach now can understand well, for although they may not have interrogated language as a means of exclusion, all realize the prejudices that are connected to race, class, and to regional or community use of language. My story and Bryan's story help my students to understand the tremendous political and social power of words. I like to think that these stories help students to understand that one form of language does not have to be privileged over others, and that language does not have to create distance and emotional schisms among and between family members. All of my comp classes begin with these stories, and with an examination of the power that language holds: the ability of words to wound.

—Patti Capel Swartz

1 1 5

You don't quit seven years of graduate school, two years of part-timing, and three years of tenure-line work all at once. There is one moment, however, that sticks in my mind. It was a Saturday afternoon, my son was playing in a Little League game, and I was in the stands, grading freshman essays. The guy next to me had a bag of ham sandwiches and offered me one. He was stretched out, enjoying the sun.

We traded professions. He repaired outboard motors.

"Ever got a machine you couldn't fix?" I asked.

"Naw," he said.

"Lucky customers."

"They come in unhappy and leave happy. But that's before they see the bill." He laughed and then was on his feet, shouting, "Way to go, Buddy!" The centerfielder waved the ball at his dad before he threw it back to the infield. Suddenly I had a vision that made me cringe. I was looking through my son's eyes and seeing his dad sitting in the stands, hunched over, marking student papers.

I work as a financial advisor now, and my customers are happy (so far), and my weekends are my own.

Told over the phone.

—Author's name withheld, remembered by Rich Haswell

116

It is fall semester, almost midterm, and a fellow tenured faculty member is returning to town and to her classes for the first time since the first week of classes. She is apprehensive, she tells me, about facing her classes again. She's talking to me because I have had a fall like hers, a fall during which my mother died of a lingering illness.

"It's not like the first-day jitters," she emphasizes. "These faces should be familiar."

They are not.

We go back over old ground. "You did the right thing," I assure her. "How could you have been anywhere else?" We talk about how impossible it is at times like these to live in two so completely different worlds. In one, we are daughters, not yet forty, caring for our mothers who will die soon: tomorrow, a week from today, two weeks. In the other world, we are professors, with pride in our records of strong teaching. We know that while the research will wait, the students do not, cannot.

How, we wonder, do we explain to our students, not the duty children have for their parents, but the exquisiteness of care, of reciprocating stroke by soft stroke what we have expected and received all our lives? How to explain that drafts dates, editing sessions, and midterms have been all but erased by the drip drip drip of morphine or the endless shhhhhh of ventilating equipment?

"My undergraduate students gave me a card," she says. "I feel relieved."

"Yes," I answer, "my graduate students gave me a card when my mother died." But what I am really thinking about are the department summaries of my teaching evaluations from that semester, the semester we adopted our second son, the semester my mother was felled by A.L.S. That semester I had two classes, an undergraduate seminar on writing about place and a graduate seminar for first-year teaching assistants. The undergraduates who didn't send a card were, in their evaluations, generous to the point of fiction. The graduate students, on the other hand, had mastered the course content. Their evaluations, according to the department summary, were clear, direct, unambiguous and damning. They noted (accurately) that I was unenthusiastic, underprepared at best, frequently absent (a month's worth to be exact—two weeks adopting a child, two weeks for my mother's death).

I promised myself not to look at the original evaluations and filed them unopened in the drawer that holds the record of fifteen years of mostly strong, successful teaching. What could I possibly learn from them? That the university has no policy for caring for sick family members? That the university doesn't support adoption, offering as it does only "sick" leave, for pregnant women who do that "sick" thing of giving birth? That I could, at the very time we adopted a sick child and needed money for travel home, take the federal family medical leave several weeks without pay?

But none of this is before me now. A grieving friend and colleague is, and such thoughts offer little solace. I search for something else to say, but my second attempts aren't much better. I want to tell her that this thing we are living will not conform to a university bulletin, that we are living drafts in progress that will become final, irreversible products, but not under the pressure of the last day to drop or the last day to withdraw.

Instead, I offer her the only timely, practical piece of advice I can think of: I counsel her not to read her semester evaluations, not even the departmental summary of them.

But she's back to her classes now, back to the semester calendar, and she is thinking about that card. I can tell she will read them and I know that someday, I will read mine.

—Janet Carey Eldred

1 1 7

About the statement that all of rhet/comp folk ought to be teaching FYC [first-year comp]—I don't think anyone would disagree. I certainly don't. Yet I seldom "get to teach" (and that's honestly the way I put it) a first-year course. What happens to us? Fifteen years ago, I taught first-year comp every semester. When I came to the University of Arizona, I was to help build a graduate program in rhetoric and composition, supervise 150 TAs, edit *Rhetoric Review*, be associate director of comp— all of you know the story because most of you, I believe—us old-timers anyway—have similar stories about our evolving/escalating careers in rhet/comp. That first semester "they" wanted me to teach a graduate seminar because the graduate students *wanted* to take a grad course from the new faculty member, I was told. And I was to be course director for our 101. I argued that I couldn't direct a first-year writing course when I'd never even taught that first-year course. So I "got to" teach 101 in fall 1987. I never "got to" again, although I've "gotten to" teach basic writing a couple of times and two upper-division writing courses since.

So what do I do? With each passing year, my responsibilities in the graduate program increase; I direct the graduate program now but have had regular responsibilities in the comp program (except for the last year). I sit in meetings all day (maybe a slight exaggeration—but not much, right?). I mentor, advise. I don't need to go on because this is a familiar story.

The point is that we start out teaching FYC and cannot imagine not teaching it. As we get heavier into writing programs and writing program administration, being responsible for teaching core graduate courses in rhetoric and composition, serving on many qualifying, preliminary, and dissertation committees, the terrain and responsibilities shift. And—perhaps like me, fifteen years later—we find that we don't teach FYC anymore.

I love to teach first-year composition. I miss it. Can I go back to those days? I doubt it.

Posted on the WPA-L, but also told to our graduate students. I always add, "You can't possibly imagine that you'll be busier than you are as graduate students—but you will be busier when you become faculty members in a writing program." They are appalled—but, later—when they do become faculty members—tell me that I told them rightly.

—Theresa Enos

1 1 8

"What goes around, comes around." Most people attach negative meaning to this expression. I, on the other hand, choose to think of it differently in this situation. Many years ago I taught elementary school. During my tenure there I had the pleasure of teaching first and fourth grades. And while I had many rewarding moments with my students, one always stuck out in my mind. She was cute, sweet, kind, considerate, with a round face and a "Dorothy Hamill" haircut. I took to her instantly. I grew to love her like she was my own. I was sad to see first grade end, knowing I might not see her again, except in the hallways.

To my surprise, three years later I was asked to transfer to fourth grade. And there, on my first day of class, was that special name and face. Kimberly Law was in my class again. I watched as she walked up the hall, with my heart in my throat. Our eyes met and a contentment filled each of our hearts. This year she became even more precious than before. I got to know her family better and we developed a bond that stayed with me for many years to come. Again, I was sad to see the year come to a close.

As is often the case, we lost touch after that year because her family moved away. And while we had no contact, I thought of her many times, wondering how she was and what she was doing with her life. Last week, while I was just about to finish rating placement essays, I decided to look down the list of names and tests yet to be rated. I could barely believe my eyes. There was the name I had not seen in nearly ten years, Kimberly Law. Immediately, a flood of memories came. I knew I had to find her. This was not as easy as I anticipated. I looked in the phone book, but the number was unlisted. I searched the Internet for her father's business or an e-mail address where I might reach her. Every time I came up short. Finally, after hours of effort, I was able to locate her phone number through the registrar's office.

Last Saturday morning, I called her. It was just as expected. She was as glad to hear from me as I was to talk to her. We spoke about the times we spent together in elementary school and what has kept her busy all these years. She had been home-schooled for the past few years and was trying to decide whether or not to attend college. She said she had been looking for a "sign" and I told her that this "looked like a neon sign to me." I met with her and her mother this week on campus and she, once again, will be in my classroom for the fall semester.

This story demonstrates how we, as teachers, can impact the lives of our students and likewise be impacted by them as well. You never know the impression you may have on any individual, yet we hope we can always have a positive result. Most students are in our lives for a brief period of time and move on. In this case, I am the lucky one to be able to share more time with her. So, "what goes around, comes around."

—Cindy Buchanan

1 1 9

The last time CCCC was in Chicago, Jim Kinneavy was retiring (a euphemism, to be sure, since I think he's still teaching as an emeritus at Texas) so we held a party for him at the Billy Goat Tavern (famous as the source of Belushi's "cheeborger cheeborger" routine) and invited everyone at the convention who had ever studied with Jim. The best count was that there were about 200 people teaching composition at some college or university who had studied with Jim. It was quite a sight to see this huge crowd at the Billy Goat, standing on chairs, singing "The Eyes of Texas Are Upon You," and doing the hook 'em horns sign.

I frequently tell this story to folks who ask what the community was like at Texas when I did my Ph.D. there and to people who want to know what it was like to study with Kinneavy.

—David Jolliffe

1 2 0

Here is an excerpt from a letter, sent five years after a student I will call Ada took my advanced writing class:

Dear Karen,

I would remind you of who I am but I know you well enough to know that you already know. What you don't know is how your advanced writing class has influenced my life.

I followed my high school boyfriend—the honors student, the Rhodes Scholar candidate, the "bright" one—to the university. I even became an English major so we could take all our classes together. I hid in his shadow quite effectively until your class, when it became clear that with all the focus on individual course goals and individual conferences that I could no longer hide behind George. We broke up that semester. I stopped going to classes just so I would not have to see him. Your e-mails and individual sessions in your office gave me the confidence to return not just to your class but eventually to the others. I graduated and moved on.

I am now a high school language arts teacher. Sounds pretty corny but I actually hear your voice when I am teaching literature or composition. "Listen to the rhythm, hear the voice, feel the texture of the writer's style—style intertwined with meaning—and what does this writer evoke for you?" My students chafe to read aloud and to think this way about other writers and their own writing, just like I did. I even laugh and tease them about hearing voices as you did. I bring my own paper drafts to class workshops for their peer review as you did. You made me feel powerful as a writer and now as a teacher. I strive to do the same for my students.

But what you did not know—what I could not face during those years—was my father's sexual abuse. Although it was not a course requirement, you encouraged us to keep personal journals as self-discovery. That one optional assignment was the beginning of a long journey of counseling and pain, which has allowed me to finally move beyond those memories and my anger. I now talk to teenagers in the area about my own story to give them the courage to tell theirs.

I just wanted to let you know. For the first time, someone wanted to hear my voice. You listened. Thank you.

Love and blessings,

Ada

I read this letter to my advanced writing students to help move them from this class is a requirement to seeing their class as an extraordinary opportunity for self-discovery and liberation, as writers and individuals. I also share this letter when I teach writing-across-the-curriculum graduate courses for the School of Education as a reminder of the humbling power of our teaching. I get tears in my eyes every time I tell this tale—and even my stoic students look at their comp class with new eyes.

—Karen Vaught-Alexander

1 2 1

One of the best things about teaching is that I love what I am doing. I remember talking with my graduate students over lunch one day. They listened intently and several of them began taking notes. My daughter was at the other end of the table, and when I looked at her, her jaw was hanging open in amazement. I have four children and when I give them my sage wisdom they not only don't take notes they usually turn away in disgust. On one occasion I complained to a colleague that the garbage collectors in New York made more than I did. "But I don't really want to be a garbage collector in New York," he responded. And, of course, I don't either. What I have always wanted to do is teach, study, and write. And one of the best rewards of such a career is when you see your graduates out there teaching, studying, and writing, and gaining distinction on their own within the academic community.

I tell this story to my colleagues who have children and to my own large, talkative family when I have a chance to get a word in.

—Win Horner

122

In my sophomore year at Brigham Young University I decided that I wanted to be an English teacher, because I wanted a life like that I thought my best teachers were living. My mother, who had taught elementary school most of her life and was now teaching teachers, was horrified; she was sure that I'd be impoverished all my life and would never, as she put it, "amount to anything." My answer was always, "Why not get paid, even if it's only peanuts, for what you love to do?" And it still seems to me, fifty-eight years later, exactly the way to think about it.

I often tell this story when the subject is choice of vocations, or "doing things for the love of the doing."

—Wayne Booth

✄ ✄ ✄

NOTES

TALE 108 (p. 140). A reminder of the gap between dominant conventions for presenting our work (in terms of area studies or dissertation topic) and the narrator's lived experience of that work, which includes reading student essays, posting journals, participating in mentoring meetings. Academic discourse and structures force us to "hide" these aspects of ourselves and our work by making them "hard" to describe. Could this be one of the reasons why we have so few tales detailing the work writing teachers put into reading and responding to student texts? (MZL)

TALE 110 (p. 141). This tale puts a spin on the impulse among composition professionals to affirm one another's career choices by positing composition as above and beyond the problematic behaviors of literature professors and students. The narrator juxtaposes scenes from his "academic journey" to remind us that composition's concerns to nurture a student's voice, set up student-centered classes, or practice collaborative learning are collective goals towards which we must work, but not always already established facts permeating our actual practices (as the narrator had initially presumed from reading composition literature). The narrator takes a tough look at the discrepancy between his expectations of the profession before entering the program and his lived experience of it. I find powerful the narrator's choice of a final scene, where he waits in the delivery room as he reads and worries about finishing his paper on time for his last course for the Ph.D. To what extent is the narrator inviting us to hear his conclusion, "still plenty of time," as not just a reference to his wife's labor but also a reference to the nature of the "labor" of collectively turning composition into a field which lives up to its ideals? Or to the labor of the narrator's finishing his doctorate? The labor of his not letting his disappointment at the past behavior of others and himself keep him from trying to act according to his sense of the best of composition? The labor of reading and writing in general? (MZL)

TALE 112 (p. 144). "The narrative of a speaker's own career within an institution," writes Linde, "may either be coherent with the founding and paradigmatic narratives or may contest them, but is always told against the background of familiar and authoritative accounts" (1997, p. 286). It is informative to set against Swartz's tale the "familiar and authorita-tive" tales of the discipline that it challenges, tales of which versions may be found in this collection: males are cold and uncaring, comput-ers help solve student writing block, athletes are troublemakin in the writing teacher's life, writing classes are a refuge of good sense in an academic world in pursuit of surface conventions, literacy instruction operates as family enhancement, language is a tool or a therapy and not a "weapon." (RHH)

TALE 113 (p. 145). A perfect illustration of the point made by all students of lifestory (see Appendix B) that the sense of one's own life is not one story but many woven together. "The authorial I doggedly works to nar-rate the Me, seeking a valid story, amidst the surrounding narrative swirl" (McAdams, 1996, p. 136). Practically every line of this tale alludes to other stories, often told by other people, from the child who needs to be taken to soccer practice to the literature colleague whose interest "seems to stop at the border of literature." We don't hear those stories narrated literally, but they are not excised either. Inclusion of other sto-ries is an inherent property of storytelling, and the reason for story-telling's distinctive quality of non-coercion. Bishop explicitly labels her tale as cautionary, yet it is the opposite of heavy-handed. To recommend her professional career with its many-strand values, she tells a many-strand tale.

For extended accounts of careers in college rhetoric and composition, see Trimmer, 1997, McCracken and Larson, 1998, and Roen, 1999. (RHH)

Tale 117 (p. 150). See "Tracking Comp Tales," p. 223. (MZL)

Tales 121 (p. 154) and 122 (p. 155). Readers at the beginning of their careers in composition might compare these tales with Don Cunningham's remembrance of Horner toward the beginning of her career, as a classroom observer (Tale 19), and with Joe Williams' remembrance of Booth as a new teacher-student, "looking down at his notes, and slowly sliding down in his chair, hoping he wouldn't be called on" (Tale 109). (RHH)

CHAPTER 11

⇆

Exiting the Story

After making up my fourth bedtime story each night, I sometimes ask my 5-year-old daughter if we can just talk awhile together, sharing events of our day. "Story, Dad!" is her typical reply: "We'll talk tomorrow morning."

—Bill Puka (1996, p. 114)

Numerologists tell us that eleven is the number of renewal. This Chapter 11, the last of the book, may not look like a celebration of renewal, but it is. The oral storyteller exits the story only to tell the story again in another performance where, because the scene is changed, the story will be different, revitalized. And even if the scene has changed so much that the story no longer emerges from it, even if the story has died, it only opens up space for new stories that have been waiting around, latent, for the right time. "Every story that is told obscures the stories that go untold," says Verlyn Klinkenborg (1992, p. 5), which is as much as to say that every story not retold allows a new one to be born. This chapter circles back to Chapter 1 and could be called "Re-entering Story."

But the re-entry into a story may not happen all at once, nor happen easily, as Tale 2 shows. The comp tales collected in this chapter seem to me to be stories a-making, caught in an Arnoldian bind between two worlds, one dying and the other struggling to be born. As such, they cast an especially long, probing, and uniquely perceptive light into the margins of the discipline, and into dark chambers in the heart of it. They show the profession a-making. We all know a good comp tale when we hear it: it fits the circumstances, reverberates with unresolved conflicts of our field, affirms the experience and furthers the lifestory of the

teller, and begs to be retold. Such are the conditions of personal anecdote in any profession. But what happens when one or more of these
conditions do not hold? Then ur-stories are told, "potential narratives"
(Linde, 1997, p. 287), stories that beg not so much to be retold as to be
resumed and renewed—stories nonetheless, powerful and compelling.

In a fundamental sense, all comp tales are re-stories. It is part of their
oral nature. All narratives told rather than written are built to deconstruct.
They are like William Gibson's famed digital story "Agrippa," whose program is encoded to erase itself as the text is played. Comp tales deconstruct so that when retold the new teller is free to better them. They
deconstruct so they can remain authentic. "The bottom line," says Gary M.
Kenyon, "is that stories are lived before they are told" (1996, p. 25). If lived
experience does not match the original experience narrated in the stories
of the trade, then those stories are not authentic and gradually die. And
new ones, more authentic, rise from the ashes. Authenticity is when you
make the story, even your own story, your own. (RHH)

᛭   ᛭   ᛭

1 2 3

I begin each term with the narrative essay. In the first freshman composition class I taught, a young Vietnamese woman wrote the story of
her family's escape from Vietnam. She described how, in the middle of
the night, her father awakened her and her siblings and instructed
them to tape all of their money and small valuables to their bodies as
they dressed and then ran through the night toward the boats. She says
the road was muddy and that she lost one of her shoes, but that her sister, running alongside her, gave her one of hers. Suddenly, that particular desk was occupied by a young woman who had once shared a pair
of shoes with her sister as they ran for their lives. I was dumbstruck.

A term or two later, a student wrote about having been "rushed"
late one night as she opened her front door and then being assaulted
on her kitchen floor. The other day, I read a diagnostic essay about a
student's closest friend from her childhood. She writes: "He listened to
me and offered support. He was fifty-two years old. He shot himself."

It's a funny thing we do, structuring our students' lives into reader-
oriented prose. I do it as an adjunct working at several colleges in
Portland, Oregon, and I am still amazed at the way my students' lives
affect me, and at how they are sometimes interconnected.

I arrived one Monday morning to teach my class at a small parochial college and found in my mailbox a memo alerting staff to the fact that one of our freshmen had been killed when hit by a drunk driver on I-84 Saturday night. Another of our freshmen had been driving the car. The driver was in my class. The other students in my class knew about the accident; the absence was palpable.

Later that morning, at a community college twenty miles away, I faced my research paper class still a bit out of sorts. We were having "press conferences," and a student was writing on drunk driving. I told the class that a student of mine had been in an alcohol-related accident that weekend. After class, one of my older students approached me to say that he was a paramedic and had responded to an accident on I-84 Saturday night.

That was in February. Eventually, my freshman returned, healed physically, and seemed to improve emotionally. In April, at yet a third college, I held conferences with students on their position papers. I sat in my office with two very young students whose antics I enjoyed more than I let on. They came to class late daily—but stampeded down the hall so the class knew they were on their way. They did as little as possible, but made sincere entreaties. They usually looked a bit glazed over. This afternoon, in conference together (they were inseparable), one was preparing to write an essay on teen drug abuse (using his friends as subjects), and the other was writing on drunk driving. Their friend, it seems, had been killed by a drunk driver one Saturday night in February, on I-84.

I tell this story when I bump into other adjuncts. I put an emphasis on bump. We don't have the same number or types of conversations that full-timers have, and many of those we do have deal with the offices we keep in our trunks and our spiraling mileages. What we really have in common is our sense of inconsistency. I tell this story when I want to show that even over my one hundred miles a day, and over a broad economic and academic range, connectedness (even in this sad instance) still exists.

—Melody Leming-Wilson

124

I served on the counseling faculty at William Rainey Harper College—a community college in Palatine, IL, just northwest of Chicago. One of the delights afforded by this position was the opportunity to teach life skills courses within the Student Development Division. My favorite course, Humanistic Psychology, integrates sociological and psychological theory with interpersonal and intrapersonal development. The small classes provide intimate environments where, once trust is established, students share significant events in their lives, and opinions on a myriad of often controversial topics.

It's the third semester I've taught the course, and we're in the fifth week. My class is a diverse lot, in ethnicity, in age, in gender, in religion. We've discussed interpersonal communication, family dynamics, and bereavement issues. Ground rules, such as mutual respect and confidentiality, have been addressed and revisited when needed. Tonight's topic: racism. Students view a short video, "True Colors," which examines the discrepancies in how blacks and whites are treated in various contexts. A pregnant, telling silence fills the classroom once the video ends. After a moderate amount of verbal prodding by me, the white students respond to what they've just witnessed. Their comments are a mixture of naïveté, incredulity, and denial: "I didn't think it was that bad." "Well, that's just one side of the story." "That doesn't happen around here—does it?" These reactions eventually become too much for the lone African American male in the class; with clenched fists and raised voice, he indicts, "Man, y'all are full o' shit! How the fuck you gonna sit here and tell me this shit don't happen? Happens every damn day. Y'all know it, y'all live it—and if we wasn't in the class, all you'd see me as is a NIGGER!" We've now moved from the philosophical to the personal, and all in the room are scared.

I tell this story, not to invoke fear in the hearts of first-year composition instructors, but to acknowledge the risks our students take in sharing significant life events and aspects of their culture with others. Multicultural education, like the art and craft of writing, is a process, one involving the head, hand, and heart.

—Rod Brown

1 2 5

The first assignment I gave in my new position as composition instructor was an old standby: the significant event. One of my favorite new students, a quiet young woman named Monique, was having trouble with her rough draft. When I sat down with her during an in-class editing session, she told me that her problem was remembering the name of the teacher she was writing about. "I can remember her face," Monique said, "and I can remember her hands, her desk, but her name is gone. Maybe I never did know it." As it turned out, the teacher's name didn't matter all that much, because the event was arresting without names. Monique was writing about a couple of weeks in her grade-school life when she and her younger brother were fed peanut butter sandwiches by a teacher who noticed that the two children were coming to school hungry. Monique could remember her mother leaving the house before sunup to catch a bus to work; she could remember the feel of her little brother's hand in her own, the teacher's room, the desk, the hand holding the sandwich. And that was enough.

But how was I, a new Caucasian faculty member at a traditionally African American university, to grade such a paper? What I could teach Monique about paragraph development and sentence structure seemed profoundly insignificant compared to what she could teach me about definitions of family. I found myself questioning my colleagues, especially the other new white faculty member in the department, about our new roles as "authorities" in the composition classroom. Almost every week since the beginning of the school year, the questions have come up between us: what authority can we command as instructors?

For me, the pretense that I can be race- and class-blind is no longer an option. My students are affected daily by race issues. They write papers on gang violence in African American communities, on the fragmentation of the African American family, and on the problems associated with rising rates of pregnancy among African American teenagers. My previous teaching job was in a private church-affiliated liberal arts college, where the "significant event" papers often involved the trauma of choosing a boarding high school; I often feel now that I have little authority to "grade" the experiences I read about in composition papers.

And as far as content goes, perhaps I don't. My new colleague also moved here from a largely white school, although his was a large public university. We share the sense that we have become the "other," and that our new position as the minority on campus will sensitize us to issues of which we have been unaware. I have never witnessed a shooting, as many of my students have, nor do I have memories of the kind of economic struggle that Monique's family experienced. We don't have to remind ourselves that we are outsiders; the content of our students' papers reminds us daily.

At the same time, of course, our self-construction as "other" to the culture of our campus often feels self-congratulatory. Suddenly, we can tell ourselves, we understand African American experience better. Suddenly, we have access to a multi-ethnicity that our personal heritage may have denied us. Late in September, I was startled when, walking into a local bar with another colleague, who is African American, I was met with ten pairs of hostile Caucasian eyes. Had I walked in alone, I wouldn't have been noticed at all.

But still—my students and I do seem to make inroads into each other's experiences. One of my students writes that he was "getting giggy" in New York, and another student looks over his shoulder to say, "You need to explain that to Dr. Kennedy. So she'll understand. You need to know that, right, Dr. Kennedy?" I stand in front of the classroom, talking about empowerment through language rather than giving the "sensitivity" talk I would have given to my boarding-school students. In a discussion of an essay about Manhattan, one of my students raises her hands to ask, "How do you, as a Caucasian person, feel about the word 'whitie' here? If I were you, I think I'd be mad." I tell her how I feel, as a Caucasian. She responds to the characterization of Harlem, as an African American. We agree, as adult human beings, and I feel the class has succeeded that day.

My new colleague, who is gay, and I, who am female, retain our old "authorities" of sexual orientation and gender, but our positions are problematized, challenged, and refigured as we encounter, and are encountered by, our students. We exist in constant identity flux: feminine/masculine?, gay/straight?, black/white?, other? As professional teachers of writing, we watch our colleagues from previous schools drop their eyes and say, "Oh, I didn't realize your new school was African American. How is that?" And we say fine, it's great, we feel right at home, which too often we don't. Except, of course, on those days when we do. . . .

This is a story that my colleagues and I discuss as white faculty at a traditionally African American university.

—*Sarah Kennedy*

1 2 6

The young woman already had a bachelor's degree, but was in my W132 for a prerequisite to get into pharmacy school. Though born in Vietnam, she was raised in a small southern Indiana town, and her English was unaccented midwestern. It was also clear, articulate, and expressive. She had no trouble talking intelligently about any of the readings I assigned, and participated in class enthusiastically.

Nevertheless, her writing was a train wreck of broken syntax, puzzling grammar, and disjointed ideas, far beyond the standard ESL troubles. She made errors on paper that she never made out loud. On top of that, she was at the end of the semester and still searching for an argument to make in her last paper. Her first draft of the researched argument had been filled with vague ramblings about problems Asian Americans felt smothered by. She was angry about a lot of things, but unable to focus clearly on any of them.

I asked her to come talk to me about this, to see if we couldn't put something together in a hurry that her research could support. It took some time, but we finally narrowed it down to her unhappiness with the way Asian families force their young to study the sciences, no matter what their interests and temperaments might be. It had something to do with living up to their own image of the model minority. When I asked if it might also have something to do with the way her parents and older sister demanded that she become a pharmacist, she emphatically said, "No. Not at all," and said it twice.

Anyway, the woman got her thesis down to a couple of sentences that went right to the point. Playing secretary, I wrote them down for her, word for word, as she spoke them. They looked great. But when I read them back aloud, she looked awestruck and perplexed. She asked, "How do you just do that, just find the words and write them down like that?" Now it was I who was perplexed. I had just taken her dictation, neither adding nor subtracting a thing; they were her words, not mine. I told her so and pointed out that the accomplishment was all her own. She looked at me dejectedly, then literally hung her head and shook it so her hair covered her face. She could not really deny this, but there was no real way for her to accept it either.

Somehow this very intelligent, articulate woman was so alienated from her ability to write she was unable to even recognize her own words when someone wrote them down for her. Was this a case for an Oliver Sachs book, or a fairly standard ESL problem? I wanted to find some way to help this student connect with her own abilities and write as well as she spoke. I thought I should know how to do that, but I was baffled. Anyway, a few days later, while I was speaking with another student, she came by and handed me a drop slip, which I signed. Then, before I could speak to her, she vanished.

An "OK, Explain This One" story I tell other teachers, usually when discussing the differences between oral and written. Finding ways to bridge this gap seems to have become more urgent as the number of ESL students increases, and the story is usually a preface to a plea for ideas from my colleagues and writers.

—Kevin Corn

1 2 7

Some students are just hanging on by a thread. I often don't know what it is that makes them decide whether to stay in a class or drop out. I had a student, Joe, who really didn't want to be in my Composition II class. He'd waited to take it his final semester in school, a semester in which he carried an overload in order to graduate. I knew his history in our composition program: he'd failed basic composition and struggled through it a second time to earn a low C, never warming to the subject.

He'd had good attendance in my class, enjoying the new Power Macs in our classroom, but he struggled with each writing assignment. He did visit my office for conferences and used the writing center to work on his papers. He seemed to need help facing down his dislike for writing and the anxiety it brought him. His anxiety was especially withering.

One day when I was standing in front of the class, talking to the students about a new writing assignment, Joe got up from his seat and left the room. I assumed he'd gone to the bathroom or had some emergency to take care of. He returned about ten minutes later and approached the podium where I was still talking. He shoved a drop slip in front of me. When I realized what it was, I stopped talking and faced him, asking, "Would you like to talk about this after class?"

"No," he said.

I signed, giving him permission to drop the class, and he left the room. About ten minutes later, he returned to sit at his computer. He stayed that day and returned every day for the rest of the semester, completing his work and earning a low C.

I tell this story to my students, sometimes at mid-semester doldrums when it seems the semester will never end, and I can tell they're interested in it. They don't say anything, but their silence signals that they're paying attention. I think it comforts them to think that if Joe could make it through composition, then they can probably make it too. Probably the most important thing the story does is to let students see that I'm not very judgmental, and that I'm willing to accept them where they are.

—Ceil Malek

1 2 8

During my second semester as a TA at a large California urban university (a decade plus ago) I taught a section of first-year composition in which I decided to incorporate journal writing.

About mid-semester, I collected the journals for a spot-check. I was reading through the pile when I got to one young lady's. She had just the previous day called me to make an appointment for a chat during office hours. She'd been somewhat vague about what she'd wanted to talk about; I thought it probably would be to go over a draft or discuss her progress in the course. I was about halfway through her journal—the usual stuff about frustrating incidents and bad dorm food and long bookstore lines—when I started reading an entry about how she'd come out of the student health center one day shocked and stunned that the test had come back POSITIVE.

A few sentences later, after reading in several different ways how "literally dazed and confused" she felt and how "everything seemed a dream," I read that the test she had mentioned had confirmed that she now had AIDS. She then went on to muse about it philosophically, eventually coming to the conclusion (or at least considering it a strong option) that she'd start "sleeping around" just for the malicious fun of spreading the guarantee of slow death to a bevy of able-bodied collegian males. After all, someone had passed it on to her, she wrote, and if she was going to die, why not take a few folks with her, particularly representatives of the gender that had issued her a death warrant? Given that she was not unattractive, I had no doubt that she could bring about a considerable amount of destruction.

And at this point I felt I was pretty sure I knew what she was coming to see me for. After all, she'd been comfortable enough to share this via the journal; she probably now wanted to follow up for some sort of advice or counsel.

Now, I'd recently gone through TA training about how we have to be sensitive to student needs, anxieties, and psychological makeups. But this was all rather intimidating to a twenty-four-year-old, extremely married, extremely monogamous, and rather naïve wannabe college instructor, whose closest thing to leading an intense counseling session had been, many years prior, to hold the hand of a former girlfriend who'd become rather ill as the result of a few too many margaritas.

I consulted with the composition coordinator, who had me consult with our counseling office, and I conferred with a fellow TA who happened to be an older female, and I got all sorts of advice so that by the time I found myself sitting in "my" office (it was mine for about two hours each week) waiting for her to show up, I was about as wound up as a garage door spring.

The Kleenex and the counseling office's phone number were placed near at hand on my desk, and my TA colleague and the comp coordinator were in nearby offices should I need to bring them in. The door was to remain wide open, I was reminded several times.

At the appointed time she came bouncing through the door, a smiling, cheerful sophomore.

A protective façade, I was sure.

"I'll bet you're wondering what I wanted to see you about," she said, and before I could heartily agree she then went on to inquire about her various paper grades. Then, she pulled out a couple of papers, and we went over some passages to see how she revised them and what she might do better on later assignments.

And then she said she was done and had to go. I asked if there wasn't something else she needed to discuss.

She gave me a quizzical look and said no.

"What about this?" I said, indicating her journal, which just happened to be on the top of the stack on my desk.

No, she said, she was pretty sure she was doing what I wanted.

"What about the entry about the health center and the test results and all that?"

Her raised eyebrows, frown, and a quick shake of the head told me she didn't have any idea what I meant, so I turned to the passage and had her read it.

She looked up, stared at me, again nonverbally saying, "So what?"

"You don't intend to do anything like that?"

"Oh, no," she said, "That's just me imagining I'm someone else. You know, sort of role-playing. I thought it sounded like a pretty dramatic hypothetical situation, and you'd said we could write anything in the journal—was that OK?"

I assured her it was, that she was doing fine in the course, and she went on her way.

I now direct a large writing center at a state university, and many of the tutors I employ go on to be TAs in our composition program. I tend to end up as an informal mentor to many of them. I tell this story at staff meetings and in my tutor training course to illustrate a number of things:

(1) Why I no longer ever assign unfocused "write what you want" journals. (2) Why writing teachers should be careful to avoid the temptation of wanting to play psychologists. (3) Why, if a lesson or assignment doesn't get the kind of response you want, you should first closely examine it before blaming the students. (4) And, finally, how I've noticed that the things I worry the most about, and thus waste lots of time, effort, and sleep on, often turn out to be much less serious than I originally anticipated.

—W. Gary Griswold

1 2 9

It was my first 4Cs, in San Diego in 1993. At that time, I was not yet aware of the significance of these events in scholarly life, having been a nontraditional, commuting graduate student who mostly just did his studying and had little contact with the life of academe. My dissertation advisor had wisely insisted that I submit something to 4Cs; and when my half-baked, last-minute proposal was rightly "dinged," she wisely insisted that I accept a chair role and come down to see what it was like. The session I was chairing happened to have a paper by a graduate student who had studied X's writings in a class on composition and had some interesting criticism to offer. None of the panelists were "stars," and indeed only one of them was then a fully employed professor; and yet the session as a whole was superb, still one of the best I have ever attended. The audience was surprisingly large (it hadn't taken me long to pick up on the dynamic by which small rooms tended to be sparsely filled and large ones packed). Anticipating an interesting discussion of the several intriguing ideas the papers had raised, I looked out over the raised hands in the audience while the applause died on the last paper, thinking about how to begin the process of a fair and varied selection among those who wanted to contribute. I never got the chance.

A well-coiffed gentleman simply began to respond to the critique of X. Eventually, I figured out that it was X himself, though he did not identify himself (I suppose only a rookie like me wouldn't have known). It also became clear afterwards that this was why the room had filled, since afterwards many more people stopped to talk to X than to any of the panelists. Using just shy of the entirety of the discussion time, X essentially embellished a point he made clear relatively early on in his critique of the critique—that the criticism was fair, but that he had changed his view to account for it, as we would all hear in his own paper later on in the conference. As the minutes dragged on, I felt badly for the authors of the other papers especially—since X was essentially praising with faint damnation the paper to which he was responding. Feeling that certainly X himself would appreciate the value of hearing other voices, I started making a slightly exaggerated (though quite tactful, I thought) point of looking at my watch. I noticed that a few audience members, picking up on what I was doing, were looking somewhat shocked but quietly amused. It did no good anyway, for by the time X finished there was time for, I recall, one more question, and even for that the session time ran out before the answer could be completed. While I tried to keep going, when people started leaving and new people started looking in to see if the room was empty, I took the hint and called the session to a close.

Later on that day, as fate would have it, I was talking to a friend and mentor, who was a close friend of X's and who happened to be waiting for X and wanted to introduce me to him. Seeing X standing just around the corner, his back turned as he talked to a few other people, my friend and mentor tapped X on the shoulder and asked if he could introduce someone to him. X wheeled about, took a good hard look at me, and turned back to his conversation. He did not turn back until after I had taken my leave.

I tell this story very quietly and circumspectly when I just can't take any more glowing praise of X.

—Author's name withheld

1 3 0

There's one story that I've told—or tried to tell—for years. I've offered the story to colleagues, to organizers of conferences, to editors of journals. Under the title "Darkness Visible: Professionalism, Censorship, Tenure," I offered the story for the 1999 CCCC Convention, like this:

"The strongest impulse of academic disciplines is to serve their members' material interests, that is, to devise methods to capture a good share of the rewards provided by academic institutions" (James Berlin).

Professional defense of professional turf takes many forms, of which two are notable: tolerance, or even support, of hierarchies of unjust privilege (academic ranks, tenure, et sim.), and intolerance, or even suppression, of criticism of professional abuses.

In consequence, talk of liberation and empowerment by transformative intellectuals has mainly benefited the talkers, who now ask, in some distress, what social good they have done and turn to "service learning," with its comforting but impossible promise of delivering students from "moral miasma." Ironically, service learning has not lessened professional contempt for service courses.

Academics with real concern for social justice should put less trust in professional societies (MLA, NCTE, CCCC) and more in unions. Academics are workers, and their natural allies are not administrators but "staff"—janitors, campus cops, book shelvers, furniture movers. United academic workers could resist the pullulating administrators, who serve neither students, staff, nor faculty, but the external powers, to whom also the professional societies make quiet obeisance.

Of course my story won't get told at the 4Cs: it was rejected. A big, long version was rejected by one of the composition journals in the spring of 1998. Several readers have said nice things about that version, but the editors wanted me to follow their party line on The Great Undefined (aka theory, which I think is largely nonsense). Now I'm offering another one-pager ("Return to Service") to another conference. As I tell the story, there's been no "revolution in composition," just a totally conventional quest for academic status and privilege in a world where the job market for Ph.D.'s in literature collapsed thirty years ago.

So my story says that the culture of compositionists is a sick culture and that the cure would be a return to the service that boss compositionists despise. What will happen to the story in this latest version? I don't know. I do know that I'll keep telling it—maybe next time with the title "De Te Fabula."

—James Sledd

1 3 1

This is a story that I first heard Cindy Selfe tell at one of the CCCC conferences.

As I recall the story, Cindy had a student in a writing class during her first year of actual teaching, who never showed up for class (or perhaps he showed up but never turned in any work.) So, of course, she gave him a failing grade at the end of the semester. He called her the following semester in great indignation to ask why he got an F. She told him that she had never seen any of his work because he had never turned any in. And his response was, "Exactly, so how can you say that I can't write?"

I probably don't have the details correct, but it's one of my favorite stories about how two reasonable people can look at the same set of circumstances and come up with two different interpretations.

I've retold this often (giving Cindy proper credit of course!) as writing teachers, and other teachers, talk about the sometimes unreasonable responses students have to what the teachers consider their quite reasonable grades.
—Linda Stine

1 3 2

In 1980, after finishing my degree at the University of Texas, I was offered my first and only job—by Art Young at Michigan Technological University. I taught summer school that year, a course in technical writing for students who had junior standing at the university. The course went well—the students bright and motivated, the subject matter focused on problems about which they knew a great deal.

At the end of the course, however, when I had to assign final grades, I noticed a name on my official roll list that was unfamiliar—a student who had signed up for the course, but never attended. This was not an unusual situation; students often decided at the last minute to take a co-op position in industry over the summer or to stay home and earn money rather than attending summer classes. Generally, however, they dropped the class they had enrolled in by mail; occasionally they forgot. I assumed that the latter situation described this particular case. The standard university procedure to be followed involved giving the student a failing grade—only students themselves were allowed to drop a class; teachers could not remove them from the rolls unilaterally. The expectation was that students, upon seeing the failing grade, would arrange to have the course dropped with the permission of the dean of students. So, I assigned the student an F.

At the tag end of summer that year, I received a telephone call from the student in question. I did not recognize his name at first mention—having never met him face to face—and had to be reminded of our connection. As I suspected, the student had indeed accepted a co-op opportunity in an engineering company that summer and had never attended class.

I was taken aback, however, by the question that followed.

"Why did I flunk the course?" he asked.

I replied, "Well, Mr. XX, you never came to class!"

The student responded indignantly, "Dr. Selfe, that's exactly what I wanted to talk to you about. How could you even think of flunking me without ever reading a single piece of my writing?"

Damned good question.

I tell this almost everywhere: it seems to strike at the heart of the silliness with which the educational system sometimes presents us.

—Cynthia L. Selfe

1 3 3

I was sixteen and riding the city bus with my uncle, to be deposited for the day at the Smithsonian. He was then Washington correspondent for the *Detroit Free Press* and an ideal person to visit for someone who had fallen unawares under the spell of words. Suddenly he stopped talking and started listening to the conversation of two men in the seat in front of us. When they got off at the next stop, he told me they had been discussing the current political scandal, which he had just written about. In fact one of them was citing from his column. "Trouble is he was getting me all wrong," he said. "But then," he added, and I saw that his eyes were no longer focused on mine, "maybe he got it right and I got it wrong."

I tell this to students to make the disturbing point that when the reader doesn't understand you, you cannot always tell who is at fault.

—Rich Haswell

1 3 4

Rhetoric teachers always tell stories about how much time they spend responding to student essays—often one hour per student paper, usually late at night or early in the morning and thus how little sleep they are getting. "I've had only five hours of sleep total in a week!" If a rhetoric teacher has 44 students per semester, the weeks that papers or speeches are due, he or she dedicates 44 hours *only* to responding, not counting time planning for the classes, doing their own graduate work, or attending to their own personal lives. They tell these stories to show how labor-intensive the teaching of writing is and how hard they are working—to gild their ethos as workhorses.

Many stories in the composition profession are victim narratives of the Rodney Dangerfield "can't get no respect" variety. Either students get "dissed" on their writing by their content area teachers (who call them stupid in the margins of their papers and cover their papers in red ink); or composition TAs themselves get humiliated in their own graduate programs either orally in class, during their comps, prospectus, or dissertation defenses, or by cruel comments or no comments at all on their papers; or if they are faculty, they get humiliated at faculty meetings when non-composition people repeatedly tell them their profession doesn't exist and that research on writing is an oxymoron.

An increasing number of victim narratives are about discipline problems in the classroom, especially first-year students challenging the authority of TAs who are young, female, and/or minority. Students openly disparage and talk back to TAs ("How would you know how to grade me, you're just a TA—you don't know quality work like mine when you see it"). This mean-spiritedness comes out most of all on midterm and final evaluations when students criticize not only their TA's grading system (because they themselves failed to get the grades they wanted), but her appearance, including her clothing. These stories are told to illustrate the obstacles TAs face and to show that with the prevalent consumerist mentality about higher education fostered by the media, students are becoming more audaciously rude.

Many victim narratives have to do with writing centers: of teachers, of both non-composition and composition courses, sending their *entire* class to the writing center because they do not want to bother with teaching writing; of students who want to drop off their papers at the writing center to get them corrected and then pick them up later; of teachers who humiliate their students by pointing out every flaw in their writing and then the writing center staff has to try to restore their egos. Writing center people tell these stories to demonstrate the multiple forces they are up against, to illustrate how much work they do (the workhorse ethos again), and to show how the rest of the university doesn't understand or respect the teaching of writing.

"Here are some stories that I've heard composition and rhetoric people tell. Many are story-types or genres." Personal letter to the editors.

—*Carol Severino*

1 3 5

Some years ago, I began asking teachers in workshops and in-service programs to create narrative cases about teaching problems that they could share with colleagues as a way to encourage reflection. These cases were much like comp tales, but longer. They were often written from the third person point of view, and usually ended with a dilemma that begged for discussion. The more complex and open-ended the dilemma, the more thoughtful the reflection and the more interesting and wide-ranging the discussion. The teachers had fun being creative with their cases, and the groups almost always found talking about them a source of professional enrichment.

In most of these workshops, someone would inevitably ask what didn't make a good narrative case for reflection. They knew, of course, that the cases had to be well-written, with believable characters, complex actions, good narration and dialogue, and a culminating problem or crisis that begged for resolution. What they meant was whether certain situations or scenes made for ineffective cases. When this question came up, I usually described a situation that for me had become a kind of "urban teaching legend." It goes like this: At one college somewhere in the U.S., a senior professor has a strange method of returning his students' papers. First he places each successful paper in front of its author, moving around the room until they're all distributed. Then he retrieves from his briefcase the papers of the students who haven't done well. These students get, deposited humiliatingly on their desks, a zip-lock plastic baggie containing the shredded contents of their paper.

The point was delightfully simple. Such an outrageous action couldn't possibly make a good case because, as the workshop attendees quickly realized, there was nothing to discuss. The guy was a creep. Everyone agreed he shouldn't be teaching. Was this story true, they'd ask? Not to my knowledge, I'd reply. Which went to the point: good cases are more subtle, like real teaching situations.

Years later, I was having coffee with a composition director at a small, private liberal arts college and we were talking about cases. When I related the horrendous urban teaching legend to her, she gasped, spilling her coffee, and looked at me in amazement. How had I heard about him, she wanted to know—the faculty member in her department who had earned a reputation on campus for the zip-lock plastic baggie routine? Equally stunned, I confessed that I had no idea. The story was apparently floating around out there in the masses of lore and legend and apocrypha of teaching. But he's real, she insisted, and went on to tell me all about her senior colleague who tortures developing writers with acts of shame and humiliation.

I used to tell the plastic baggie story to show that some scenarios are so one-sided or outrageous that they make lousy cases. Now I use the story as a case—a case that's symptomatic of an unresolved problem happening out there in the teaching world. It's called hateful teaching. The question is: what are we going to do about it?

The discussion can last for years.

—Chris Anson

1 3 6

When conducting orientation workshops with new writing teachings and writing across the curriculum workshops, I have often begun by asking participants to write about a memory of writing that stands out in their minds, for whatever reasons. This invitation often elicits memories of writing in school and prompts participants to put themselves in the role of learners and writers. I write along with everyone, and to open the discussion, I have often told the following story from my own childhood:

In sixth grade, my teacher gave us an assignment to write a fictional story about anything we wanted. My choice was to write a story of a young boy being taught to sail by an older man. As I recall it now, it was a less than gripping story of my own experience learning to sail from a man I respected greatly. I invested a great deal of time and care in writing the story and illustrating it and my teacher praised me for it.

The experience of writing that story still stands out vividly in my memory, and I have told the story as testimony to the personally meaningful function writing can serve to recreate an experience and relive feelings associated with it. And, I have pointed to the importance of being given choice as to my topic and of feeling that I was writing to a teacher I could trust. But when I have told this story at workshops in the past, particularly before groups who don't know me well, I have moved it closer to nonfiction than it already was, making the narrator a little girl, not a little boy.

Why this re-coding? I think now that it was in part embarrassment at my earlier self, at my seemingly too obvious projection into a male role when I would later identify as a lesbian. And, I write now self-conscious that I may be perceived as making too much of a little pronoun and should perhaps let this reflection stay in memory, not move to print. Linked to my own internal embarrassment was a desire to control how I would be perceived in the moment by workshop audiences. I wanted to pass, not call attention to myself by invoking in their minds a heterosexist stereotype that a lesbian is just a female who wants to be a male, the same stereotype that prompted my own embarrassment. I wanted to submerge these intertwined personal/social issues and focus their attention on a neatly packaged point about writing as a way of re-valuing and even re-shaping personally important experiences. Ironically, telling the story as written, with "he" as narrator, would have made that point even more strongly. Telling it now as written makes another point that my deliberate re-coding of the narrator submerged: my re-storying of my past story was intimately connected to how I wanted to position myself in present moments and my perception of how the story would be heard in relation to pervasive social discourses.

I write this story now invoking the persona of truth telling, of setting the record—if not the person—straight, but I do so aware that it is my recollection for this moment, for this time. In contrast to my position at those earlier workshops, I tell this tale out of comfort with myself, out of a feeling that the times call for openness about my sexual orientation, and out of a feeling that this collection invites critical re-examination of the stories we tell and retell. This re-examination leaves me all the more aware of the multiple perceptions and forces that shape the stories we tell in our professional lives—in workshops, conference sessions, published writings. I'm wondering about how susceptible we are in these public venues to simplifying and shaping our stories in relation to the image of ourselves we want to project and in relation to the theoretical perspective we choose to foreground. Some theories—for complex and intertwined personal/social/cultural/political reasons—are safer than others to validate through one's person. The theoretical perspective that I didn't validate through my telling foregrounds the psychological and social dynamics and the interactions of power and desire that shape what tales get told in public in our professional forums and in our classrooms.

—Anne Herrington

᭐ ᭐ ᭐

NOTES

TALE 123 (p. 160). I appreciate the tension achieved by the narrator's efforts to convey both her sense of the inconsistencies in the everyday life of an adjunct and the connections she perceives in the lives about which her students are writing in three very different institutional settings. This tale would work well with Tale 15 (p. 21) to examine the unequal distribution of office space across faculty ranks and its effect on teaching and learning. See also "Tracking Comp Tales," p. 215. (MZL)

Tale 123 (p. 160). To this teller, the "reader-oriented prose" of the classroom seems somehow inauthentic. But the stories that she knows are authentic have no analogues, no familiar tales to authenticate them for listeners. Her students' essays, and her own tale, then, are what James C. Scott calls "offstage transcripts," hidden scripts that resist the public scripts, parts of a "discourse of dignity, of negation, of justice" (1990, p. 114). Scott's terms are chosen with care. The ur-tales of this chapter make worthy of respect experiences of the narrator that the storybook of the profession treats as undignified. They negate the paradigms and stereotypes that often appear in stock tales. And they call for a more just account of professional lives that have been neglected, such as adjunct teaching in the community colleges. (RHH)

Tale 124 (p. 161). I take the narrator to be asking teachers to examine the source of that fear and what we are going to do about it. I am often scared in similar situations because they raise questions I am still struggling to address. First, this is one of those classroom situations where the "lone" African American appearing student would have no choice but to risk sharing his view on racism. Living it, this student would have to have been aware that racism has most likely predisposed the rest of the class to view him as the spokesman of his race. Had he remained silent, his silence would have been perceived as "speaking" the same incredulity and denial as his peers. Moreover, his unspoken denial would have been taken as speaking for all African Americans rather than as being spoken by this particular student as a result of specific life events he has encountered. For the same reason, even if he did share his peers' opinion that racism was not "that bad" or "doesn't happen around here" as it is portrayed in the film, he'd still have to negotiate the assigned task of being expected to speak for other African Americans with different experiences than his. Tales like this one remind us to acknowledge the different, extra risks taken and the different, extra work performed for the course by the "lone" African American (or female, return, gay and lesbian, etc.) students in classrooms explicitly aiming to combat the very systems which discriminate against these students.

Secondly, this student clearly wants us to consider that "[we] all live [racism]." Yet, because racism has predisposed us to assume that Euro-

American appearing persons have no race and therefore, do not "live racism" unless they are publicly committing hate crimes, we often find it easier to hear his statement as a personal attack accusing the rest of us (in that room) of being racists, and immediately launch into a series of earnest denials or angry protests. As a teacher, I would want to make sure that I and my Euro-appearing students would honor the risk taken by this student in at least two ways. We would rigorously examine the multiple ways racism has predisposed us to "see" an African American male, even though very few in the room probably have, would have, ever actually used the word NIGGER in our conscious thoughts or to others behind this student's back. And I would want to ensure that we examine the complex levels in which we indeed "live" racism, even if and especially when a part of that lived experience often leaves us feeling that racism "does not happen around here" rather than that it "happens every damn day." Done right, such a class discussion and the series of writing assignments which might proceed from it can move the course further and deeper than any discussion or writing assignment in response to any other published text or film. But I cannot be sure that I would have the wit and expertise to always make this kind of teaching and learning take place. It demands literacy skills we seldom get from our professional training. I myself often have to rely on the literacy skills of the "lone" student from the margins to sustain me through such teachable moments. (MZL)

TALE 125 (p. 162). This tale is so rich that it can be used with a variety of tales to highlight a series of issues relevant to the teaching and learning of writing. For instance, it joins tales such as Tale 37 (p. 45) to examine the challenge of "grading" the experiences about which students write. The local bar scene could be used with tales similar to Tale 124 (p. 161) to explore our invisible experience of living racism, such as the exemptions from hostility we automatically obtain by not appearing to be African American and not appearing in the company of persons who look African American. The classroom scene on discussing the essay on Manhattan would work with Tale 124 to explore the experience of being the "lone" other when sharing with the class one's response to a textual representation of one's own "kind." See also "Tracking Comp Tales," p. 213 and p. 215. (MZL)

TALE 126 (p. 164). This tale seems to join Tale 58 (p. 70) to pose yet another purpose for comp tales: a preface to a plea for ideas from colleagues and writers on how to address a concrete situation. It is thus the listener's responsibility to ask: How would I have responded if the plea were addressed to me? I think a side of me would immediately jump to the conclusion that this narrator needs to be updated on composition scholarship which has explicitly examined and offered teaching strategies for addressing the issues I see surfacing from the narrated event. I hope though that were the occasion to arise, I would be able to hold this side of me back and listen, instead, carefully to what more the narrator might have to say about the situation. For my guess is that even if this narrator might indeed benefit from this scholarship, knowing the scholarship alone is not going to be enough for either the narrator or myself to fully meet the challenge arising from the actual event. Rather, we might both learn by using the event to also locate issues overlooked in current scholarship or where the suggested strategies do not fully apply. (MZL)

TALES 126–128 (pp. 164–167). In biology, researchers say that they have achieved a "story" when separate experiments can be connected with an explanatory scheme, usually a causal sequence. In that sense, these three tales don't achieve story and, not surprisingly, it is separate facts about their students whom the narrators can't connect (see Chapter 6, especially Tale 58). From their genre study of personal narratives, J. R. Martin and G. A. Plum would categorize these three tales about students not as "stories," which have a sense of resolution or dénouement, but as "recounts," which merely record a sequence of events (1997). But the reasons we recount may be very important—to take stock, for instance, or to assess losses, or to step back in order to better leap forward. (RHH)

TALE 128 (p. 167). Told alongside Tale 98 (p. 122), we are reminded of the danger of conflating writing with living, even as we strive to present writing and living as mutually constitutive. (MZL)

TALE 129 (p. 169). Like Tale 24 (p. 33), it unpacks the behavior of leading figures to pose alternative imagoes for the self and the profession. (MZL)

TALE 130 (p. 170). This tale asks us to consider the collaborative work we receive (and often take for granted) from some of our "invisible" colleagues: custodians, campus cops, furniture movers, secretaries, etc. It also raises questions on how and why certain stories are privileged more than others at given institutional sites, including by the apparatus of this book and my reading of the tales. (MZL)

Tales 131 and 132 (pp. 171–172). People tell other people's stories all the time, of course, though understandably contributors were not inclined to submit re-tells to this collection. Stine's version of Selfe's story matched Selfe's version remarkably well. But as Selfe explained to us, she has changed since she first started telling the story. "I think this student had hold of something about writing instruction (even though I also think he was scamming me) that eluded me at that early point in my career. In 1981, I flunked this student. Now? I think I have come to a belief that the system is probably much more problematic than the student and I thought." She has re-storied her own story, and for her it now ends with an unanswered question rather than with a resolution. An essential motive for many of the stories in this chapter, then, has to do with a mismatch between an old self and a new self and with a need to re-story one's own life. "We seek restorying when our current lifestory (inside at least) no longer coheres within itself" (William Randall, 1996, p. 238). (RHH)

Tales 133–134 (p. 173). Three tales that are about our own tales, prodigal sons, returning to us, changed. By telling them, do the authors authorize and further the change others have made in the stories? (RHH)

Tale 135 (p. 175). A powerful reminder of the responsibility of the audience. The life of a story depends not only on how we tell and retell a story but also on what we do, are going to do, in situations similar to the narrated event. See "Tracking Comp Tales," p. 222–223. (MZL)

Tale 135 (p. 175). The discussion, at least the storytelling, will last as long as individual members of the profession keep growing. In a forgotten article published a quarter of a century ago, Mina Shaughnessy outlined a four-stage plot of professional development common among comp teachers. First they concentrate on protecting the academy, then they commit themselves to filling the students with knowledge, then, baffled at their indifferent success, they begin observing their students' and their own behavior, and finally they admit that they themselves are students with much to learn. Shaughnessy calls these stages Guarding the Tower, Converting the Natives, Sounding the Depths, and Diving In (1976). This story, as well as many of the other tales in this chapter, strike me as rising out of the diving in. (RHH)

Tale 136 (p. 176). This tale suggests that how we shape and reshape the narrated event is related to the specific conditions of the narrative event:

one's changing sense of how one wants to position oneself, of public reception of that position at a given time and place, of the pervasive social discourses and the effect these discourses might have on how one's audience would hear one's story, and of the kind of story and storytelling favored by the audience. See also "Tracking Comp Tales," p. 213 and p. 216. (MZL)

Taking In Comp Tales

⇔

Richard H. Haswell

The anecdote consists, ever, of something that has oddly happened to someone, and the first of its duties is to point directly to the person whom it so distinguishes.

—Henry James,
Preface to *The Reverberators* (1908)

1 ADVENT

For the second morning in a row, I saw her standing in the driveway, looking independent and forlorn. Jan and I had been thinking about a cat. We guessed this one was about six months old, a blue-tip Siamese, elfin, lapping up the saucer of milk. It was near Christmas and she carried herself with a certain elegance, so we named her Grace. Gracie, though, turned out not exactly the package we might have wished for. She had hookworms and an intestinal infection. She converted the medicine into permanent stains in the dining room rug. She tested positive, the vet warned us, for feline leukemia. Six months old or not, sick or not, she spent an awesome portion of her days pacing and yowling around the house in heat. Had we taken her in, or had we been taken in by her?

I'm thinking of Gracie because it was about the same time that the first comp tales started coming in, and they were looking a dicey lot. As I sized up our first returns, I wondered what exactly Min-Zhan and I had asked in. To begin with, none seemed birds of a feather. The first twenty, ragtag and motley, sorted into twenty different pigeon-holes. They ranged in length from a sentence to three single-spaced pages, and some came from the oddest experiences—pondering trash on a California beach, teaching in prisons, helping with necropsy at a local zoo. And while all showed the oral-tale bloodline, they were some degrees removed from the classroom or faculty-lounge anecdotes we laugh at and shake our heads over. Not that they weren't appealing and insightful stories. By the first twenty, I knew that all we needed was more of the same before we would have the book we envisioned. Nor were they trivial, since they dealt with the central preoccupations of our trade. Nor passionless, since as most narratives of human experience they staked their claim near to the heart. Indeed, some were almost alarmingly raw, like four-legged alley creatures prowling around in verbal rut. But at the time it seemed to me that something was missing. They felt, well, lightweight. They just didn't seem to go very far. What they didn't have were those ideas—they appear in every issue of the trade journals— that pull together or light up or transform whole chunks of our understanding about the profession.

Actually, I was wrong. I just didn't know what to make of what we had. I was just better at taking in a composition article than a comp tale.

2 Adventure

Two months later, Gracie's vet told us a comp tale. Gracie had escaped the house, returned a couple of days later, and we decided to have her spayed. Now we are back at the clinic, and the doctor is trying to diagnose Gracie's post-operative distress—wheezing, lung congestion, maybe a temperature. I ask if feeling the nose is a reliable gauge of an animal's temperature. He looks at us and his slightly apologetic air changes to one of interest. "It will do in a pinch," he says, smiling. "But you're both English teachers, aren't you?" And as he continues to manipulate Gracie's tender underside:

> It was an English teacher who brought in a cat with the highest temperature I've ever seen. Rushed in with it, I should say. 110°— it would have killed a mature cat. Fortunately, it was just a kitten. The woman said she had been sorting clothes from a dryer and putting in a new load and the kitten had been playing in the piles of clothes.

"Uh-oh's" from Jan and me.

The phone rang, and she threw in the rest of the load, started the dryer, and ran to answer. She said it was a student. I can't remember exactly the problem, but it had to do with a paper he had written or was writing, something. He went on for a long time. She said she was thinking that his ideas just weren't going together, that they were banging around in his paper like that pair of tennis shoes in the dryer. Then all of a sudden it dawned on her, wait a minute, there weren't any tennis shoes in that laundry.

Jan, "Oh, my goodness!" Rich, shaking his head.

Well, we gave the kitten an ice bath and brought it around. When it was clear that it was going to be okay, she told me, "You know, I don't even think I hung up the phone."

We laugh. And he, as if the story were not over yet,

I don't think I mentioned, but this time Gracie's test for leukemia came out negative.

I had two thoughts about the vet's story. Almost before he had finished telling it, I was telling myself that it had to go in this book. The second thought came that night—a kind of click experience—as I was reading, of all things, a study of vernacular narratives. The essay was about Israeli soldiers who had refused to participate in the Lebanese war of 1982–1985 or later in the Intifada, how some had continued their resistance in jail by publishing narratives of their moral decision. The author, Ruth Linn, writes that this kind of soldier "tells a narrative that is not constructed in a lonely manner but in regard to other people's moral narrative" (1989, p. 109). It occurred to me that the vet's story and the comp tales were deeper than I had thought.

The story of the kitten in the dryer was funny but it was moral as well. And it was not just told "in a lonely manner" but interwoven with the stories, also moral, of many people. Beside the story of the kitten's fate, there was the story of the teller, how he, the good vet, had saved the kitten. There was the guilty story of the woman, who had saved the kitten as much as he had and whose obligation to her student had been preempted by her obligation to her pet. And there was the story of the student whose call for help his comp teacher so abruptly left on hold. As we will see, there are other stories entwined in the vet's tale.

What I finally realized was that comp tales will seem lightweight if we do not try to extend their meaning in ways native to their genre. That genre is narrative, but it is also personal and vernacular and oral and social. Two ways of extending comp tales are by looking for moral directive (always there) and for embedded tales (always there), but those are not the only ways. There are others as crucial and as illuminating, and a little thought about them could well save many a comp tale from my initial misapprehension. Above all it can show how a professional genre as plebeian as oral anecdotes of personal experience provides a rich and singular understanding of the profession. It can show, I hope, how *Comp Tales* turned out far better than the book I originally envisioned.

But first, an aside. In a recent book featuring some extended English-teacher narratives, John Trimmer (1997) makes the same point but from the teller's angle. Storytelling, he says, is a distinctive way of making knowledge. It is a way the profession not only understands but furthers itself. But Trimmer adds that his experience with narratology, or the formal study of narrative practices, is of little use in interpreting teacher stories. That did not turn out to be my experience. I have found wonderfully fruitful the last three or four decades of exploration of narrative, in fields such as anthropology, cognitive science, communications, ethics, folklore, history, literature, personal development, psychotherapy, sociolinguistics, and study of organizations. That narrative is not only stories but a mode of understanding to itself—a mode constituting as well as representing reality, as Jerome Bruner insists (1986)—is a notion owing to the formal studies, for instance, of philosophers such as Paul Ricoeur, developmentalists such as Mark Freeman, historians such as Louis O. Mink, sociolinguists such as Barbara Johnstone, and psychologists such as Jerome Bruner himself. To this many-disciplined exploration, my understanding of the oral sharing of narrative knowledge in composition—comp tales—is heavily indebted (see Appendix B).

Perhaps I should also add, as a warning, that in my list of ways to appreciate comp tales, you will not find reading for formal plot structure. Many of us can remember, if dimly, Vladimir Propp's classic "morphology" or underlying structure of the European folktale (1928/1968). Probably we can't name all thirty-one of his invariant plot features, but the major ones are familiar enough: (1) an initial situation wherein (2) a protagonist (3) reacts to some misfortune or lack, (4) leaving home to battle an antagonist and (5) to be assisted by a magic agent or donor, (6) with whose aid the hero solves the lack and (7) returns home to triumph over disbelievers and to live happily ever after. I'm not saying that this structure is dead. It's an adventure plot-line that keeps coming back, with more lives than a cat. No doubt you can find examples of it in these comp tales (I'd recommend looking at the stories of comp careers in Chapter 10). But I have found structure search as one of the least rewarding of tools to open up comp tales. Let's put Propp and his numerous structuralist followers away for a while and look instead in a direction with more recent appeal. Instead of structure, let's focus on performance. And to protect any one *Comp Tales* contributor from the burden of excessive analysis, let me focus on the vet's tale.

(1) By way of initial situation, *comp tales don't set a scene but rather emerge out of one.* Perhaps it takes a recorder of on-site storytelling such as folklorist Richard Bauman to recognize it, but an oral tale consists second of the storyline (the "narrated event") and first of the context of the telling (the "narrative event"). The telling comes first in the sense that the past events to be told are not told until a present event calls for them (1986, p. 2). The conversation takes a certain turn, a story is recalled, the moment seems right for it, the signals for storytelling are sent ("But you're both English teachers, aren't you?"), the listeners signal back that they are willing to give to the would-be raconteur their usual allotted space in the turn-taking of conversation, and then, and only then, the story starts. It starts as a second chapter, as a continuation of the larger storyline of the original conversation. All comp tales thus begin *in medias res.* The vet's story is finally and originally not about the saving of the kitten nor the salvation of the kitten's owner but rather about the doctoring of Gracie ("I don't think I mentioned, but this time Gracie's test for leukemia came out negative"). While collecting our comp tales, Min-Zhan was especially aware of the importance of the narrative event, and she wisely insisted that we ask contributors to tell not only the tale but the circumstances when they tell it. Indeed, you can almost say that it is the circumstances that tell the tale. Donna Dunbar-Odom's experience was not unique among contributors, in being unable to think of any stories to send and then soon after finding herself relating one in class (Tale 22).

(2) But if the circumstances of the telling are in some ways first, then in some sense *the teller is always the protagonist.* The comp tale may report the adventures of heroes, anti-heroes, or fallen heroes, but the teacher teller always perceives a need and always sets out in quest to resolve it. Helpful here is Bronwyn Davies and Rom Harré's notion of "positioning" in everyday conversations. As they put it, positioning "is the discursive process whereby selves are located in conversations as observably and subjectively coherent participants in jointly produced story lines" (1990, p. 48). People assume all kinds of positions during conver-

sation: indulgent parent, slighted youngest child, sincerely confused student, overworked department chair. An oral comp tale assumes a position for the teller but also a position for the listener, who can challenge and alter it. By his story Gracie's doctor positioned himself as the cool-headed veterinarian, and positioned us as the less than professional English teachers, which it would have been easy to alter in mid-story ("Whoa, diagnosing over the phone! I never do that. Do you?"). Had we done so, the story would have changed, at least the telling of it. And stories do change with time and circumstance. "Today's horror on the highway," notes William L. Randall, "becomes tomorrow's tragedy, next week's exciting adventure, next month's amusing anecdote, and old age's illustration of the irony of life" (1996, p. 235), each story assuming a different footing for the storyteller. Positioning allows entry into some of the more fascinating complexities of comp tales, for instance where one tale comes in several variants (e.g., Stine's version of Selfe's story, Tales 131 and 132), or where master teachers tell stories of themselves making mistakes to an audience of apprentice teachers (e.g., most of the tales in Chapter 2), or where stories contain other contradictory stories (as most obviously in Tale 2).

(3) So the narrator, now the protagonist, of the oral comp tale sets forth out of a *sensed lack or sensed misfortune of the listeners*. That presumed need is always more than just a yen to be entertained. It may be a need to find compadres in resistance to the establishment (James C. Scott, 1990), to be part of cultural fantasies (Ernest G. Bormann, 1985), to understand an argument (Walter Fisher, 1987), to trust a new boss (Charlotte Linde, 1996), to feel a member of a profession (Joanne Martin and Melanie E. Powers, 1983), to understand origins (Frank Kermode, 1967), to mend a moral relationship (James M. Day and Mark B. Tappan, 1996). It is easy to find all of these needs in the comp tales, with the help of the contributors' commentary. The immediate needs of the audience are as varied as happenstance and social relationships, but what remains constant is the willingness of listeners to open up their lacks and misfortunes to the healing charm of the teller's story. And as listeners we do open up. Jan and I had brought Gracie in with a lurking fear that the operation had gone awry, worse that the vet and his veterinary practice would not find something routine and curable. And the doctor told a story salving those fears. All three of us wanted the situation to work, to make sense. There lay the dovetailing of our need to hear and the doctor's impulse to tell. That is why, says Peter Brook, that all narratives take the "form of desire" (1984, p. 37). That is why comp tales— even the frothiest coffee-klatch gossip—finally cannot be shallow or triv-

ial. "It is the complicity of the listener," says Freema Elbaz, "which allows the story to repel the threat of meaninglessness" (1991, p. 6). When the professional paper lacks that complicity of writer and reader, *it* is the discourse form that deserves the word "lightweight."

(4) But if the tale proceeds in complexity, it does so also in *deep conflict*. The need shared by teller and listener goes beyond them and it goes deep. The captivating surface movement of the story (this and then this and then this) is constrained by faultlines, entrenched and active. This itself is an old story, told by all the core studies of twentieth-century narrative: Freud on fantasy as rooted in unresolved traumas, Jung on dreams as messages sent from one part of the psyche alienated from another, Levi-Strauss on myths as holding clashing social forces in suspension (1979), Fredric Jameson on prose fiction as class-conflict reflections of social contradictions (1981), Sam Schrager on folk history as containing "opposing versions of truth" (1983, p. 89), Tamotsu Shibutani on rumor as a public means to cope with the social uncertainties (1966), Antonio Ferreira on family myths as a family's defense mechanism to handle internal and external conflicts (1963), Joanne Martin, et al. on stories told in organizations as "reducing tension by expressing it" (1983, p. 448), Elbaz on teacher stories as masking "the fragmented nature" of their lives (1991, p. 5).

In comp tales, faultlines are easy to detect. Within the story performed by the vet, Jan, and myself, beneath the smiles and laughter and gestures of entente, lie stubborn clashes in point of view: scientist and belletrist, practitioner and educator, doctor and client, teacher and student, male and female. As all oral anecdotes, comp tales constantly risk offending people because so often their content is precisely those cultural clashes that political correctness tries to hide. A comp feminist would not likely appreciate the vet's portrait of the dingbat, housewife English teacher, nor would a member of the SPCA be likely to repeat the story of the kitten's fate. Perhaps not so easy to detect in oral stories, though, is the way social and cultural conflicts appear in the form of counter stories. A comp tale, as I have said, always holds other tales. We now see that hand-in-hand with the stories of the woman drying the kitten, the woman abandoning the student, and the vet saving the day, go stories of the vet performing a clean operation, of Gracie defeating leukemia, and of the field of veterinary science outperforming the field of English. And there are yet at least two other major tales.

(5) One is the *saving grace of experience*. In setting out to tell a story, the storyteller always takes a chance. All of us know the subliminal heart-skip just as we launch publicly into an anecdote. There is, of

course, the chance that the listeners will become bored, or not get it, or have heard it before, or worse than those—if it is a story of personal experience—not believe it. But there is a deeper risk, underpinning every story ever told. And that is the risk that the story won't work as a story. Won't work in two ways. Won't somehow find a way to deal with the faultlines exposed by the narrated events, if not bridge them at least offer an explanation or a way around them. And won't somehow fill the lack or soothe the misfortune of the listeners. How does the narrator make the story work? At bottom, the only way is to convince listeners that the tale is being told out of experience. Experience, *ex periculum*, through peril. The very act of telling the story says that the narrator has been through and has learned—even a story of personal failure, even a story of the narrator being saved by someone with more experience, even a story that happened to someone else. Experience is the token or talisman that certifies the teller and therefore the tale.

All oral stories that work, ultimately, celebrate the storyteller. But only if they work. Our vet's story clearly tells of his success as a veterinarian. But notice that the success is not in the tale but in the telling. If he had told the same story in exactly the same way to a couple whose pet had just died under his care, it would not work. It would not even be a story, since it would not make sense. Only experience allows it to make sense. Charlotte Linde notes that in a California research institution, non-participant stories—tales of events that the narrator knows only second-hand—are usually told by people with the most experience in the organization (1996, p. 335). Narrative skill may be the gift that allows the storyteller to convey a story, but experience is the gift that makes it a story. And that is the second-to-last tale inside the vet's tale of the kitten, the tale of how the event itself became a part of the vet's experience that authenticated his telling of it.

(6) The last story, of course, is his telling of the story. The telling itself tells a story, distinct from the narrated events, and that story is the *ongoing life history of the teller*. In some ways it is the founding adventure, the one story that has the most claim to moral jurisdiction. An event may happen to us, but we will never tell it if we do not have the experience to understand it or do not have the experience to add it to our understanding. But even if an event becomes part of our experience, we will not tell it as long as we do not need it to maintain the experience or need it to continue our growth as a person (e.g., comp tales that contributors no longer tell, such as Tale 77). The anecdotes we tell help constitute the story we construct of our lives. And if we retell an anecdote differently, as we do periodically, it is because we are reshaping

our autobiography or life history, as we do periodically (Donald P. McAdams, 1996; Mark Freeman, 1996). The stories we choose to tell, the way we tell them, the position we form for ourselves in telling them, and the particular experience we project as an answer to the needs of our listeners all fit the image we are creating of ourselves traveling through life. With every story we tell, we celebrate our "autonomous, unique self" (Johnstone, 1996, p. 56) and show that self to others as coherent and creditable.

Every time the vet tells the tale of the kitten, he is successfully continuing to write the story of himself as a competent, cool-headed professional with a sympathetic and humorous outlook. It's important to recognize that this story is ethical at root. Merely by telling the story, the vet is arguing that this is the way he should be and by extension the way others should be. A number of students of narrative have asserted that morality inheres in the very form of the narrative. Brook (1984) argues that in establishing the expectations of resolution from the start the narrative assumes the shape of an ethical act. Alasdair MacIntyre goes further and provides an argument connecting ethics with narrative, life-history, and practices such as veterinary science (and the teaching of writing, I presume). He argues that virtues, such as truthfulness or courage, exist only as acts that sustain human practices *and* sustain the lives of people who make up the practice. An act is virtuous only if it helps build the actor's sense of a self "whose unity resides in the unity of a narrative which links birth to life to death" (1981, p. 205). It does not follow, of course, from the claim that human virtue is essentially narrative, life-constructive, and practice-maintaining that any story told by a professional will foster virtue. But to the extent that people feel in control of their lives, especially their professional lives, then the stories they tell, which help shape those lives, will assume a moral cast.

(7) "Moral" cannot be the last words to a fable, however. "The end" cannot be the last words to a story, not one that works. Comp tales live happily ever after *as long as they are retold*. They will be retold by the tellers as long as the telling remains a vital part of their life history. Charlotte Linde remembered a friend's old story about being so disgusted by a senseless task of mice dissection that he changed his goal from scientific experimenter to technical editor, but she discovered that he had forgotten the story since he had switched back to a career in science (geology) and the story no longer worked, no longer fit his self-history (1993, p. 32). A story, it seems, may live on even after the original teller has forgotten it if it continues to work for other tellers and other listeners. I told the vet's tale the next day to a composition class and for the

rest of the semester we referred to disconnected ideas in a draft as "tennis shoes in the dryer." Especially within institutions—clubs, support groups, professions, corporations, families, whole societies—stories live on, sometimes undergoing metamorphoses as strange as Ovid ever put into hexameters (see Ralph L. Rosnow and Gary A. Fine, 1976; Charlotte Linde, 1997; Elizabeth Stone, 1989; Daniel Bertaux and Paul Thompson, 1993; Martin, et al., 1983; Harrison M. Trice, 1993, pp. 82–89; Alan L. Wilkins, 1983). The narratives and narrative performances within institutions make fine reading.

As will the comp tales in this book, if they are read right. I am arguing that just as Min-Zhan and I asked contributors "to write the stories in the same spirit that you actually tell them," a reader will do well to read their stories in that same spirit, the spirit of oral performance. To do so will reject them as the lightweights of the professional discourse genres and little more than conversation filler. Obviously, contributors did not give us their stories in the raw, oral form. They re-composed their tales into written form, some narrators more so than others, but usually for the first time and usually for a new audience, the implied readers of this book. But if these tales are not the vernacular, they are from the vernacular. As such, they render a particularized and immediate situation, in both the story and the telling. As such, they preserve the true nature of the oral story as a vibrant node of tangent tales, as an answer to some calling lack, as the voice of authentic experience, as something told that asks to be retold. And as such they open their own personal door to the landscape of teaching college composition. Perhaps to a greater degree than other discourse modes, they capture the profession alive, with a sense of breathing the air and treading the ground, a sense of what it means to be active in an active field. Sensitive as a seismograph, offhand and throw-away only on the surface, these tales reenact the dynamics of a changing profession, and will continue to do so as long as the tellers keep changing and keep changing the tales.

3 Venture

It follows that the best way to read a comp tale is to tell one of your own. Alas, easier written than done. I would be remiss if I ended this praise of professional storytelling without noting how risky that venture is.

Paul Ricoeur argues that as a distinct mode of discourse the narrative expresses our felt sense of time. It puts into words the experience of our selves put into a body and into a world moving inexorably through time (1984). The work of writing teachers, it occurs to me, is unusually involved with time. We get to class on time, give timed writings, ask students to give quality time to the course, beg them to revise time and time again, give them more time to turn in their work, imagine them constrained by the time of their life, hope to teach the course better this time around. The bulk of our writing on the job is narrative: syllabi, course descriptions, grading standards ("To earn an A, you must . . ."), letters of reference ("I have known this applicant for two years . . ."), essay assignments ("Read the following three essays and . . ."), tests ("You have thirty minutes to . . ."). The narratologists tell us that all people live "storied lives" (Richard L. Ochberg, 1994) but comp teachers earn an especially storied living. You might say that our job is one comp tale after another.

But let's not get taken in by our own fictions. As Henry James notes, an anecdote is "something that oddly happens to someone," and the truth is that most of our professional life is the opposite of odd. Our hours may be storied but it is only the odd hour that turns up a story. Twenty years ago, when specialists from every field were arguing that all was narrative, including logic, communication, scientific knowledge, and memory itself, Barbara Hernstein Smith raised a hand of caution. "Our knowledge of past events is usually not narrative in structure or given in story-like sequences; on the contrary, that knowledge is most likely to be in the form of general and imprecise recollection, scattered and possibly inconsistent pieces of verbal information, and various visual, auditory, and kinesthetic images" (1981, p. 225). Stories have to be lived before they are told, and good stories don't happen to everyone. I am not above suspecting that good storytellers sometimes arrange their lives so that they can tell about it later.

Indeed, we should not forget that in any institution willing and expert raconteurs are not a dime a dozen. It takes a stout heart to venture a tale, a story of personal and professional experience, while listeners await, all ears, or in the case of *Comp Tales*, all eyes. You do it with your fingers crossed, banking on intuition that it is going to be right for the occasion, that it will meet some need of your listeners, that it is faithful to your lived experience of the field, that it affirms and develops your historical and moral being. What riskier test for both folk hero and teller of the tale than that moment when they ask to be taken in?

After surviving leukemia and the operation, Gracie has turned into the kind of cat to whom the word curious does not much apply. She has some weird ways, such as lying on her back in the middle of the living room, surveying the life around her, legs sticking up like shipped oars— but that hardly makes a tale. My efforts to teach her to ride on the back of Luna (the dog) have not achieved success. As Gracie, most of us spend a lot of time waiting for a story to happen. In the meantime, we can be instructed and entertained by the lucky and brave ones in this volume who have tales to tell and who have told them.

Tracking Comp Tales

Min-Zhan Lu

The premise of this book project is that who we are, how we act, and what we think inform and are informed by the stories we tell. At the same time, the stories we tell (and do not tell) shape and are shaped by the material conditions of our work. Therefore, the ambition of the book is that individual readers will use it not merely as a source of the stories college writing teachers tell and retell and our storytelling practices. Rather, readers might use it to explore alternative ways of telling, listening to, reading, and writing stories about our work. With this in mind, in the following two sections, I pose some ways for using *Comp Tales* to continue parts of the project it has begun: to collect, compose, and disseminate comp tales aimed at critically intervening in the conditions of our work and our storytelling practices. My intention here is not to exhaust how individual readers might use this book but to start a critical dialogue across diverse groups of college writing teachers about how to reshape our selves and our work in the process of tracking comp tales.

PART ONE—COMP TALES: COMPOSITION AND DISPOSITIONS

Comp Tales aspires to be a collection of the stories about work that college writing teachers tell and retell. It is a book resulting from a series of negotiations between the editors, publishers, reviewers, and (potential and actual) contributors. Therefore, *Comp Tales* is not a mirror reflection but, at best, a partial representation of the dynamic struggle for representation within the profession of teaching writing. How does each tale represent this struggle over who we are, what we do, and how we might best change as a collective? How does each tale represent the way we use storytelling to participate in this struggle? These questions need to be considered in relation not only to the tales which have made it into the book but also to the ones which have been left out. One possible route is to consider the dispositions—the powers to dispose of (and bestow) and the prevailing tastes (and distaste)—affecting the composition of this book. To initiate this line of inquiry, I posit four possible points of departure.

Signatures

As Pierre Bourdieu puts it in *Language and Symbolic Power*, "in the struggle to impose the legitimate vision, agents possess power in proportion to their symbolic capital, i.e. in proportion to the recognition they receive from a group" (106). *Comp Tales* is in part made possible—enabled and disabled—by the recognition the editors receive, i.e. their "signatures" (Bourdieu, *The Field of Cultural Production* 75).

In collecting stories about work that college writing teachers tell and retell, *Comp Tales* inevitably legitimizes certain representations of who we are, what we do, how we might change. However, the question of what gets consecrated by the book is significantly mediated by the reputations of those editing the book. Publishers, reviewers, readers, and potential contributors might "take the book seriously" (or not) depending on their sense of the stature of the editors or what is known of their other works. For instance, in answer to Longman's question on the strength and limitation of the book project, one reviewer of the book's prospectus speculates: the different styles of the editors—"funny and sad"—might make the book "show the human side of teaching." Another reviewer asks: "What experience does she have as a trainer of GTAs? That is not the work she is known for." Each editor's reputation for having particular propensities might elicit different decisions from publishers, reviewers, and potential contibutors or readers on whether to endorse, contribute to, buy, read, or teach *Comp Tales*. Seeing the two editors as "funny and sad" could predispose potential contributors to accent the "human side of teaching" (and thus gloss over the "institutional side"?). Knowing one editor's lack of experience in GTA training, other potential contributors might anticipate a lack of appreciation in that editor for GTA training stories and submit stories concerning only those areas of work "she is known for." These decisions affect not only how one writes down the stories but also how one selects which story to write down and submit.

Thus, the often multi-layered, contradictory "reputation" of each editor is one place for examining what stories are present or absent in *Comp Tales*. If a signature ensures the power to consecrate—legitimize particular stories about our work and our storytelling practices—then it can also predispose of other stories and storytelling practices which are vital to the actual struggle for representation within the field. Readers might use their sense of the dominant themes, plots, and styles surfacing from the tales printed in this volume as a map for tracking stories left out by this collection: for recollecting and collecting stories which could and would have been better represented in a similar book project bearing a different set of signatures.

Prospectus and Calls

During different stages of this book project, Rich and I put out several versions of our Call for Submissions. When needing more copies of each version, I did the photocopying myself by making a special trip to school on weekends. I did not want the work-study students to see the one-page limit we had imposed for the submissions. I'm known on my campus for strictly refusing to assign page limits in writing assignments. "It should be as long as it takes you to say what you are trying to say, in the way you are finding it best to be said," I'd maintain. But I don't think it was the fear of revealing to my students the contradiction between my practice as a teacher and as an editor which kept me from using the office staff for duplicating the Calls. Rather, it was my continuing inability to come up with a quick answer to how and why Rich and I agreed on the one-page limit.

In retrospect, it seems that, when drafting and revising the book prospectus and the various calls for submission, much of my correspondence with Rich concerned reaching an agreement on the length of individual tales. Our deliberations over the appropriate length helped me to recognize a conflict between my view of whose voices among college writing teachers I am most interested in "collecting" and my view of what is involved in the act of writing down a story one tells and retells. Therefore, a seemingly simple and straightforward editorial guideline like the one-page limit is a good place for examining some of the silences potentially resulting from our vision for the project.

Any story about work inevitably functions as both a portrait of who we are and a proxy: speaking as, to, about, on behalf of certain constituencies among college writing teachers (see Spivak). Any limit set on the length of the submissions would set constraints on not only what kinds of comp tales would appear but also whose interests or perspectives would be voiced. Furthermore, the act of writing down the stories we "tell and pass on" involves negotiating the differences between oral and written forms of representation. Restrictions on the length of the submissions would thus also affect how potential contributors went about addressing these differences when "transcribing" the stories they tell and retell.

As editors, Rich and I wanted to collect "what is out there": the stories which are actually being told and retold by people in the field. We hoped to bring to print these stories in "the same way and in the same spirit" people actually tell them. In short, we were interested in stories passed along in snippets of time. Along with our interest in the actual was our concern to be inclusive. We knew from the start that we wanted to collect a whole range of stories from *all* writing teachers, including those traditionally camped under such rubrics as experienced teachers vs. novice GTAs; senior vs. beginning professors; WPAs vs. composition theorists; tenure-tracked or adjuncts; two-year and four-year college teachers; minority, gay and lesbian, ESL teachers vs. "teachers," meaning, by implication, the "regular" and "normal" teachers. While we knew that all in composition tell and retell stories, we also presumed that not all stories and all forms of storytelling practices within composition have received equal representation in print. For instance, because of the unequal distribution of work among college writing teachers, many among us may simply not have had access to the time and energy required to produce the kinds of texts concerning storytelling currently populating many composition journals and books. I also suspect that there are a significant number of others who have deemed it important to put their energy and time into producing different kinds of work: program building, service, teaching, or different types of research. We hoped that a different length might lure more contributions from writing teachers whose voices are currently under-represented in composition journals and books. And then, there is the simple logic—the shorter the individual submissions, the more submissions we would be able to squeeze into the volume. The one-page limit seemed an appropriate means to achieve our goals of both capturing the "actual" stories told and being inclusive.

Personally, the concern to bring in the voices of the under-represented writing teachers stems from my interest in autoethnography. I wanted the book to offer a sense of what is actually out there. But by "out there," I envisioned a collection of stories which captured not only the subjugated nature of the teaching of writing but also the unequal distribution of power across different college writing teachers. I wanted the book to serve as a place where those put out there—marginalized by the official representations of the work of college writing teachers— could speak back, pose their own sense of themselves and their work against the texts by those better "established" (i.e., more published) members. I hoped the one-page limit might bring counter-stories to the ones legitimized by those of us with the time, energy, and interest to produce the kind of "scholarship" currently in print.

Yet, the one-page limit is also highly problematic. Among other things, it puts significant constraints on how potential contributors would go about answering our call for the actual. While the language surrounding the page limit made clear that we were after "tales that you actually tell and pass on," it is far less clear from our call what that "actual" might entail. The need to write down an oral tale inevitably raises the question of what the story of actual storytelling is. Anyone who has told stories in face to face settings, the kind we were after, knows that storytelling is highly dialogical. It is contextually marked, collaboratively mediated, and provisional. As Walter Benjamin puts it in "The Storyteller," the storyteller is a person who has "counsel," but that counsel is less "an answer to a question" than "a proposal concerning the continuation of a story which is just unfolding" (86). The narrative event—the occasion for storytelling, the physical setting, the audience, the perceived need of the audience from the point of view of the storyteller, the listener's view of and relation to the storyteller, the call and response between the teller and listener, etc.—is a constitutive part of the counsel or the life of the story, of how the story will unfold both during the exchange and afterwards. If the telling of the same narrated event—the incident being described—often varies from narrative event to narrative event, then to write down the story we tell and retell in the spirit and manner we actually tell it would necessarily involve the challenge to capture the variety of narrative events and the provisional nature of each telling of the same narrated event in the life of a story.

To acknowledge the provisional, collaborative, and contextual nature of storytelling, we built into the Calls a two-part structure for each submission. We asked for a story as one "actually" tells it and an explanation of the customary context in which one tells it, a reflection on "when, where, to whom, and why" one likes to tell it. We hoped the call for an explanation might generate attention to the multiple narrative events and their function in shaping the story one fashions and refashions out of a single narrated event. We also hoped to use the two-part structure to contest common conceptions of lore which, in emphasizing its word-of-mouth transmission and its attention to "knowing-in-action," tend to overlook the "critical element" in how people actually generate and use stories (Phelps 872). As many in composition have argued, lore has become the operative term for the underside of a string of generic and institutional binaries: practitioner/researcher, description/reflection, direct message/complex analysis, straight talk/theory talk (Bartholomae, Phelps, Horner). We hoped that calling for an explanation of when, where, to whom, and why one likes to tell particular stories would help us explore the critical, theoretical work performed by storytelling.

At the same time, the two-part structure leaves open how individual contributors would go about defining the story or the context and go about proportioning the narration and the explanation within the space of a page. For instance, should context refer to the more objective aspects of "what is" or to the more subjective aspect of "how those in it perceive it"? Or to both? Since the teller's definition of the context would inevitably affect one's choice of self representation and the content and style of the story, then one's choice of explanation of the context would also affect one's choice of description of the story (*Stories Lives Tell* 196–197; Bauman 101, 105, 112).

When seeking a submission from someone who has regularly swapped stories with me at the 4Cs, I reminded him that we were merely looking for stories no more than a page in length. "Shouldn't take more than a couple of hours from your busy schedule," I assured him. He replied that, in fact, he'd already sat down many times and tried, but after fiddling for hours at a stretch, ended up not liking anything he'd written. This experience of one potential contributor suggests that composing a no-more-than-one-page tale took much more time and energy than I was claiming. I think part of that comes from the need to define the story and context of storytelling. The writer also has to decide how many versions and which of the multiple versions in the lifetime of a story and how much explanation of the complex contexts of storytelling one can possibly squeeze into the space of a page. It is one thing for Rich and me, in our desire to get people hooked on to the project, to state in an earlier Call: "Five minutes at the computer, then hit the send button, that's all the time it will take." It is entirely another to presume that the act of transcribing a story which takes no more than five minutes to tell is natural, spontaneous, and therefore easy and non-labor intensive. Rather, the effort to textually capture as much of the provisional and collaborative nature of oral forms of storytelling is extremely labor-intensive and intellectually as well as stylistically challenging. The need to capture the dynamic and complex life of a story within the space of a page is even more constraining, delimiting not only what story can be written down and how it is written out but also who will have the time, energy, and interest to meet the challenge.

Not liking any of the written versions he had produced, none of the stories regularly told by my 4Cs friend made it into *Comp Tales*. Reading *Comp Tales* with the editorial guidelines in mind can help us appreciate the complex labor put into the seemingly brief and chatty scripts gathered here. It can also incite us to listen more attentively for other stories which seem to defy the confines of this project, and to try out other ways of writing down these stories.

Composing a Comp Tale

To explore from a different angle how and why many stories we regularly tell and hear might be absent from this collection, let me share with you my own failed attempt to compose a tale for this book.

"First Publication"

One version of the events surrounding my first publication goes something like this: in 1985, I was taking a graduate seminar from David Bartholomae. One of our assignments for the seminar was to use our own experience as a writing student to theorize about the nature of writing education. David encouraged me and several other graduate students in the seminar to revise and submit our papers for publication. I sent mine to *College English*. I sometimes tell this version to express my admiration for Bartholomae as a teacher and a mentor. I also tell it to emphasize the importance of assignment writing, the ways in which a well designed assignment can take student writers places—both institutionally and intellectually—with lasting effects.

Version Two of the story of my first publication focuses on my initial difficulty getting a positive review for my essay. One reviewer, claiming it to be "an essay about China," rejected it because the "topic is too narrow." A second reviewer found "the narrative moving" but "too personal," and therefore inappropriate for a scholarly journal. I've used this version to make two points. First, the reception of a text is mediated by the reader's horizon of expectations, which is in turn shaped by the discipline's legitimized content and style. Second, during the past decade, composition has changed its attitude towards the place of personal narrative in scholarship. On yet other occasions, I have raised the possibility that explicit textual references to my foreign, graduate student status might have led the reviewers to dismiss out of hand the article's relevance to the teaching of English in the U.S.

Version Three extends the second version by detailing the careful readings the same essay received from a second round of reviews. Both reviewers recognized the theories of language and writing pedagogy embedded in the narrative of my educational experience. In fact, one reviewer began his review with: "This is not about China. It is about the nature of language and the teaching of English in the U.S." I tell this version to colleagues and graduate students depressed by rejections which seem to have misread their work, to inspire them to keep on sending their work out. Lately, I have been telling it when I and others complain about the amount of time we spend reviewing for various journals—my way of reminding myself to take seriously those "weird," "hard to place" submissions.

Version Four tells of the two revisions I did after the second round of reviews. I was first asked to make explicit the theoretical frames embedded in the narratives of my earlier experience as a student of writing. After this revision was accepted, I was asked to take out some of the theoretical discussion for the final print. Sometimes I tell the story to suggest the possibility that I had to first demonstrate my command over theory to prove that I, a foreign graduate student, was indeed aware of what the reviewers perceived me to be doing. At other times, I tell it to emphasize the positive outcome of this seemingly unreasonable and wasteful exercise. Having to first put the theory in and then take it out made me grasp more firmly why I was invested in the project and helped me formulate ideas for another essay.

Version Five fills in the gap between Versions Two and Three by explaining how the essay got a second round of reviews from *College English* after it had been rejected. New Orleans. My first 4Cs. Three people in the audience, and one of them, a leading figure in the field, liked my paper. "You should try to get it published," she urged. When I told her about the rejections I had just received for a longer version of my talk, she promised to persuade the editor to send the manuscript out a second time to a different set of reviewers. I tell this version to newcomers to substantiate the belief that 4Cs is a good place for newcomers to expose their work, and that composition is an open field, with lots of supportive old-timers.

Version Six contains details I am comfortable sharing only with a very select audience. This version mentions by actual name several others (in addition to the leading figure who had attended my 4Cs panel) who had also pressed the editor of *College English* to reconsider my submission. They had heard about my essay through my mentor. I told this version to very few people during the first years of my career for fear that others might think less of my work if I acknowledged the break I got through access to institutional networks. I tell it more and more through the years, usually to remind those of us who have "made it" to not forget the advances we gained by having the right people speak for us at the right moments in our careers, and therefore to have a less inflated view of the quality of our work. I am more reluctant to share this version because it implicates others in ways they might not welcome. But most of all, I fear it might further the already debilitating myth that one just can never make it in the academy without the right network, leading so many promising newcomers to waste so much energy and time networking that they could have spent in other areas of work.

I believe there is another version embedded in the events surrounding my first publication which, if told right, could be used to make several other points I would like to spread. Point One: It is important to have the practical know-how to make an impression on others in a position to advance your work, but that alone cannot make or break a career if one does not have other work to sustain it. Point Two: Those in positions of power to network for a newcomer need to take care that, in helping to get exposure for that person's work, they do not lead the person to perceive the help as a personal favor. It is important to spell out for that person what particularly about her work interests the helpers and why. (I was fortunate to have that pointed out to me by all those who spoke on behalf of my article.) Point Three: The support one gets for one's work can sometimes come from those who have "misread" as well as those who have "understood" exactly what one is trying to do. To tell this version right is to make all three points together. I still have not quite got this version down.

It took me three sittings to compose "First Publication." And, like my friend, I did not end up liking what I'd come up with. I know that my friend would have felt the same about this comp tale, since he'd heard me tell almost all six versions on various occasions. I think of my friend as an integral part of the life of this story. But I wasn't quite able to bring him back into the text.

Not one single version of the story in this script was told in the manner I regularly tell it. At one point in composing it, I tried to capture at least one version of it, as it was told on one specific occasion with this friend in the audience. I tried to depict the call and response I've learned to expect from him and the physical surroundings in which we usually gather during the 4Cs. Then I scrapped that version because it was taking up too much space. Instead, I opted for a fuller explanation of the range of people to whom I tell the story and my motives. The end result makes me wonder, as many contributors expressed in their submissions, if this tale was at all "what the [editors] had in mind." After all, it turned out to be (how?) many pages longer than the one in the samples attached to the Calls. I decided not to submit this tale for *Comp Tales*.

However, this failed attempt has other outcomes. It has made me much more aware of the complex labor individual contributors have put into composing their tales. I gain a firmer grasp of the actual amount of time and energy individual contributors may have invested in their compositions. And I become sensitive to the thematically and stylistically innovative choices individual contributors have made to capture the complex and dynamic life of a story. I am more attentive to the vivacity and efficiency achieved by some contributors when detailing the people and actions involved in the narrated events. And I am more attentive to the challenges facing other contributors in their attempts to capture the flux in the life of the story: the changes in the life of the narrator, in his or her view of a particular event, and in how she or he tells that event. The ability to capture this constant flux is all the more impressive since some of the stories span more than ten, twenty years. Others move back and forth from four-year universities to community colleges and from white to black colleges. Other stories evolve as the narrator talks to students and colleagues in all sorts of settings, including, in one case, literally bumping into fellow adjuncts who are also compelled to keep office in their cars. Yet other stories take on new turns as the narrator anticipates a change in the audience's attitudes towards racial or sexual differences. Finally, composing "First Publication" has also given me a more concrete sense of the kinds of constraints the Calls pose on how different writing teachers might go about keeping track of the stories we tell and retell.

For these reasons alone, I urge readers to compose a tale or two as if you were going to submit them to a book project similar to *Comp Tales*. Hopefully, as a result of this exercise, your assessment of how and why which of your stories would (or would not) "work" within the confines of the book can open up new directions for appreciating the comp tales appearing in this book and for tracking the stories left out there.

Submitting to *Comp Tales*

Besides my dissatisfaction over how I handled the tension between the narrated and narrative events, I had several other reasons for hesitating to submit "First Publication" to *Comp Tales*. I share four of them to mark another possible point of departure for examining what might be missing from this collection.

Reason One: "It Is Too Familiar!"

My reasons for telling the story of my first publication are too common. Like many others I know, I tell it to support or dispute a point others have made about our work, about how the field works, and about what has worked or not worked for certain members. I tell it to address a need—fear or desire—I perceive in others and myself, to reveal or hide an aspect of my work, and to pay tribute to or criticize the actions of the better established. Both in terms of content and style, I have merely replicated the familiar genre passed around by myself and others in writing as well as through word of mouth. This tale would make me come across as someone working comfortably within, rather than uneasily against, existing conventions. Definitely not an image I am interested in projecting.

Reason Two: "This is Hardly Worth the Time and Energy!"

This has taken far more time to compose than I or anyone else would have expected. I might as well save it for another occasion, working it into an article or something so that at least I'd get the return it deserved. Even if the tale is accepted by the editors, I still won't be able to list it as a publication. The word "tales" in the title of the book and the average length of the tale would automatically disqualify it as such in the eyes of any tenure or promotion committee.

In fact, I'm not even sure I would have bothered to compose a tale for this type of a book project, especially if it were edited by someone whose name is not "respected" in my circle.

Reason Three: "Mine Is Not the Voice Needing to be Heard!"

Judging from the accounts of stories and storytelling practices already in print, the voices of people like myself have already been overprivileged. To get a fuller sense of "how composition shapes and is shaped by narratives," we need to give room to those whose work has so far been excluded from such a database. I need to hear tales by others working in different circumstances and with different goals.

Reason Four: "I Can Only Submit One Tale!"
I am much more likely to submit a tale such as "How Do You Inline Something?" (see Tale 39) than "First Publication." Tale 39 is shorter. It touches on my sense of the best of writing and teaching: a commitment to listen to one another and to our students, to problematize established conventions of reading, writing, and learning, to examine the politics of literacy practices, to learn from and theorize daily experiences in extra-professional settings.

In comparison, "First Publication" touches on several aspects of the worst of the field, including the need to network and the power of both sloppy and careful reviewers. Because the story acknowledges the often unpleasant and mindless work we do to get published, I worry that, when repeated in the wrong context, it would only create more anxiety, skepticism, and opportunism among colleagues already overwhelmed by the official dictum of "publish or perish."

Furthermore, there is also the issue of self-representation. Tale 39 presents me as just another person in the trenches. I prefer this image because it eases my sense of guilt over my privileged institutional location. It could counteract the impression I fear many in the profession already have of me as someone only interested in research and high theory. It puts out a more "realistic" picture of my work. It impresses on others that undergraduate teaching is important to me. I have chosen to work in an institution with a three/three, exclusively undergraduate teaching load, and I teach what I preach.

Last but not least, Tale 39 also gives me a forum to spread the message I am most invested in at this point in my career. That is, it is best to examine the politics of reading and writing not only in terms of content—what we say and do not say—but also in terms of style—the way we do things, ranging from how we use words and construct sentences to how we mark up a text. I believe composition needs more stories along this line. Besides, there is a "teaching tip" embedded in the story. It is more practical and therefore probably a more effective way of getting my point across.

All my reasons against submitting "First Publication" are symptomatic of my immediate location in the field, and therefore collective as well as personal. Listing the reasons has helped me get in touch with the networks of power, concerns, and desires I am likely to bring into my efforts to write and read a comp tale. This has in turn taught me to appreciate how others have addressed similar institutional forces in their storytelling practices. For instance, the sheer fact that over two hundred writing teachers have chosen to contribute to the book indicates that institutional rules are made and broken by agents in the field. That is, despite the official dictum of "publish or perish" and existing institutional guidelines for what qualifies as a publication, many in the field are willing to devote their hard-earned time and energy to composing a tale for submission. Several contributors risk revealing aspects of self and work which defy dominant notions of what college writing teachers and the teaching of writing should be like. Together, they pose diverse, innovative ways of addressing the challenges of writing down an oral tale against the grain of dominant networks of power, concerns, and desires.

I hope this account persuades you, as readers of *Comp Tales*, to compose a few tales you might have submitted to a similar book project and to make your own list of reasons for submitting (or not submitting) each tale. As a result of this exercise, individual readers might become more alert to the different networks of power, concerns, and desires motivating the reader and motivating diverse contributors to read, write, tell and listen to competing stories of our work. Such attention might in turn incite individual readers to recollect and compose stories which speak to power relations, concerns, and desires which remain under-represented or absent in the book.

In positing a set of dispositions potentially shaping the composition of *Comp Tales,* I hope to initiate a conversation on how individual readers might use what is included in the book to examine what has been excluded by it. To turn *Comp Tales* into the beginning rather than the end of a collective search for alternative ways of tracking stories, we need also to explore ways of reading and rewriting the stories out there, those needing to be told by diverse college writing teachers as well as those currently marginalized by various official forms of symbolic circulation (including books such as this one).

Part Two—Comp Tales: Interpretations and Revisions

Keeping track of all the stories within the community gives us all a certain distance, a useful perspective, that brings incidents down to a level we can deal with. If others have done it before, it cannot be so terrible. If others have endured, so can we.

The stories are always bringing us together, keeping this

whole together, keeping this family together, keeping this clan together.

—Leslie Marmon Silko, "Language and Literature
from a Pueblo Indian Perspective" 86

The work space and the space of creation is where she confronts and leaves off at the same time a world of named nooks and corners, of street signs and traffic regulations, of beaten paths and multiple masks, of constant intermeshing with other bodies'— that are also her own—needs, assumptions, prejudices and limits.

—Trinh T. Minh-ha, "Cotton and Iron" 335.

In this section, I pose some ways of reading and rewriting the comp tales collected in this book in the interest of creating a work space against the grain of established accounts of who we are, what we do, and how we should live. In "Language and Literature from a Pueblo Indian Perspective," Silko argues that keeping track of all the stories within the community can bring us together. It can give us a useful perspective, one which brings incidents down to a level we can deal with. Silko is referring to the storytelling tradition of a subjugated social group—the Pueblo Indians—and to family stories which keep the clan together because they counter in both content and form the official Dick and Jane stories taught at the Bureau of Indian Affairs school.

Storytelling within the community taught the young Silko to distrust "words which are detached from the occasion and the audience," to re-attach recitations such as "Robins are flying south for the winter" to where the textbook companies are situated in the physical and social geography of America, and to locate a Pueblo perspective for coping with her "worry" that the robins in Laguna had not left in the winter (83, 91-92). In short, Pueblo storytelling helps members of the community find a position which is convincingly experienced and from which the community can begin to be known against the grain of the dominant. These stories and storytelling practices remind students like Silko that there is indeed a very vital area of social experience which is lived but does not get incorporated, is neither spoken to nor even recognized by official—e.g., Bureau of Indian Affairs—accounts. Pueblo storytelling legitimizes social experiences which get neglected, ignored, and at times repressed by the conqueror's language and literature (see Williams, *Marxism and Literature* 130-131; *English Novel* 192).

I take Silko to be invoking the Pueblo Indian storytelling tradition because, as Trinh T. Minh-ha puts it, it is the kind of work space where one can confront and leave off at the same time a world of named nooks, beaten paths, assumptions, prejudices and limits. Silko's analysis of the Pueblo Indian storytelling tradition poses interesting questions for keeping track of all the stories within the community of writing teachers. It reminds college English teachers of our need to confront the fact that ours is a community of "the dominated among the dominant" (Bourdieu, *Language* 245). When trying to keep track of and pass on the stories we tell about our work, we need to grasp our potential for working in complicity with as well as against the official, established, master narratives. Collectively, this potential for complicity as well as resistance needs to be explored on at least two levels: our location as cultural producers within the larger social, economic scene and our location as teachers and writing teachers within the academy and English studies. Individually, this dual potential is further complicated by the unequal power relations across college writing teachers and one's specific but ever changing location within such a collective at a given time and place.

It is essential for those of us interested in contesting our "subaltern" experience to confront the fact that we are working for a "social order opposed to the one that is supporting [our] own undertaking" (Chow 12). Instead of wallowing in "self-subalternization," the question to address is how to struggle against a hegemony which already includes us (13, 16). Rey Chow suggests that we use the Chinese term for "crisis" (weiji), which is made up of two characters—"danger" and "opportunity"—to frame our efforts to deal *with* and deal *in* dominant cultures (25). That is, we might practice the understanding "that opportunity is molded in danger and danger is a form of opportunity." To read *Comp Tales* with such a frame of mind would mean that, instead of merely searching for stories which preserve a sense of identity between self and others and a sense of continuity between the past, present, and future, we might also search for stories and search for ways of reading, retelling, and rewriting these tales which create a sense of "crisis." We would want to keep more careful track of stories which move us beside ourselves: stories which make us "feel beside ourselves" with worry, anger, empathy and thus place us "beside, alongside, among, in common with, with the help and favor of, in the midst of" the most subordinate groups within and outside the community (Jarratt 57, 71).

Reading *Comp Tales* for "crisis" would involve the labor of dis-membering and then re-membering cultures, lives, and selves one calls one's own. We would use the tales to confront our power-fullness as well as our power-lessness. *Nosotras*, not *Nos/otras* (Anzaldúa and Lunsford 7–8). Instead of dichotomizing dominance and subordination, us and them, we

learn to think in terms of the us in them and the them in us. To bring college writing teachers together, we must search for positions of reading
and writing which are convincingly experienced and from which one can
try to know oneself and others, ourselves with others, under very specific and active and continuing pressures (Williams, *English Novel* 187).

For Silko, finding such a position involves paying attention to differences: differences in one's own and others' geographical locations (winter in Laguna and in Boston), in the social experiences across Indian
tribes (between Pueblos, who were not relocated, and other Native
American groups who were torn away from their ancestral lands), in the
educational experiences across diverse subaltern groups (between
African or Caribbean people and Pueblo Indians in terms of their different exposure to the Western literary canon at colonial schools). Silko
learns to know her community by listening to the ways in which different stories and storytelling forms suppress or speak to these differences
and to the very specific, active, and continuing pressures of a Pueblo
Indian woman writing in English. If we are to use *Comp Tales* as a means
of knowing the community of college writing teachers and of knowing it
in ways which do not preserve but bring to crisis both ourselves and our
work, then we must find a position where the different but specific pressures experienced by each of us are grasped as a danger which molds
opportunity for new possibilities.

To do so is to refuse to treat *Comp Tales* as a dictionary, as a set of universal codes of "what works in composition" and of "how composition
works" or as codes capable of functioning outside the constraints and without the assistance of specific situations (Bourdieu, *Language* 48). Instead
of recitation or replication, we need revision: ways of reading, retelling, and
rewriting these tales within the constraints and with the assistance of the
very specific but different situations facing each of us. This would mean
reading each tale not to ask what this story "means" but what particular
relations of power render the story meaningful and what needs to be done
to change unequal relations. In the interest of crisis, I suggest three trajectories for reading *Comp Tales*. Hopefully, these trajectories would serve
as beaten paths for individual readers to "confront and take off from."

Fashioning a Nonce Taxonomy
What kind of a person should (or should not) be found among college writing teachers? This is a question explicitly or implicitly addressed by all the
tales in this collection. We might read each tale to analyze the specific taxonomy of college writing teachers it poses. We could then examine how
such a taxonomy addresses the differences among college writing teachers.

In the Introduction to *Epistemology of the Closet*, Eve Sedgwick argues that while categories such as gender, race, class, nationality, and sexual orientation are "indispensable," the strange relations of our work, play, and activism prove that even people who share all or most of our own positionings along these axes may still be different enough from us, and from each other, to seem like all but different species (247). To "survive," everyone needs and probably has a "nonce taxonomy" for mapping out the possibilities, dangers, and stimulations of their human social landscape. By "nonce taxonomy," I take Sedgwick to have in mind those stories which are often dismissed by orthodox, official taxonomies as relevant only "for the nonce" and "at the nonce": relevant for *the* expressed purpose and at *the* very moment rather than for *all* purposes and at *all* times. To put it in another way, "nonce taxonomy" is often rendered nonce by orthodoxy exactly because it acknowledges differences and contingencies within a particular social site and thus brings to crisis official accounts of what kind of persons should or should not be found at that site.

Historically, the art of gossip is devalued in part because it is a central form of nonce-taxonomic work and because people with the experience of oppression or subordination have the "most *need* to know it" (Sedgwick 247). Gossip enables the creation of categories for making sense of those purposes and those moments in the lives of the powerless which are convincingly experienced but systematically repressed by the official taxonomy. It is a tool of subordinate groups for surviving and even thriving within the dominant's power to story their lives. Given the subjugated location of college writing teachers within the academy and the academy's official dictum of "publish or perish" policy, it shouldn't be surprising that the kinds of word-of-mouth stories gathered in this book have long been perceived by both those who tell them and those who dismiss them as "academic gossip." However, when exploring the potential of "academic gossip" for nonce-taxonomical work, we need to also keep in mind that it is indeed "academic"—the gossip of intellectuals or of the dominated within the dominant. That is, we need to examine each piece of academic gossip in terms of its ability to speak not only to those purposes and moments suppressed by those more power full than writing teachers but also to those purposes and moments often inadvertently suppressed by the more power full among writing teachers.

What taxonomy of college writing teachers is posed by each comp tale? What particular relations and positions within and what provisional hypotheses about college English teaching does such a taxonomy legitimize or prohibit? These questions are useful even for those tales seemingly focusing on our students rather than ourselves. For instance, many in the field have observed the fact that a significant number of stories told by writing teachers tend to portray students who "misinterpret" academic codes of commenting—"tense," "awk.," or "jargon"—or students who make "weird" demands of teachers and writing center tutors as confused "foreigners." Such stories often depict these students as having physical appearances and dress codes used by TV commercials to represent "athletes," "rednecks," or "housewives." These stories pose an orthodox taxonomy which renders as nonce those persons, relations, purposes, experiences, and concerns which do not directly conform to institutional definitions of what type of person belongs in college writing classrooms.

To actively sustain a nonce taxonomy, we must not only refuse to recite these stories but also actively recollect and collect stories which present these "foreigners" as active and contributing members of the community. For instance, Tale 1 (p. 5) features a "large man, with scarred face and imposing tattoos" who proves to be a competent, conscientious, and resourceful student of writing. He has managed not only to have himself enrolled in a writing course but also to have kept up with all the work he had to miss while in jail by seeking the collaboration of his sister and jailer. This is the kind of nonce taxonomy which can increase our resistance to the dictation of orthodox taxonomy over the lives of our students and, indirectly, our lives. For in ostensibly targeting the students, such orthodoxy inevitably also renders as "foreign" teachers with certain types of physical appearance, dress codes, and backgrounds.

Examining the taxonomy of each tale can also alert our attention to the nonce-taxonomical work performed by some of the malicious gossip we hear passed around concerning big names in the field. Such gossip often poses through repulsion and satire provisional, alternative hypotheses on how to conduct oneself after getting established in the field. Interest in nonce taxonomy might also help us recollect pieces and sites of gossip we know and participate in but which are absent from or underrepresented by *Comp Tales*. And it might help each of us compose stories concerning those experiences which, as several of the contributors mention in their comp tales, we have never told others. For instance, we might read the anonymous contributor of Tale 41 (p. 50) to be asking: How common is it for writing teachers to use their knowledge of the handwriting of students to identify the author of individual class evaluations? If such a "violation" has led this narrator to understand the extent to which evaluation forms might expose the teacher to (negative and positive) comments which students might otherwise hide from or not care to directly express to the teacher, then shouldn't we be talking more about when, where, how, and why some of us might have, or might want to, engage in such behavior? Or, if a significant number of us do indeed engage in such behavior, shouldn't we create more public forums for talking about such behavior? Researching the importance of nonce-taxonomical work might even motivate us to compose stories which we know we might not be ready to share with anyone for some time to come and certainly not for print in a book such as this one.

We might also explore ways of retelling the events narrated in some of the comp tales with a different taxonomy, to put back in the landscape those relations, purposes, and moments neglected by a majority of our comp tales. For instance, reading some of the comp tales alongside Tales 125 (p. 162) and 136 (p. 176), I couldn't help wondering why it is that when telling stories and when writing down the stories we tell, heterosexuals like myself are more likely to categorize ourselves as having gender and professional rank but seldom as having sexuality. The same question seems to also apply to issues of race. Orthodox taxonomy tends to name minority racial, ethnic, or class identities only when depicting students with "problems." However, in Tale 125, the narrator learns to see herself as reading, writing, teaching, colleaguing "as a Caucasian person" with sexual orientation as well as gender rather than just a writing teacher teaching African American students and having African American and gay colleagues. She reminds me to retell and rewrite some of my stories, so that I learn to see myself as heterosexual and a Chinese-born naturalized citizen of the U.S. teaching writing rather than just seeing my students as gay, lesbian, Vietnamese, or as "normal"—having presumably no race, sex, or nationality. As the student in Tale 124 (p. 161) reminds us, we all live racism. We need a nonce taxonomy which presents *all* writing teachers and students as having to deal with unequal relations along the axes of race, sexual orientation, ethnicity, gender, nationality, and class. Moreover, we need a taxonomy which acknowledges the infinite differences among persons positioned under each of these indispensable categories.

Recitations and Revisions

In *The Practice of Everyday Life,* de Certeau argues that citations of stories and the interminable recitation of stories are two of the three senses in which "[s]ocial life multiplies the gestures and modes of behavior *(im)printed* by narrative models" (186). How might each of us cite and re-cite the comp tales collected in this volume for the purpose of bringing into crisis the current structures of institutional spaces, including the academy, English studies, composition, or rhetoric?

One way would be to explore reasons for needing to refuse to cite or recite individual comp tales in specific situations. This exercise might involve jotting down not only what particularly in the story's taxonomy of college writing teachers might harm the work and lives of which group within and outside college writing teachers, how, and why. It would also involve detailing the specific occasions where one might be expected to recite such tales and the "dire consequences" of refusing to recite them (Smith and Watson 13). As Tale 85 (p. 104) attests, a student taking an ESL teacher certification failed five times until she "collaborated" by citing—reciting—a fictional story about her past from the point of view of a nineteen-year-old and with events based on cable TV reruns. Therefore, we need to not only track the tales we will refuse to recite but also develop a firm grasp on why, when, where, and with what consequences we practice such refusals.

Remaining silent is not the only form for refusal. One alternative would be to re-cite by removing an individual tale from its original situation. Telling a comp tale appropriate for one situation in another could confound the grounds of its credibility and thus make it work against itself. Or, one might re-cite with excessive earnestness, flamboyance, sarcasm—i.e., with alternative intonations and rhetorical gestures—to dislodge the normative relation between story and speaker. For instance, we've all found ourselves in situations where the sharing of stories about individual students' misunderstanding of our teacherly jargon, even when initially told to stress the importance of clarifying to our students the intended meaning behind our commands, soon escalates to a oneupsmanship on who can tell a story with the wittiest pun (with the dirtiest connotation) to earn the heartiest laughter from listeners. That is, we descend into competition among teachers at the expense of the students. Refusal to contribute on such occasions might take the form of retelling a story similar to Tale 17 (p. 28) with sarcasm or exaggerated earnestness. The audience would then be reminded not only of the fact that teachers often have problems comprehending the jargon other teachers use to name jargon in students' papers. They would also be reminded of the fact that in laughing with rather than laughing at the uncomprehending newcomers, old-timers have often failed to laugh at themselves, at their own propensity for using jargon in the very act of remonstrating against it. Because such re-citations often risk making the speaker appear "confused," "mad," or "naïve" (Smith and Watson 13), it would also be useful to examine when, where, how and why such risks are costly but nevertheless necessary given one's immediate and specific conditions of work and political vision.

Refusal to recite can sometimes also take the form of creative counterposing: composing tales which function as a "but . . . also" to the tales circulating at the center. For instance, in situations where one is expected to share stories of student plagiarism which make the student appear dumb and lazy, one might honor the topic but disrupt the spirit of the occasion by repeating a story similar to Tale 90 (p. 108). This tale not only posits alternative reasons for student plagiarism—"to hoodwink the system"—but also illustrates the energy, deliberation, and creative collaboration family members put into coming up with the best product to be "stolen" by the narrator's brother. A story such as Tale 90 can bring into crisis some of the standard assumptions over how and why students plagiarize.

Creative counterposing often involves form as well as content. In both content and form, Tale 123 (p. 160) illustrates the "sense of inconsistency" common to adjunct teachers working at several colleges and keeping offices in car trunks. This tale suggests that to an extent, the coherence in plot and message we often take pride in achieving when telling our stories might have more to do with the consistent work conditions some of us accrue from our privileged institutional locations than with our artistic skills. Likewise, Tale 125 (p. 162) takes us from scene to scene as the narrator grades papers from one course, discusses a student text in another classroom, spends time with new colleagues at school and a local bar, and converses with old colleagues. Holding the story together is her sense of crisis over her authority as a teacher of writing and her confidence in certain goals and methods of teaching as she learns to see herself as not just a writing teacher but also a "Caucasian person" with a specific gender and sexual orientation. To look for suspense and resolution to this story of crisis when telling it could only result in using a quick fix to dissolve our accountability for (rather than turning the crisis into an opportunity for changing) our existing ways of living the differences among writing teachers and between writing teachers and students, in a time and place deeply riven by a long history of racism, sexism, homophobia. We need to recollect stories which depart from standard notions of good storytelling and appear convoluted, strange, or unfinished in comparison. And we need to more self-consciously explore a variety of occasions and audiences for reciting these counter-stories.

Toni Morrison offers a powerful metaphor for creating critical dialogue across readers and writers socially placed and self-identified as in similar positions of subordination. Morrison reminds us that the Mississippi River has been "straightened" in places to make room for houses and livable acreage (305). When the river is flooding, "it is remembering. Remembering where it used to be" (305). Morrison uses the metaphor of flooding to argue that when reading the narratives of African American life by other African American writers and when composing one's own narratives of that life, African American writers need to remember where and how "we" have been straightened out. For instance, earlier slave narratives must shape the experience of slavery "to make it palatable to those who were in a position to alleviate it." As a result, "they were silent about many things, and they 'forgot' many other things" (301). In trying to compose alternative narratives of that experience, writers like Morrison must "flood" those places "straightened" by readers, editors, publishers. The metaphor of flooding is useful for reading, retelling, and rewriting comp tales since writing teachers are often in positions of less power within the academy. At the same time, we need to keep in mind that as *college writing* teachers, we embody both the power and interest of civil engineers: the pressure to "straighten out" is simultaneously within and outside oneself. So we need to learn to flood against the dispositions of ourselves as well as others.

Tale 136 (p. 176) enacts such a flooding, as the narrator retells of her decision in sixth grade to compose a story of a young boy being taught to sail by an older man. She remembers what she had earlier straightened out when telling the same story to workshop audiences, when she recoded the event by making the story she composed that of a girl being taught to sail. She had recoded the event out of fear that the real story might invoke in her audience the heterosexist stereotype that a lesbian is just a female who wants to be a male and out of a desire to focus the audience's attention on a neatly packaged point about writing.

In encouraging one another to compose and tell counter stories, we need to also recognize that there might be a variety of reasons why certain stories are "unspeakable" and cannot, should not be shared at a given time and place. For instance, as the narrator of Tale 136 reminds us, she is setting the record straight because she feels that "the times" and the particular occasion of writing down this tale calls for an openness about her sexual orientation. Furthermore, as many cultural critics have argued, the negotiation of everyday narratives is an ongoing process rather than a certain achievement (Smith and Watson). Resistance to a stereotypical communal notion of the unspeakable, such as rape or incest, can be co-opted and reordered into the community's normative patterns of speakability. How, when, where we choose to go public with our counter-stories is an ongoing and complex process which would vary from person to person, moment to moment, place to place. But the composing of such stories in and between oral and written forms could still go on, even if we are aware at the moment of composition that it might not be a story one would share in more public forums.

Reworking Habitual Reactions

Another way of seeking critical intervention is to use our habitual reactions to others' stories about their and our work to revise some of our culturally constructed tastes. To offer some points of departure for this line of work, I put together three composite reactions from my own experience reading some of the comp tales and from the responses of others to some of the sample tales Rich and I sent out.

Reaction One: "Too Much is Lost in the Written Transcript!"

I experienced and heard others repeatedly express this sense of something important having been lost in the process of writing down an oral tale. This reaction speaks in part to a healthy skepticism among college writing teachers about the unequivocal value of writing. I call it healthy because it aims to counter the historical devaluation of orality in modern and post-modern Western societies, it puts a premium on the contingent and provisional nature of meaning and the making of meaning, and it expresses concern over the further diminishment of face-to-face verbal interaction in a world increasingly dominated by cyberspace and virtual reality. At the same time, to keep this skepticism a healthy one, we need to explore ways of using the perceived inadequacy of writing to revise how we go about composing comp tales in both oral and written forms. This also means resisting the common tendency to dismiss the written version and the effort to write it down in the name of preserving the putative authenticity of an univocal "oral tradition." Put another way, we need to dismantle the binary of writing and speech, rather than merely inverting the hierarchy and thus inadvertently preserving it. Instead of wallowing in some sort of nostalgia for a more authentic mode of communication, a nostalgia which most likely speaks more to our own certified access to writing, it is more constructive to use this skepticism to revise both how we use writing to keep track of the stories we tell and how we retell the stories we've written down.

When discussing the importance of writing for black storytelling, Michael Eric Dyson calls writing a central project of African and African American peoples (Dyson and Dobrin). First, writing is central because it breaks the links between the binaries of orality vs. writing, body vs. intellect, and black vs. white. Given the history of slavery, it is central that "[African American] ideals are *not only* mediated through speech *but* constituted in very powerful ways through the very act of writing" (146). To argue for the centrality of writing for African American story-telling is not to dismiss the centrality of oral forms of storytelling. Rather, it is to urge those social groups historically designated as only capable of having an oral tradition to also exert their central place in written discourse. While it is dangerous to wallow in self-subalterniza-tion and thus assume an absolute equation between the division of race along the axis of literacy and orality and the division between researchers and teachers along the axis of writing and teaching, it is nevertheless necessary that college writing *teachers* become vigilant towards our own and others' automatic distaste for any attempt by writ-ing teachers to write down the stories we tell and retell.

Secondly, writing is central because the "physical weight of writing" enables a different and necessary form of work than oral storytelling (Dyson and Dobrin 145–46). The very physical act of having the paper to refer to offers a different kind of material density. It enables African American storytellers to "contrast" their own words against not only what other writers have said but also "what slave narratives have been *talking* about" (145, my emphasis). If we interpret "talk" to mean both oral and written forms of narrative, then we might argue that such a convergence can be not only trans-historical and trans-racial but also transgressive of the written/oral divide. To apply Dyson's argument to *Comp Tales*, we might think of writing as enabling a critical reflection on the distance between what the writer is saying on paper when transcribing the story and what the writer has been saying and will say when telling the story.

The question is how to use our sense of the differences between written and oral forms of storytelling to dismantle the binary of literacy and orality as well as the assumptions and distastes resulting from such binary thinking. The challenge is to turn our reading of the written tales into an occasion for making possible the critical convergence of differ-ent voices, between one's oral and written voices as well as between our own and that of others. If, as Rey Chow reminds us, the battles intellec-tuals fight are battles of words, then the battles writing teachers fight are battles of writing (17). Part of that battle would involve using writ-ing to explore the different functions of written and oral storytelling and to use the crises we experience when negotiating those differences as opportunities for revising our oral and written practices.

Reaction Two: "This Does Not Represent My Experience!"
College writing teachers work within drastically different material condi-tions. Making a list of the kinds of comp tales I have an aversion toward

has helped me grasp not only the specificity of my immediate situation but also my need to listen more responsively and responsibly across the differences among us (Royster). In "Age, Race, Class, and Sex: Women Redefining Difference," Audre Lorde argues that women must struggle to "relate within equality"—"root out internalized patterns of oppression within ourselves" (286). That is, women must learn to use each others' differences to enrich their visions and their joint struggles. The same challenge faces college writing teachers committed to ending all forms of oppression within and outside the academy. One starting point for learning to relate within equality would be to confront one's own powerful positions when listening to others' stories about their and our work.

For instance, I have always been aware of my strong visceral discomfort toward any story concerning plagiarism. And I know much of this distaste comes from my aversion to the smug tone with which these stories are often told and to the frequency with which the student is made to appear simply dumb, lazy, and dishonest. Reading some of the comp tales on plagiarism has helped me to more systematically examine my position on the topic. Plagiarism highlights a contradiction between my interest to promote intertextuality and collaboration and my interest in protecting the intellectual property of individual authors. To effectively fix this conflict on a day-to-day basis, I arrive at this counsel for myself and others: "Instead of wasting time catching plagiarized papers, put energy into making sure that each student is required to identify the arguments and stylistic choices he or she has made in an original paper and write a revision which tries out alternative arguments and choices." My rationale: the revision would force the student to labor over the "stolen" paper and thus make it his or her "own." This student would have learned something about reading and writing in the process of first having to perform a close reading of the "stolen" text and then experimenting with alternative thoughts and stylistic choices.

Contrasting my tendency to treat revision as an antidote to plagiarism with the approaches described in some of the comp tales in this book, I realize that part of my impatience with some of the tales stems from a tendency to mine stories for useful tips. To a certain extent, my impatience comes from my sense of how little the situation they are dealing with and in applies to my immediate concerns as a teacher. While I'm still convinced of the need to refuse recitation of those tales which denigrate students, I am also more aware of the ways in which the immediate conditions of my work have an impact on my distaste for others' seeming obsession with catching and punishing students for plagiarism. For instance, in presenting revision as an antidote to plagiarism, my counsel also assumes the availability to all writing teachers of a set of material conditions, including smaller class sizes and a reasonable teaching load, which makes more possible a sustained engagement with each piece of writing produced by individual students, and which ensures the necessary time and energy for the teacher to compose revision assignments after reading each batch of student papers. These are not conditions of work yet available to many college writing teachers in spite of repeated position statements by various professional organizations. Furthermore, to "rise above" others' concern for plagiarism is also an option requiring a certain sense of institutional security, the knowledge that one is in a position to ignore or weather the complaints and pressures from administrators and colleagues holding different views towards institutional guidelines on plagiarism. More obviously, my solution—revision as antidote to plagiarism—certainly does not speak to the needs and experiences of many writing program administrators charged with enforcing institutional gatekeeping policies and having to deal with issues surfacing from the classrooms of a dispersed staff. As the narrator of Tale 46 (p. 54) reminds us, some of us work in institutional conditions where one feels grateful any time all the teachers in the program finish the semester. Other tales caution me to take more seriously the lack of institutional support experienced by some among us having to deal with the threat of lawsuits (or pit bulldogs) which might follow one's charge to carry out such gatekeeping policies. These perspectives in turn shake my confidence about my strategy for dealing with issues of plagiarism.

In the future, when offering advice such as use-revision-as-an-antidote-to-plagiarism, I need to question my tendency to pass this around as a universal teaching tip. That is, I need to highlight the ideal working conditions assumed by my advice while acknowledging current unequal access to such conditions among college writing teachers. I also need to explore ways of retelling others' stories on plagiarism so that the immediate and often unreasonable working conditions embedded in these tales are not only acknowledged but also challenged. Instead of using our distaste for others' stories on topics such as plagiarism to deny the inequality and differences among us, we need to experiment with ways of using these stories to enrich our visions and our joint struggles for more reasonable working conditions for all.

"This does not speak to my experience" is also a sentiment behind the concern of several reviewers that most of the TAs taking the graduate teaching seminars they offer might not relate to a significant number of the sample comp tales Rich and I sent out with the book prospectus. That is, some of the tales might more effectively serve as a general introduction to the field of composition and rhetoric than be useful to teachers looking for concrete solutions to concrete classroom situations. I read the reviewers to be reminding us that the term "college writing teachers" is used by this book project to refer to both a dispersed and subjugated work force and an academic field. For instance, a significant number of writing teachers perceive themselves as only a temporary part of the work force but not a part of the field: teaching of writing is something they do while they work to credential themselves in other fields of interest, including creative writing or literary studies. Some among this temporary work force have little interest in telling and hearing stories concerning the field, its operation and positions within English studies or the academy. "How does this tale address my immediate situations, interests, and concerns?" This question is inevitably at the back of our taste or distaste for certain types of comp tales. To relate within equality, we need also to consider the extent to which such reactions advance or impede our efforts to break the divisions and hierarchies between research, teaching, and service and between composition/rhetoric, creative writing, and literary studies.

For instance, those of us who perceive ourselves as *in* the field of composition and rhetoric might rework our distaste towards simple teaching tips by recollecting alternative stories of classroom practices. And we might explore ways of retelling teaching-tip-tales so that they speak not only to the interests of those worried that "all this teaching is getting in the way of my real work" (Tale 111) but also to the institutional divisions and hierarchies driving such interests and worries, as well as to the difference in "our" and "their" sense of the reality of college writing teachers. This might also help us examine the actions we have taken and not taken in the process of credentializing ourselves and the field of composition, actions which might have directly and indirectly caused an institutional need for and the often undesirable conditions of work conditions faced by a temporary work force.

Those of us perceiving ourselves as temporary teachers of writing but interested in contesting asymmetrical relations of power might recollect instead stories concerning the operation and institutional locations of composition/rhetoric or of the work of WPAs. Such research would be especially important in the long run, if and when one eventually moves out of the writing classroom into the center of one's "real" field of interest—literary studies or creative writing, say—where much cutting edge work is devoted exclusively to issues of border and hybridity. We might then use our previous, lived experiences as teachers of writing and our knowledge of the field of composition to make ourselves accountable for the ways we deal with and deal in the hierarchies in teaching, research, and service and in composition, literary studies, and creative writing.

Reaction Three: "This Is Way Too Traditional!"

"Traditional," meaning "conservative," is a judgment I and others often make to voice our disappointment at some comp tales, especially those seemingly out of touch with "cutting edge" scholarship. We need to be particularly vigilant towards such predispositions because dominant discourse in composition tends to use "traditional" as a code word for "oral," "unenlightened," "common," "ordinary" (Horner). "Traditional" often functions as an operative term protecting the binary between the "written critiques" of researchers and the "tacit knowledge" of practitioners.

Given such a collective disposition, we need to keep in mind that no story is inherently liberatory or repressive: all can be co-opted or be used as a source of resistance (Smith and Watson 17). Instead of focusing attention merely on what makes a story "traditional," we might consider also how and why this story continues to be meaningful to individual writing teachers. Likewise, it would be counterproductive to simply view others' interest in "traditional" stories as evidence of their (lack of) knowledge of "cutting edge" work or as a sign of the presumed apathy among practitioners towards theory. Rather, we can use "traditional" stories to examine the specific, material conditions making these stories meaningful, to grasp the discrepancy between the ideal conditions of work we desire and the actual, different conditions facing individual writing teachers at a given place and time.

As Tale 135 (p. 175) reminds us, stories such as the one recounting a teacher using a plastic bag to return to the student writers the shredded pages of their "bad" paper in front of their peers might seem lousy (and I might add, dated) because they are so one-sided and outrageously out of touch with what some of us perceive as standard scholarship on teaching practices. Yet, as the narrator realizes after visiting a campus where the plastic baggie approach is still being practiced by a senior member of the faculty, such stories are often symptomatic of unresolved problems happening out there in the teaching world. They refer to real situations many of us have to reckon with on a daily basis.

Tale 135 stimulates me to rework several of my initial reactions to some clusters of comp tales. For instance, given current scholarship on the danger of simplistic approaches to issues of gender and the danger of stereotyping our students, I initially found "traditional" those stories illustrating the need for female teachers to negotiate authority with their big-bodied, white, male students. On the one hand, my heard-this-done-that reaction towards recitations of familiar stories of sexism in the workplace might express a healthy vigilance towards the tendency to let an established genre and theme reduce the full complexity of specific, lived events and relations across the gender divide. On the other hand, as Tale 135 reminds us, what we can get out of a story depends to a large extent on the question we take to it. What particular material conditions make sexism an unresolved problem recurring across a variety of classrooms? What are those of us who view such tales as traditional going to do about these conditions? For instance, my interest in nonce taxonomy, an attempt to confront the tendency to essentialize one another's identity and life, requires that I resist any attempts to stereotype "student," "female," or "male." At the same time, I need to keep in mind that categories such as gender or race remain an indispensable part of the taxonomy of the powerless, especially in contexts where sexism and racism continue to dictate judgments on what kind of persons should have the authority to teach what kind of persons. I need to confront rather than dismiss the crisis these "traditional" tales bring to my sense of relevance. That is, I need to examine what needs to be done to make anti-essentialist critiques address issues some of us feel the field has already moved beyond but which remain unresolved in situations encountered daily by others among us.

A second cluster of tales concerns weird-things-which-have-happened-to-me. These tales often strike me as "traditional" because they touch on issues of teaching—such as the discrepancy between the tutee and the tutor's uses of language—which have been explicitly addressed for some years by a variety of scholarship in the field. I reread the tales to examine the specific material conditions of work captured in each story. In fact, these tales often speak more about the narrator's concern to prepare new teachers and tutors for the specific material conditions they are likely to face than the narrator's seeming fixation on recalling "weird" student behaviors and demands. Rereading these tales, I have to wonder how implicated some of us are in the fact that new TAs often end up being the ones assigned to "basic" writing courses and writing centers—worksites where the institution houses students with "weird" behaviors or demands. For instance, when was the last time any of us sent such a student to the writing center or placed the student in a basic writing course staffed by new teachers? When was the last time any of us has actually tutored at a writing center? What are we going to do about the fact that, as Tale 117 (p. 150) reminds us, some of us are holding positions which literally no longer allow us to work in the "trenches"?

A third cluster of "traditional" stories involves teachers who behave in ways which have long been critiqued in current scholarship. However, the narrators seem totally uncritical of such behaviors, both in how the narrator narrates the event and construes the moral of that event. For instance, a senior faculty observing the teaching of a new TA "took over" the class to demonstrate to that TA and her students the "right" way of conducting a class. The narrator tells the event to illustrate the useful lesson about teaching she learned from such a takeover. We, the reader or listener, may be twitching in our seats over the insensitivity of the observer. To an extent, in taking over, the observer can be seen as publicly delivering to the TA, in the plastic baggie of his teaching demonstration, her shredded "bad" teaching. And yet, such an "insensitive" teaching practice seems to have nevertheless remained meaningful to this particular TA. The question to be explored when reworking our visceral repulsion to such tales is to examine how and why ostensibly the same teaching practice can be productively meaningful to some while being an instance of supreme insensitivity to others.

Sometimes, stories appear "traditional" because they convey a sense of resignation towards existing relations of domination. But resignation does not necessarily imply the teller's "false consciousness" or blind ideological support for the dominant. As James Scott argues in *Weapons of the Weak*, "resignation to what seems inevitable is not the same as according it legitimacy, although it may serve just as efficiently to produce daily compliance" (324). A certain tone of resignation is entirely likely in the face of a situation that cannot, in the short run, be materially altered. It often speaks to the "rational understanding of what is achievable in a given situation" (Scott, *Weapons* 326) or the subordinate people's understanding of "credible options" (West, in De Alva *et al.,* "Our Next Race Question" 57). To rework our disappointment at the tone of resignation in some comp tales, we need to examine individual narrators' sense of credible options given the situations as they experience them.

What are the "credible options" for teachers who tell and retell stories which seem resigned to unfair working conditions, teaching loads, class size, banal gatekeeping policies, etc.? For instance, Tale 12 (p. 19) recounts an instance where a beginning teacher in a community college is assigned a "remedial" course contracted by the local sheriff's office for employees who had failed a placement test. To resolve the resentment students openly displayed at being assigned the course, the teacher involved students in setting "realistic goals," given "what time they had in and out of the classroom and what would encourage them to leave their sidearms at home." On the one hand, the tale suggests a resignation to the "reality of classroom and student circumstances." On the other hand, this does not necessarily mean that either the students or the teacher approve of the reality of placement testing or of an obsession with quick, cheap, quantifiable fixes embedded in the move by the sheriff's office to contract a "remedial" writing course. Rather, it conveys teacher and student effort to arrive at an understanding of their credible options—of what is achievable in the given situation. It reminds readers like myself to examine the different realities constraining the work of the teacher and those students and the work of me and my students.

Told by itself or on certain occasions, a story similar to Tale 36 (p. 44) could be construed as simply illustrating the passive compliance of ESL students to teacher obsessions with issues of grammar. Yet, we might gain an entirely different understanding of the seeming resignation in the action and voice of the ESL student from Africa and his teacher if we accompany this story with stories similar to Tales 47 and 48. In Tale 47 (p. 62), we encounter thirty English professorial hands reaching into thirty suit/sport coat pockets to remove thirty red pens and begin circling typos in a memo handed out at a department meeting. Tale 48 (p. 62) testifies to the lived experience of a job candidate from England who was rejected in part because of a "comma splice" in his letter of application. These tales might help us grasp not only the credible options facing the ESL student from Africa and his writing center teacher in given institutions but also the need of readers like myself to become more accountable for our actions outside the classrooms or the writing centers, at department meetings and in reaction to the writing of our colleagues, actions which might have indirectly contributed to the lack of credible options facing that student and writing center teacher. To become more accountable for our own actions, we need to recollect comp tales which do not depict what one does and thinks others should do but also what one has failed to do to make the same credible options available to all.

I believe my list of composite reactions is symptomatic of both the general conditions of the field and my specific dealings in and with it. I hope it will persuade individual readers to compose their own list of habitual reactions and to use my discussion to detail alternative modes of reading and writing comp tales in the context of their own immediate situations and political visions.

Conclusion
In "Composition's Imagined Geographies: The Politics of Space in the Frontier, City, and Cyberspace," Nedra Reynolds argues that turning to

cultural geography might help us question the relationships between material conditions and imagined territories. She urges us to "attend to the negotiations of power that take place across and within a number of spaces: regional or topographical, domestic or institutional, architectural or electronic, real or imagined" (13). I hope my thoughts in both parts of this afterword offer some points of departure for reworking the politics of space in and with which college writing teachers deal when telling, listening to, reading, and writing the stories of our work.

To keep track of the stories we tell beyond the scope of this book and this afterword, we need most of all to experiment with a variety of forums for writing down the stories we tell and for sharing our written and oral versions of individual stories. In *Teachers' Stories: From Personal Narrative to Professional Insight*, Mary Renck Jalongo, Joan P. Isenberg, and Gloria Gerbracht urge teachers to keep a journal of stories they might not have thought about for years but "resurrected" in the process of reading or listening to someone else's stories (183). Sharing stories with trusted colleagues through regular mail and e-mail or working face to face with a small community of teachers in graduate seminars, in faculty workshops, self-initiated writing or reading groups, co-teaching and mentoring arrangements, varied professional development activities, task forces and in-house journals are also good ways of exploring the work of storytelling. That is, I trust readers to move beyond the scope of this essay, which treats acts of reading and writing as the primary means for tracking comp tales, by creating new means and forums for extending the life of the stories we tell.

To keep track of the stories we tell and of our storytelling practices, we need to continually draw and redraw maps of the world, of named places and paths with and in which we deal. Further, we need to use these maps to bring to crisis established conditions of that world and established understandings of and relations to those conditions, so that with each crisis, opportunity is molded in danger, and danger becomes a form of opportunity.

APPENDIX A

Call for Submissions

The call for contributions to *Comp Tales*, first posted in October 1997, went through several versions, but the one printed below was probably seen by the most people.

We can imagine other versions used for other purposes. Susanmarie Harrington at Indiana University–Purdue University at Indianapolis and Jeff Sommers at Miami University of Ohio have used the call for in-service faculty workshops before classes begin. Teachers, old-timers and new-timers, write a tale before the session, read it aloud at the session, and everyone discusses. As Sommers writes, "this activity was an excellent format for bringing our faculty together to talk about teaching values."

THE CALL:

Rich Haswell and Min-Zhan Lu are editing a book titled *Comp Tales*. It will be a collection of the stories about work that college writing teachers tell and retell. *Comp Tales* will gather together oral narratives from the field, stories that are actually told in the classroom, in the halls, over the tutor's table, in committee rooms, on street corners, over the kitchen table, wherever.

These stories can evolve around students, courses, programs, teachers, colleagues, departments, administrators, conferences, graduate school, the public—anything connected with college composition.

Obviously, we are not after just the kind of stories that emerge from the coffee klatsch or the gripe session. We want the whole range of professional tales. But they must be tales that you actually tell and pass on.

That is the bottom line, the distinctive genre that will make our collection unique.

So we would like for you to write the stories in the same way and in the same spirit that you actually tell them. Most of the tales we have received are less than a page in length. We would also like for you to explain the customary context in which you tell the story—when, where, to whom, and why you like to tell it. This will be useful for exploring how composition shapes and is shaped by narratives.

Your stories will be seen by only the two of us until publication, and those not used will never be seen by anybody else. You can name names or use pseudonyms and circumlocutions (e.g., "a young comp researcher once . . ." or "a large public university in the Midwest"). You can remain anonymous if you choose. In short, we are aware of the need to protect everyone's privacy.

APPENDIX B

~

Bibliography of Oral
Tale and Composition

Richard H. Haswell

All fields of study have taken a turn toward narrative in the last thirty years. And many of their paths converge on the conversational anecdote. Beginning, then, with the oral-based comp tale, we are led in every sort of interesting direction. The following sources, largely books, are chosen because they serve as useful trailheads. The complete bibliographic entry can be found in the Works Cited.

TEACHING

Coles, Robert. *The Call of Stories: Teaching the Moral Imagination.*

Dyson, Anne Haas, and Celia Genishi, eds. *The Need for Story: Cultural Diversity in Classroom and Community.*

Elbaz, Freema. "Research on Teachers' Knowledge: The Evolution of a Discourse."

Jalongo, Mary Renck, et al., *Teachers' Stories: From Personal Narrative to Professional Insight.*

Meyer, Richard J. *Stories from the Heart: Teachers and Students Research their Literacy Lives.*

THE TEACHING OF WRITING, K-12 AND POST-SECONDARY

Anson, Chris M., et al. *Scenarios for Teaching Writing: Contexts for Discussion and Reflective Practice.*
Clifford, John, and John Schilb. *Writing Theory and Critical Theory.*
McCracken, H. Thomas, et al., eds. *Teaching College English and English Education: Reflective Stories.*
Roen, Duane, ed. *Living Rhetoric and Composition: Stories of the Discipline.*
Stock, Patricia. "The Function of Anecdote in Teacher Research."
Trimmer, John, ed. *Narration as Knowledge: Tales of the Teaching Life.*

WRITING TEACHER LORE

Corder, Jim. "Argument as Emergence: Rhetoric as Lore."
Harkin, Patricia. "The Postdisciplinary Politics of Lore."
North, Stephen M. *The Making of Knowledge in Composition: Portrait of an Emerging Field.*

LITERATURE

Brooks, Peter. *Reading for the Plot: Design and Intention in Narrative.*
Lanser, Susan Sniader. *The Narrative Act: Point of View in Prose Fiction.*
Martin, Wallace. *Recent Theories of Narrative.*

LITERACY AND FAMILY STUDIES

Harste, Jerome Charles, et al., eds. *Language Stories and Literacy Lessons.*
Moss, Beverly J., ed. *Literacy Across Communities.*
Pillari, Vimala. *Pathways to Family Myths.*
Stone, Elizabeth. *Black Sheep and Kissing Cousins: How Our Family Stories Shape Us.*

HISTORY

Carr, David. *Time, Narrative, and History.*
Ricoeur, Paul. *Time and Narrative.*
Schrager, Sam. "What is Social in Oral History."
White, Hayden. *Metahistory: The Historical Imagination in Nineteenth-Century Europe.*

ETHICS

MacIntyre, Alasdair. *After Virtue: A Study in Moral Theory.*
Tappan, Mark B., and Martin J. Packer, eds. *Narrative and Storytelling: Implications for Understanding Moral Development.*

COMMUNICATION AND SOCIOLINGUISTICS

Bamberg, Michael G. W., ed. *Oral Versions of Personal Experience: Three Decades of Narrative Analysis.*
Bauman, Richard. *Story, Performance, and Event: Contextual Studies of Oral Narrative.*
Fisher, Walter. *Human Communication as Narration: Toward a Theory of Reason, Value, and Action.*
Johnstone, Barbara. *Stories, Community, and Place: Narratives from Middle America.*
Young, Katharine Galloway. *Taleworlds and Storyrealms: The Phenomenology of Narrative.*

SOCIOLOGY/POLITICAL SCIENCE

Polanyi, L. *Telling the American Story: A Structural and Cultural Analysis of Conversational Storytelling.*
Rosnow, Ralph L. and Gary Alan Fine. *Rumor and Gossip: The Social Psychology of Hearsay.*
Scott, James C. *Domination and the Arts of Resistance: Hidden Transcripts.*
Shibutani, Tamotsu. *Improvised News: A Sociological Study of Rumor.*

INSTITUTIONS

Linde, Charlotte. "Whose Story is This?: Point of View Variation and Group Identity."
Martin, Joanne, and Melanie Powers. "Truth or Corporate Propaganda: The Value of a Good War Story."
Pondy, L. R., et al., eds. *Organizational Symbolism.*

PSYCHOLOGY

Mandler, Jean Matter. *Stories, Scripts, and Scenes: Aspects of Schema Theory.*

McAdams, Dan P. *The Stories We Live By: Personal Myth and the Making of the Self.*

Pearson, Carol. *The Hero within: Six Archetypes We Live By.*

Schafer, Roy. *The Analytic Attitude.*

White, Michael M., and David Epston. *Narrative Means to Therapeutic Ends.*

LIFESTORY

Bamberg, Michael, ed. *Narrative Development: Six Approaches.*

Birren, James E., et al., eds. *Aging and Biography: Explorations in Adult Development.*

Freeman, Mark. *Rewriting the Self: History, Memory, Narrative.*

Linde, Charlotte. *Life Stories: The Creation of Coherence.*

Sarbin, T. R., ed. *Narrative Psychology: The Storied Nature of Human Conduct.*

APPENDIX C

⤺

Index of Topics
in the Tales

Richard H. Haswell

Works Cited

Anson, Chris M., Joan Graham, David A. Joliffe, Nancy S. Shapiro, and Carolyn Smith. *Scenarios for Teaching Writing: Contexts for Discussion and Reflective Practice.* Urbana, IL: National Council of Teachers of English, 1993.

Anzaldúa, Gloria, and Andrea Lunsford. "Toward a Mestiza Rhetoric: Gloria Anzaldúa on Composition and Postcoloniality." *JAC: A Journal of Composition Theory* 18 (1998): 1–27.

Bamberg, Michael G. W., ed. *Oral Versions of Personal Experience: Three Decades of Narrative Analysis.* Special issue of *Journal of Narrative and Life History* 7, nos. 1–4 (1997).

Bamberg, Michael, and R. Damrad-Frye. "On the Ability to Provide Evaluative Comments; Further on Children's Narrative Competencies." *Journal of Child Language* 18 (1991): 689–710.

Bamberg, Michael, ed. *Narrative Development: Six Approaches.* Mahwah, NJ: Erlbaum, 1997.

Bartholomae, David. Review of *The Making of Knowledge in Composition: Portrait of an Emerging Field*, by Stephen M. North. *Rhetoric Review* 6 (1988): 224–28.

Bauman, Richard. *Story, Performance, and Event: Contextual Studies of Oral Narrative.* Cambridge University Press, 1986.

Benjamin, Walter. *Illuminations.* Trans. Harry Zohn. New York: Schocken, 1955.

Bertaux, Daniel, and Paul Thompson, eds. *Between Generations: Family Models, Myths, and Memories.* International Yearbook of Oral History and Life Stories, vol. 2. Oxford University Press, 1993.

Birren, James E., Gary M. Kenyon, Jan-Erik Ruth, Johannes J. F. Schroots, and Torbjorn Svensson, eds. *Aging and Biography: Explorations in Adult Development.* New York: Springer Publ. Co., 1996.

Bormann, Ernest G. *The Force of Fantasy.* Southern Illinois University Press, 1985.

Bourdieu, Pierre. *Language and Symbolic Power.* Ed. John B. Thompson. Trans. Gino Raymond and Matthew Adamson. Cambridge, MA: Harvard University Press, 1991.

_____. *Outline of a Theory of Practice.* Trans. Richard Nice. Cambridge University Press, 1977.

_____. *The Field of Cultural Production: Essays on Art and Literature.* Ed. Randal Johnson. London: Polity, 1993.

Briggs, Charles L. (1997). "Sequentiality and Temporalization in the Narrative Construction of a South American Cholera Epidemic." *Journal of Narrative and Life History* 7, nos. 1–4 (1997): 177–83.

Brooke, Robert. "Underlife and Writing Instruction." *College Composition and Communication* 38, no. 2 (1987): 141–53.

Brooks, Peter. *Reading for the Plot: Design and Intention in Narrative.* Cambridge, MA: Harvard University Press, 1984.

Bruner, Jerome. *Actual Minds, Possible Worlds.* Cambridge, MA: Harvard University Press, 1986.

Byrne, Robert. *Advanced Technique in Pool and Billiards.* San Diego: Harcourt Brace, 1990.

Carr, David. *Time, Narrative, and History.* Bloomington: University of Indiana Press, 1986.

Chow, Rey. *Writing Diaspora: Tactics of Intervention in Contemporary Cultural Studies.* Bloomington: Indiana University Press, 1993.

Clifford, John, and John Schilb, eds. *Writing Theory and Critical Theory.* New York: Modern Language Association of America, 1994.

Coles, Robert. *The Call of Stories: Teaching the Moral Imagination.* Boston: Houghton Mifflin, 1989.

Corder, Jim. "Argument as Emergence: Rhetoric as Lore." *Rhetoric Review* 4 (1985): 16–32.

Crawshaw, Ralph. "Gossip Wears a Thousand Masks," *Prism* 2 (1974): 45–47.

Davies, Bronwyn, and Rom Harré. "Positioning: The Social Construction of Selves." *Journal for the Theory of Social Behavior* 20 (1990): 43–63.

Day, James M., and Mark B. Tappan. "The Narrative Approach to Moral Development: From the Epistemic Subject to Dialogical Selves." *Human Development* 39 (1996): 67–82.

De Certeau, Michel. *The Practice of Everyday Life.* Trans. Steven F. Rendall. Berkeley: University of California Press, 1984.

Dyson, Anne Haas, and Celia Genishi, eds. *The Need for Story: Cultural Diversity in Classroom and Community.* Urbana, IL: National Council of Teachers of English, 1994.

Dyson, Michael Eric, and Sidney I. Dobrin. "Race and the Public Intellectual: A Conversation with Michael Eric Dyson." *JAC: A Journal of Composition Theory* 17 (1997): 143–82.

Eiseley, Loren. *All the Strange Hours: The Excavation of a Life.* New York: Scribner's, 1975.

Elbaz, Freema. "Research on Teachers' Knowledge: The Evolution of a Discourse." *Journal of Curriculum Studies* 23, no. 1 (1991): 1–19.

Ferreira, A. J. "Family Myth and Homeostasis." *Archives of General Psychiatry* 9 (1963): 457–63.

Fisher, Walter. *Human Communication as Narration: Toward a Theory of Reason, Value, and Action.* Chapel Hill: University of South Carolina Press, 1987.

Freeman, Mark. *Rewriting the Self: History, Memory, Narrative.* London: Routledge, 1993.

Funkenstein, Amos. "The Incomprehensible Catastrophe: Memory and Narrative History." *The Narrative Study of Lives*, Vol. 1. Ed. Ruthellen Josselson and Amia Lieblich. Newbury Park, CA: Sage (1992). 21–29.

Gluckman, Max. "Gossip and Scandal." *Current Anthropology* 4 (1963): 307–16.

Haas, Jack. "Learning Real Feelings: A Study of High-Steel Ironworkers' Reaction to Fear and Danger." *Sociology of Work and Occupation* 4 (1977): 147–169.

Harkin, Patricia. "The Postdisciplinary Politics of Lore." *Contending with Words.* Ed. Patricia Harkin and John Schilb. New York: Modern Language Association of America, 1991. 124–38.

Harré, Rom. "'He Lived to Tell the Tale.'" *Journal of Narrative and Life History* 7, nos. 1–4 (1997): 331–34.

Harste, Jerome Charles, Virginia A. Woodward, and Carolyn L. Burke. *Language Stories and Literacy Lessons.* Portsmouth, NJ: Heinemann, 1984.

Hill, Carolyn Ericksen. *Writing from the Margins: Power and Pedagogy for Teachers of Composition.* New York: Oxford University Press, 1990.

Horner, Bruce. "Tradition and Professionalization: Reconceiving Work in Composition." Forthcoming, *College Composition and Commmunication.*

Jalongo, Mary Renck, Joan P. Isenberg, and Gloria Gerbracht. *Teachers' Stories: From Personal Narrative to Professional Insight.* San Francisco: Jossey-Bass, 1995.

Jameson, Fredric. *The Political Unconscious: Narrative as a Socially Symbolic Act.* Ithaca: Cornell University Press, 1981.

Jarratt, Susan C. "Beside Ourselves: Rhetoric and Representation in Post-colonial Feminist Writing." *JAC: A Journal of Composition Theory* 18 (1998): 57–75.

Johnstone, Barbara. *Stories, Community, and Place: Narratives from Middle America.* Bloomington: Indiana University Press, 1990.

_____. *The Linguistic Individual: Self-Expression in Language and Linguistics.* New York: Oxford University Press, 1996.

Josehs, Ingrid E. "Talking with the Dead: Self-construction as Dialogue." *Journal of Narrative and Life History* 7, nos. 1–4 (1997): 359–67.

Kenyon, G. M. "The Meaning/Value of Personal Storytelling." *Aging and Biography: Explorations in Adult Development.* Ed. James E. Birren, Gary M. Kenyon, Jan-Erik Ruth, Johannes J. F. Schroots, and Torbjorn Svensson. New York: Springer Publ. Co., 1996. 21–38.

Kermode, Frank. *The Genesis of Secrecy: On the Interpretation of Narrative.* Cambridge, MA: Harvard University Press, 1979.

Klinkenborg, Verlyn. "Introduction." *Turning Toward Home: Reflections on the Family from Harper's Magazine.* Ed. Katharine Whittemore and Ilena Silverman. New York: Franklin Square Press, 1993. 1–8.

Küntay, Aylin, and Susan Ervin-Trip. "Narrative Structure and Con-versational Circumstances." *Journal of Narrative and Life History* 7, nos. 1–4 (1997): 113–20.

Labov, William, and Joshua Waletzky, "Narrative Analysis: Oral Versions of Personal Experience." *Essays on the Verbal and Visual Arts: Proceedings of the 1966 Annual Spring Meeting of the American Ethnological Society.* Ed. J. Helm. Seattle: University of Washington Press, 1967. 12–44.

Lanser, Susan Sniader. *The Narrative Act: Point of View in Prose Fiction.* Princeton: Princeton University Press, 1981.

Levi-Strauss, Claude. *The Raw and the Cooked.* Trans. John Weightman and Doreen Weightman. New York: Octagon, 1979.

Linde, Charlotte. *Life Stories: The Creation of Coherence.* New York: Oxford University Press, 1993.

_____. "Whose Story is This?: Point of View Variation and Group Identity." *Oral Narrative Sociolinguistic Variation: Data, Theory and Analysis.* Ed. J. Arnold, R. Blake, B. Davidson, S. Schwenter, and J. Solomon. Stanford, CA: Center for the Study of Language and Information, 1996. 333–45.

_____. "Narrative: Experience, Memory, Folklore." *Journal of Narrative and Life History* 7, nos. 1–4 (1997): 281–89.

Linn, Ruth. "Soldiers' Narratives of Selective Moral Resistance: A Separate Position of the Connected Self?" *The Narrative Study of Lives*, Vol. 5. Ed. Amia Lieblich and Ruthellen Josselson. Newbury Park, CA: Sage, 1997. 94–112.

Lorde, Audre. "Age, Race, Class, and Sex: Women Redefining Difference." *Out There: Marginalization and Contemporary Cultures*. Ed. Russell Ferguson, Martha Gever, Trinh T. Minh-ha, and Cornel West. Cambridge, MA: MIT Press, 1990. 281–87.

MacIntyre, Alasdair. *After Virtue: A Study in Moral Theory*. 2nd. ed. Notre Dame, IN: University of Notre Dame Press, 1984 (1981).

Mandler, Jean Matter. *Stories, Scripts, and Scenes: Aspects of Schema Theory*. Hillsdale, NJ: Erlbaum, 1984.

Martin, J. R., and Plum, G. A. "Construing Experience: Some Story Genres Interviews," *Journal of Narrative and Life History* 7, nos. 1–4 (1997): 299–308.

Martin, Joanne, and Melanie Powers. "Truth or Corporate Propaganda: The Value of a Good War Story." *Organizational Symbolism*. Ed. Louis R. Pondy, Peter J. Frost, Gareth Morgan, and Thomas C. Dandridge. Greenwich, CN: JAI Press, 1983. 93–107.

Martin, Joanne, Martha S. Feldman, Mary Jo Hatch, and Sim Silkin. "The Uniqueness Paradox in Organizational Stories." *Administrative Science Quarterly* 28 (1983): 438–53.

Martin, Wallace. *Recent Theories of Narrative*. Ithaca: Cornell University Press, 1990.

Maruna, Shadd. "Going straight: Desistance from Crime and Life Narratives of Reform." *The Narrative Study of Lives*, Vol. 5. Ed. Amia Lieblich and Ruthellen Josselson. Newbury Park, CA: Sage, 1997. 59–93.

McAdams, Dan P. "Narrating the Self in Adulthood." *Aging and Biography: Explorations in Adult Development*. Ed. James E. Birren, Gary M. Kenyon, Jan-Erik Ruth, Johannes J. F. Schroots, and Torbjorn Svensson. NY: Springer Publ. Co., 1996. 131–48.

McAdams, Dan P. *The Stories We Live By: Personal Myth and the Making of the Self*. New York: Morrow, 1993.

McLeod, Susan. "Tales from the Field." *Rhetoric Review* (Fall 1990): 186–187.

McCracken, H. Thomas, and Richard Larson, with Judith Entes. *Teaching College English and English Education: Reflective Stories*. Urbana, IL: National Council of Teachers of English, 1998.

Meyer, Richard J. *Stories from the Heart: Teachers and Students Research their Literacy Lives.* Mahway, NJ: Erlbaum, 1996.

Morrison, Toni. "The Site of Memory." *Out There: Marginalization and Contemporary Cultures.* Ed. Russell Ferguson, Martha Gever, Trinh T. Minh-ha, and Cornel West. Cambridge, MA: MIT Press, 1990. 299–305.

Moss, Beverly J., ed. *Literacy Across Communities.* Cresskill, NJ: Hampton Press, 1994.

Murray, K. M. Elisabeth. *Caught in the Web of Words: James A. H. Murray and the Oxford English Dictionary.* Oxford: Oxford University Press, 1979.

North, Stephen M. *The Making of Knowledge in Composition: Portrait of an Emerging Field.* Upper Montclair, NJ: Boynton/Cook, 1987.

Ochberg, Richard L. "Life Stories and Storied Lives." *Exploring Identity and Gender: The Narrative Study of Lives*, Vol. 2. Ed. Ruthellen Josselson and Amia Lieblich. Newbury Park, CA: Sage: 1994. 113–44.

Pearson, Carol. *The Hero within: Six Archetypes We Live By.* San Francisco: Harper and Row, 1989.

Phelps, Louise Wetherbee. "Practical Wisdom and the Geography of Knowledge in Composition." *College English* 53 (1991): 863–85.

Pillari, Vimala. *Pathways to Family Myths.* New York: Brunner/Mazel, 1986.

Polkinghorne, Donald E. *Narrative Knowing and the Human Sciences.* Albany: State University of New York Press, 1988.

Polanyi, L. *Telling the American Story: A Structural and Cultural Analysis of Conversational Storytelling.* Norwood, NJ: Ablex, 1985.

Pondy, L. R., G. Morgan, P. J. Frost, and T. C. Dandrige, eds. *Organizational Symbolism.* Greenwich, CT: JAI Press, 1983.

Prendergast, Catherine. "Race: The Absent Presence in Composition Studies." *College Composition and Communication* 50 (1998): 36–53.

Propp, Vladimir, *Morphology of the Folktale.* Bloomington: Indiana University Press, 1956.

Puka, Bill. "Commentary." *Human Development* 39 (1996): 108–16.

Randall, William L. "Restorying a Life: Adult Education and Transformative Learning." *Aging and Biography: Explorations in Adult Development.* Ed. James E. Birren, Gary M. Kenyon, Jan-Erik Ruth, Johannes J. F. Schroots, and Torbjorn Svensson. New York: Springer Publ. Co., 1996. 224–47.

Reynolds, Nedra. "Composition's Imagined Geographies: The Politics of Space in the Frontier, City, and Cyberspace." *College Composition and Communication* 50 (1998): 12–35.

Ricoeur, Paul. *Time and Narrative.* Vol. 1. Trans. Kathleen McLaughlin and David Pellauer. Chicago: University of Chicago Press, 1984.

Roen, Duane, ed. *Living Rhetoric and Composition: Stories of the Discipline.* Mahway, NJ: Erlbaum, 1999.

Rosnow, Ralph L, and Gary Alan Fine. *Rumor and Gossip: The Social Psychology of Hearsay.* New York: Elsevier, 1976.

Royster, Jacqueline Jones. "When the First Voice You Hear Is Not Your Own." *College Composition and Communication* 47 (1996): 29–40.

Sarbin, T. R., ed. *Narrative Psychology: The Storied Nature of Human Conduct.* New York: Praeger, 1986.

Schafer, Roy. *The Analytic Attitude.* New York: Basic Books, 1983.

Scholes, Robert, and Robert Kellogg. *The Nature of Narrative.* New York: Oxford University Press, 1966.

Schrager, Sam. "What is Social in Oral History." *International Journal of Oral History* 4 (1983): 76–98.

Scott, James C. *Domination and the Arts of Resistance: Hidden Transcripts.* New Haven, CT: Yale University Press, 1990.

——————. *Weapons of the Weak: Everyday Forms of Peasant Resistance.* New Haven, CT: Yale University Press, 1985.

Sedgwick, Eve Kosofsky. "Introduction." *Epistemology of the Closet.* Berkeley: University of California Press, 1990. Repr. *The Cultural Studies Reader.* Ed. Simon During. London: Routledge, 1993. 244–68.

Shaughnessy, Mina P. "Diving In: An Introduction to Basic Writing." *College Composition and Communication* 27 (1976): 234–39.

Shibutani, Tamotsu. *Improvised News: A Sociological Study of Rumor.* New York: Bobbs-Merrill, 1966.

Shotter, J. "The Manager as a Practical Author: Conversations for Action." *Conversational Realities: Constructing Life Through Language.* London: Sage, 1993.

Silko, Leslie Marmon. "Language and Literature from a Pueblo Indian Perspective." *Critical Fictions: The Politics of Imaginative Writing.* Ed. Philomena Mariani. Seattle: Bay Press, 1991. 83–93.

Smith, Barbara Herrnstein. "Narrative Versions, Narrative Theories." *On Narrative.* Ed. W. J. T. Mitchell. Chicago: University of Chicago Press, 1981. 209–32.

Steedman, Carolyn Kay. *Landscape for a Good Woman: A Story of Two Lives.* New Brunswick, NJ: Rutgers University Press, 1987.

Stock, Patricia. "The Function of Anecdote in Teacher Research." *English Education* (Oct., 1993): 173–87.

Stone, Elizabeth. *Black Sheep and Kissing Cousins: How Our Family Stories Shape Us.* New York: Penguin Books, 1989.

Tappan, Mark B., and Michael Packer, eds. *Narrative and Storytelling: Implications for Understanding Moral Development.* San Francisco: Jossey-Bass, 1991.

Trice, Harrison M. *Occupational Subcultures in the Workplace*. Ithaca, NY: ILR Press, 1993.

Trimmer, John, ed. *Narration as Knowledge: Tales of the Teaching Life*. Portsmouth, NH: Boynton/Cook, 1997.

Welch, Nancy. "Sideshadowing Teacher Response." *College English* 60, no. 4 (1998): 374–395.

White, Hayden. *Metahistory: The Historical Imagination in Nineteenth-Century Europe*. Baltimore: Johns Hopkins University Press, 1973.

White, Michael, and David Epston. *Narrative Means to Therapeutic Ends*. New York: Norton, 1990.

Wilkins, Alan L. "Organizational Stories as Symbols which Control the Organization." *Organizational Symbolism*. Ed. Louis R. Pondy, Peter J. Frost, Gareth Morgan, and Thomas C. Dandridge. Greenwich, CN: JAI Press, 1983. 81–92.

Wilson, Janelle L. "Lost in the Fifties." *The Narrative Study of Lives*, Vol. 5. Ed. Amia Lieblich and Ruthellen Josselson. Newbury Park, CA: Sage, 1997. 147–81.

Young, Katharine Galloway. *Taleworlds and Storyrealms: The Phenomenology of Narrative*. Dordrecht: Martinus Nijhoff, 1987.